*For Elly, Joe and Jake, with everlasting love and
in the hope that this dedication makes up for
all the embarrassment.*

And in loving memory of Allen Viner (1916-1976)

'Before I got married I had six theories about bringing up children; now I have six children and no theories.'

John Wilmot, second Earl of Rochester (1647–1680)

'Fathers should be neither seen nor heard. That is the only proper basis for family life.'

Oscar Wilde (1854–1900), *An Ideal Husband*

'Daddy, my daddy.'

Roberta Waterbury (Jenny Agutter)
in *The Railway Children*, 1970

Prologue

It is probably unwise to risk alienating your target audience in the first sentence of a book, but let me at least pose the question: could it be that, on the whole, the moment of conception is the first and last time in the parenting process that a father takes more of the strain than the mother?

After all, it is the mother, in the overwhelming majority of households, and whether or not she goes out to work, who will do most of the feeding, ministering, nourishing and nurturing until her fledgling flies the nest. And in the earliest stages of parenthood, it is the mother who carries her offspring for around nine months, often succumbing to all kinds of physical discomforts and indignities, such as indigestion and swollen ankles, before enduring the excruciating pain of childbirth, which itself usually heralds a further set of discomforts and indignities, such as cracked nipples and piles.

The main physical burden on the father, during all this, is that he doesn't get as much sleep or as much sex as he would like, although in fairness, he also suffers some mental turmoil. For instance, when his partner follows her health visitor's advice to insert cabbage leaves into her bra to relieve painful mastitis during the weeks and months of breastfeeding, the father has to judge whether a coleslaw joke will make her laugh or turn her violent. It's a challenging time for both parties.

Of course, new dads get stuck in more than they used to. Times have changed since the expectant father sat in the King's Head or the Queen's Arms waiting to hear whether the missus had given him a son or a daughter. I was born in October 1961, and it would have been at least as surprising then to hear that a father-to-be had been present at the birth, perhaps even stepping up to cut the umbilical cord, as it would be now to learn that he'd been in his local, on his fourth pint of lager and second bag of crisps, waiting for a telephone call from the hospital to determine when he could start wetting the baby's head with another round of drinks and handing out the cigars. Nevertheless, ours is the easy bit, not only by comparison with what the mother goes through, but also compared with the Herculean efforts our spermatozoa make to set the whole show on the road.

This is what I mean by the father taking more of the strain at the moment of conception. I'm not talking about the actual coital act, which, depending on what position you favour, can be at least as tiring for the female. No, I mean the astounding subsequent journey of the successful sperm, and actually I'm mixing up my mythological heroes, for the sperm is not so much the Hercules as the Odysseus of the human body.

When a man ejaculates, typically producing, at an average velocity of 28 mph, enough semen to fill a teaspoon (in the admittedly unlikely event of anyone wanting to), that small amount of semen contains up to 300 million sperm. Yet of these, fewer than 100,000 make it through the cervix, and only the strongest 200 or so then manage to navigate the fallopian tubes. In *The Odyssey*, Homer's epic poem about the eventful journey home from the long Trojan War of the mythical King of Ithaca named Odysseus, our hero and his men are thwarted by terrible storms, a tribe of cannibals, an angry giant, a malevolent goddess, a six-headed monster, a fierce whirlpool, a catastrophic shipwreck and an oversexed sea nymph. After all these tribulations, only Odysseus himself remains. And yet, when considered alongside the obstacles confronted by the sperm on its arduous and dangerous journey, his was a gentle saunter to the corner shop.

Conception, not *The Odyssey*, is the ultimate story of the survival of the fittest. If sexual congress is to result in pregnancy, the ovum or egg must be fertilised by one of the 300 million sperm that set off on their formidable journey, with all of them worrying – at least as Woody Allen saw it, in his 1972 film *Everything You Always Wanted to Know about Sex, But Were Afraid to Ask* – that they are being despatched on their epic voyage in the cause of masturbation rather than procreation.

In the case of the latter, even when a few hardy sperm get there, fertilisation remains less than straightforward. Several of them might break through the ovum's outer membrane. But only one of them will penetrate its innermost part. It is at this point, finally, and surely with whatever might be a sperm's equivalent of an exhausted but triumphant cry of 'You beauty!', that fertilisation occurs. From the ovum and the sperm a new cell called a zygote is formed, and it develops a thick wall to keep out any other sperm. Another tired but heartfelt spermy cry goes up: hands off my family. The mighty adventure of fatherhood has begun.

In this book, I follow that adventure for the all-important first twenty years or so, which embraces my own experience of fatherhood so far. On the basis that the responsibilities of fatherhood begin with conception rather than birth, the opening chapter ponders our role before we have a baby to coo over; the book then meandering more or less chronologically through those next two decades. However, in the concluding chapter I step away from my own experience and briefly ponder fatherhood as it is yet, for me, to be.

As well as exploring my own life as a father of three, a daughter and two sons, I also borrow extensively from the experiences of others: friends, family and perfect strangers, one of whom is former Prime Minister Gordon Brown, who outside 10 Downing Street following the general election of May 2010, just before being whisked off to Buckingham Palace to offer the Queen his resignation, rather movingly said, 'As I leave the second-most important job I could ever hold, I cherish even more the first, as a husband and a father.'

It was agonisingly characteristic of the accident-prone Brown that the most pitch-perfect speech he ever gave as Prime Minister should have been at the moment of his departure. I will always think of him fondly for the dignity of that resignation speech, and for his evidently sincere declaration in front of the world's media that fatherhood is the most important job that even an important man does. Is it, though? If you're a bomb disposal expert, or a brain surgeon, or a commercial airline pilot, or a teacher, or a bus driver or for that matter a prime minister, are your fatherly skills really more important than those that make you competent in your day job? Or is the line about fatherhood being more important than anything actually just a glib platitude, likely to win applause and even jerk a few tears but as devoid of real meaning as the flimsy sentiments on the insides of greeting cards?

It is certainly true that politicians are masters of the glib platitude, and that male parliamentarians these days rarely miss an opportunity to remind the electorate that they are fathers first and cunning politicos second.

In his memoirs, Gordon Brown's successor as Chancellor of the Exchequer, Alistair Darling, recorded that at the height of the banking crisis he was about to hotfoot it to the Treasury when he got a text from his daughter, Anna, who was travelling in South America with her friend, Catriona. 'It opened with the perennially hair-raising line "Hey dad, no worries but . . ."' wrote Darling, adding that the pair were stranded on the Bolivian border; that Catriona's passport, money and credit cards had been stolen; and that they were wondering whether it was OK to slip the border guard the bribe he'd demanded to let them into Peru. 'No it wasn't; but I was thousands of miles away,' Darling recalled, following up with the zinger: 'Just because you're Chancellor doesn't mean you're not still a father.'

Well, no, it doesn't, and it's not really a fact that has ever needed emphasising, yet Darling seemed uncommonly pleased with his ability to multi-task, to be a chancellor and a dad at the same time. In a jaunty diary column in *The Spectator*, in November 2009, he described a text message he'd received from his daughter during her gap-year travels. It was the same daughter, possibly even the same gap year, but a different message. This time she was 'far, far away from any major city. And far, I had thought, from being in a position to comment on the Budget. She simply asked: "Hey dad . . . is it true you've wrecked the economy?"'

Now, I wouldn't dream of suggesting that Darling made these things up, or even that he was exploiting young Anna's texting habits to demonstrate his jokey, self-deprecating human side to folk more interested in his questionable hold on the nation's purse strings; that and the frankly alarming contrast between his snowy-white hair and his jet-black, hairy-slug eyebrows. But could it be that, if only subliminally, he was offering his jolly good relationship with his daughter as redemption for being just a bit crap at balancing the books?

All of which brings us back to Gordon Brown's assertion that fatherhood is the most important job any man ever does. It is easily enough undermined, for if for instance an air traffic controller were making some almighty cock-up bringing planes in to land at Heathrow, which of us would find consolation in the sight of a 'Best Daddy in the World' mug on his desk? But then there are daytime jobs and lifetime jobs, and indeed there was Steve Jobs, the late co-founder of the Apple corporation, who was quoted shortly after his death in October 2011 as having said in his final, cancer-ravaged days that fatherhood was 10,000 times better than anything else he'd done in his life.

The many people who mourned Jobs as a visionary genius who had changed the world probably applauded this as a dying man's sentimental and wholly under-standable parting shot, while not for a second believing it themselves. How could fatherhood have been the greatest achievement, by 10,000 times, of the man who brought us the iBook, the iPod, the iPad, the iPhone? And yet, how could anyone possibly contradict him? Either way, I don't suppose there was ever the slightest chance of Jobs declaring on his deathbed that his entre-preneurial triumphs had been 10,000 times more rewarding than fatherhood. He was singing, as he prepared for his own, more visceral exit, from the same hymn sheet as Gordon Brown. And on the whole, I'm in tune with Gordon too. Good fathers seem likely to have been raised by, and in due course to raise, good fathers, and that's manifestly a cycle from which the whole of humanity can benefit, even more than we benefit from the iPhone.

But this book isn't really about being a good father. Even though it includes breezy snippets of advice, it is not a how-to manual. It is perhaps closer to being a how-not-to manual. However much I agree with those noble sentiments of Gordon Brown's, I'm even more inclined to endorse a remark made by the second Earl of Rochester more than three hundred years ago. 'Before I got married I had six theories about bringing up children,' he said. 'Now I have six children and no theories.'

Quite. There's nothing like the actual experience of parenting to explode all the theories, to rip apart all the textbooks. But this book, I hope, will at least provide some insight into the strange and yet common, the unique yet universal, condition of fatherhood. And perhaps it will also offer a few crumbs of comfort. After all, if you have a teething baby or an eighteen-year-old stop-out giving you sleepless nights, or a recalcitrant toddler driving you demented, or a cheeky eight-year-old giving you lip, or a sullen teenager ignoring you, and if she or he is equally capable of filling you with boundless love, joy and pride, then welcome to the club.

1

The Thin Blue Line

*Becoming a father doesn't necessarily make you less
of a child.*

One Saturday morning in the late autumn of 1992 I experienced what novelists call a cocktail of emotions, after a thin, rather faint but unequivocal blue line on a Boots pregnancy testing kit had confirmed what my girlfriend Jane already suspected: that we were going to become parents.

The overwhelming flavour of the cocktail was ambivalence. It was undoubtedly nerve-wracking to think that I was about to embark on an adventure from which there would be no turning back, that a new phase of my life was beginning, that after a lifetime of more or less pleasing myself I was at last on the verge of signing up to proper adulthood.

On the other hand, I'd always yearned to be a father at some stage in my life, I'd found a woman I loved, and I was thirty years old, which seemed a good age for it. Moreover, I had a steady if not especially well-remunerated job as the features editor of a local newspaper, while Jane was earning better money as a BBC radio producer, and we had already decided that we were going to get married. It had never been an objective to have kids out of wedlock, in the old-fashioned phrase, but knowing that we might not conceive for a while we had made the bold decision to dispense with contraception. All the same, I had looked forward to at least a year of regular, unsheathed sex before hitting the jackpot.

Actually, hitting the jackpot is a singularly inappropriate metaphor for conceiving a child, a development which also marks the beginning of the end of a chap's freedom to do what he likes with his own money. In February 2010 it was reported that the average cost of parenthood during the course of a child's first twenty-one years, starting with the smart Maclaren pushchair and ending with the horrible hike in car insurance, had for the first time broken through the £200,000 barrier.

To be callously precise, it had reached £201,809, of which the overall cost of childcare was calculated to be £54,696, food £17,490 and clothing £14,035. Education was reckoned to set the parents back £52,881, and that's not assuming posh private schools, but state primaries and secondaries, with all those years' worth of uniforms, sports kits, after-school clubs, school runs, school trips, packed lunches and so on. If Jane had called me into the bathroom that morning to scrutinise not a little stick with a blue line on it but a forward-dated demand for £605,427, the estimated cost of raising not one but three of the little cherubs, I suppose I might have run out of our small flat and continued running, like Forrest Gump.

Anyway, there it was, the stark message from Boots the chemists that I wasn't, after all, going to get a year or maybe even two years of energetically attempting to conceive. I had always enjoyed the story Jane told me about her newly married female Latin teacher, at Kirk Balk comprehensive in Hoyland, South Yorkshire, who one day in 1975 had solemnly announced to her class that she would be leaving school to 'try for a baby'. Why it should have been necessary for this woman to give up work remains a mystery. Just how many times a day did she intend to have intercourse? Perhaps, as a Latin teacher, she was cheerfully planning one never-ending session of coitus non-interruptus. Or, more likely, she was worried that the stress of trying to interest Kirk Balk's third-formers in gerunds, ablative absolutes and the works of Pliny the Elder – a battle always destined to fail, from what I gather – might not be physiologically conducive to conception. That I can understand.

Whatever, I don't know how long it took the Latin teacher and her husband to conceive, but it took us about a week.

Why did we do it? Were we giving in to a biological impulse, or a selfish one? Is procreation the ultimate act of egocentricity, or of selflessness? Or, paradoxically, a bit of both? Either way, I quite like the idea that it is also a way for us to see things through a new set of eyes, just as the spectacle of life, metaphorically and often literally, is beginning to get a tad blurred. By the time many of us reach the procreating years, we have become slightly cynical about the world. It's good to introduce a fresh, impressionable take on matters, which is what J. B. Priestley was getting at more than seventy years ago, when he reflected on the pleasure of delighting a child with what had once delighted him. 'I would rather see one of my children's faces kindle at the sight of the quay at Calais,' he wrote, 'than be offered the chance of exploring by myself the palaces of Peking.'

But seeing things through your children's eyes can be a hazardous business. Once, when my eldest child, Eleanor, was about three, I was sitting on a train somewhere between London and Manchester. As we passed a field full of livestock, I jabbed a forefinger at the window and cried out 'Sheep!' It took about two seconds, during which the man in the seat opposite peered over his *Financial Times* at me with an expression registering a mixture of amusement, contempt and downright fear, before I remembered that little Eleanor was at home with her mummy, and recognised in my neighbour's look the suspicion that he was sharing a carriage with a potentially dangerous simpleton.

Something similar happened to a friend of a friend, who was at the same stage of fatherhood when, in an important meeting over lunch, and to his own absolute horror as well as that of his business acquaintance across the table, he realised that he had unconsciously leant over and started cutting up the other fellow's food.

I would guess that many fathers of babies and toddlers have experienced similar embarrassments. Mothers too. I know a woman who once, at the exit of a London Underground station, and quite without thinking, wiped a rogue bogey off the lip of a stranger from whom she was asking directions. But men are more often prey to this embarrassment because it is more often they who, in the early stages of parenthood, must plunge back into the adult outside world.

I know for sure, because I've seen it with my own eyes, that I'm not the only man to have stood at a bus stop on my way to work, exhausted after a largely sleepless night, and still swaying gently from side to side trying to rock a phantom baby off to sleep. It's the same phenomenon as the sailor who takes his sea legs onto dry land after a long voyage, and if you hang around at enough bus stops or on enough train platforms in areas where there are plenty of young families – in my own case back in the mid-1990s, in Crouch End in north London – I guarantee you'll see it for yourself.

But I am getting well ahead of myself. Having stared at the pregnancy testing kit in the same kind of dazed stupefaction with which I imagine lottery winners look at their lucky tickets, wondering for a few moments whether it's some kind of optical illusion, or maybe a cruel practical joke, and then trying to process the bewildering prospect of life never being the same again, we sat down and began to absorb the extensive ramifications of what we'd done. For a start there were our respective parents to tell, which in Jane's case would be a pleasure, since her mother had already confessed to being a teeny bit disappointed when we'd called for silence at a family gathering and announced our intention to get married. She later admitted that she'd thought, and hoped, we were going to announce a bun in the oven.

Actually, she didn't put it quite like that. Jane's mum has lived all her life in South Yorkshire, and therefore has an innate suspicion of the coy euphemism, so she would never have said 'bun in the oven'. Nor would she have aired the hope that Jane might have enrolled in 'the pudding club', or have started 'eating for two', or be 'expecting the pitter-patter of tiny feet' or found herself 'in the family way'. I doubt whether any other country has quite so many polite terms for the condition of being pregnant, but in Britain there is a long-standing tradition of circumnavigating the direct reference, doubtless to spare the blushes of sherry-sipping maiden aunts, who understand, even if they'd rather not, that pregnancy is still, even in these days of syringes, test tubes and Petri dishes, almost always a consequence of sexual intercourse. Buns and puddings and eating for two do not seem even the slightest bit related to the penis and the vagina.

Telling my own mother was going to be slightly trickier. More than a decade older than Jane's mother, she belonged to the generation who felt that marriage vows should come before maternity wear. So for that matter did Jane's 91-year-old grandma, the small and round yet formidable miner's widow Nellie; but she, sitting in the corner armchair in which she spent her every waking hour (and which was mechanically sprung to help her get up, but was at first set too powerfully, firing her across the room like a cannonball), had taken the news with a cheerful, 'Ah well, worse things 'appen at sea.' I didn't expect my mother to be quite so philosophical. It seemed to me that she might take the view that, actually, the fate of the *Titanic* and the cruellest excesses of Somali pirates notwithstanding, worse things don't happen at sea. And so it was that the first challenge of my new life as a dad was how to tell my mum.

It was a challenge I flunked. As Jane remembers it, I made the mistake of starting the announcement with 'I'm afraid that . . .', and my mother duly responded with a terse 'Oh dear.' If it's true that when you become a parent you become less of a child, the metamorphosis clearly hadn't quite begun. I was scarcely less anxious about conveying the news that I was soon to be a father than I had been about telling my mother that I had broken an antique vase during a cushion fight with my friend Jem when I was ten years old. That said, I can't honestly believe I did say that I was 'afraid that . . .' Even if I did, once we were respectably wed, by which time Jane had been a fully paid-up member of the pudding club for three months and whose bump was accommodated on our wedding day in the Derbyshire town of Bakewell by an empire line wedding dress, my mum had entirely forgotten the stigma and was properly looking forward to the pitter-patter of her first grandchild's tiny feet.

By then, we had seen those tiny feet, or at least some blurred white blobs we were told were feet, on the photograph handed to us at St Mary's Hospital, Paddington, following Jane's twenty-week ultrasound scan. The ultrasound photo is one of the earliest catalysts in the father-to-be's transformation into one big gooey bag of sentimentality, a condition that in my own case still makes me a sucker for the bit in *The Sound of Music* when Fraulein Maria finally manages to wear down Captain Von Trapp's authoritarian approach to fatherhood, and he starts crooning in front of his children. Before embarking on the adventure of fatherhood myself, I had watched *The Sound of Music* plenty of times – there was simply no avoiding it back in the days of only three TV channels, especially at Christmas – without being remotely moved by that scene. Yet suddenly it seemed to connect directly to my tear ducts.

Maybe that's just me. I know *The Sound of Music* isn't everybody's cup of over-sweetened tea. It wasn't even Christopher Plummer's, who played the aforementioned Captain Von Trapp and rudely called it *The Sound of Mucus*. Similarly, the ultrasound picture doesn't have a dramatic effect on all men, either. Some look at it and see not their unborn son or daughter but a Martian on a radar screen. These men understand the absurdity of whipping out of their wallets a photograph that might be a foetus in their partner's womb, but might equally be a still from *Alien 3*.

However, they are surely in a minority. The ultrasound photo, after all, is the first baby picture a father gets to show to his friends. 'Look, there are its little arms,' he will say, tenderly, standing at the bar of his local pub and passing on the information received that afternoon from the ultrasound nurse. 'And we think that might be a willy, but we're not sure.' For some reason, expectant mothers are usually less soppy about ultrasound pictures, maybe because they are the ones whose bellies have been smeared with cold gel, and they recognise it more as a medical practicality, and less as an exercise in family portraiture.

This is not the only way in which men and women diverge as they await childbirth; indeed the divergence can be dismayingly wide. According to my friend Avril, a health visitor in the Welsh Marches, in homes where there is already a level of domestic violence a marked increase often occurs during the months of pregnancy, a consequence of the man feeling neglected.

Needless to add, this book is not targeted at the kind of man who might thump his pregnant partner because she won't oblige him in bed, or wants to lie down instead of making him a cuppa, yet it is surely true that even in loving, supportive relationships during pregnancy, rarely do both parties have quite the same hopes, dreams, fears, anxieties, ups and downs. Rarely, too, do they have an equivalent understanding of the miracle unfolding inside the woman's body. As a general rule, the bloke is a little sketchy on the detail, not entirely sure about the differences between the uterus, the cervix, the placenta, and all those other internal bits and pieces with Latin names, and their role in delivering his firstborn.

Compared with his father or grandfather, though, he is practically a professor of gynaecology. Ante-natal care and instruction began in earnest in Britain in the years after the First World War, but husbands were resolutely excluded from the process, which I have no doubt was absolutely fine by them. In the 1980s that began to change, oddly enough at about the same time that the study of gynaecology became less of a male fiefdom. Only a few years earlier, the American anthropologist Margaret Mead had waspishly observed that men had long since taken over obstetrics and had even gone and invented a tool, the vaginal speculum, that allowed them to look inside women. 'You could call this progress,' she wrote, 'except that when women tried to look inside themselves, this was called practising medicine without a license.'

As more women rose to top gynaecological jobs in hospitals, so did more men start going to ante-natal classes. But there were still plenty who didn't. My good friend Ian – now married to Avril, the health visitor

– was an expectant father in the mid-1980s, in rural north Herefordshire, but laughs now at what his expectations were of parenthood. 'I was completely naive,' he recalls. 'I thought I'd have a couple of sleepless nights and might not get to the pub quite as often. I really didn't see how fatherhood was going to change my life.'

Ian's then-wife attended classes at the local hospital while he stayed at home, or more likely went to the pub. He could have done with US patent 4531919, otherwise known as the Empathy Belly, or in Britain, the Empathy Belt. This is a strap-on garment designed to stimulate more than twenty symptoms or effects of pregnancy, including mild foetal kicking, backache and pressure on the bladder, intensifying the desire to urinate. But in Herefordshire in the mid-1980s, as elsewhere in the UK, there were very few men even aware of the Empathy Belt, let alone prepared to wear one. All we needed to intensify the desire to urinate was another couple of pints.

Still, if the Empathy Belt represents one end of the spectrum, or perhaps in this instance the speculum, and Ian *circa* 1985 the other, then by the 1990s an unprecedented number of men were occupying a new middle ground roughly half-way between expertise and cluelessness, getting more involved in pregnancy and childbirth than any previous generation of fathers-to-be, by accompanying their wives and girl-friends to classes organised either at the local hospital or health centre by the National Health Service, or by support groups and parenting charities, of which the biggest and most vigorous was the National Childbirth Trust. It was the NCT's ante-natal classes for which Jane and I signed up, in the spring of 1993.

The NCT started life in 1957 as the Natural Childbirth Association, inspired by the theories of an obstetrician called Grantly Dick-Read, and if there's not a joke there somewhere I'd be very surprised. There was, by contrast, no joking at all at the classes we went to in a leafy north-west London suburb, attended by five couples who were very nice but also exceedingly earnest, and us. And actually we were pretty earnest about it all too, even though we kept reminding ourselves that women had been giving birth for centuries, millennia even, without breathing exercises and birth plans involving scented candles and Van Morrison tracks, not to mention bean-bags and mugs of peppermint tea in a large semi-detached house in Brondesbury Park every Wednesday evening.

The NCT, certainly in north London, was and doubt-less still is an overwhelmingly middle-class phenomenon. In our case, the large, semi-detached house belonged to a woman – I'll call her Jasmine – who was no older than the rest of us but happened to have given birth sooner, and had then trained as an NCT instructor. She seemed a bit joyless, but then the NCT isn't about joy. At one session, she asked us what we were all most looking forward to when we got home from hospital with our newborn baby. We were sitting in a semi-circle, and Jane was the nearest to her, so she had to answer first. 'I'll put the baby down and pour myself a really big, strong gin and tonic,' she said.

She wasn't kidding, either. For months her intake of booze had been limited to the odd glass of wine, and a stiff G & T, with ice and lemon, was a proper heartfelt ambition. Jasmine gave a tight, disapproving smile. 'You should keep off alcohol if you're breastfeeding,' she said, and moved on to the next person, who insisted – I swear this is true – that her first act on arriving home would be to sit down at the piano with her baby and play some Chopin. There was a general murmur of approbation, while Jane felt like an unreconstructed lush and I snorted inwardly.

Nevertheless, our NCT classes undoubtedly plugged some of the gaps in our understanding of what we had in store, and Jasmine, in a stab at light-heartedness that was unprecedented and certainly never repeated, furnished me with my all-time favourite fact about the physiological differences between men and women, jauntily informing us that if a man's bladder were powered by a muscle as strong as the uterus, he would be able to pee across the Thames. The weaker sex? I don't think so.

Not only is this my favourite fact gleaned from ante-natal classes, it is also the only one I remember. Everything else is just a distant blur. I dimly recall something about Braxton Hicks, but not enough to distinguish it from Duckworth-Lewis, or Keegan-Toshack, or even Fisher Price. With her graphic imagery illustrating uterine power, my opinion of Jasmine rocketed. Her opinion of me, by contrast, plummeted when I skipped the session on breastfeeding, partly because it seemed to me that the finer points of getting a baby suckling successfully was very much the mother's department, and partly because on the same Wednesday evening there was a big football match on the telly. England were playing Holland in a World Cup qualifier at Wembley: hapless manager Graham Taylor and his obsequious assistant Phil Neal were the only tits preoccupying me that night.

In the two decades since, I've been given very little reason to believe that breastfeeding is a topic that men should embrace. In fact in 2003 I got into trouble embracing it, having related what I thought was a funny story in my column in the *Independent*. We had recently thrown a house-warming party, and hired a professional caterer to provide some of the food. I went to her house to pick it up, and as I was loading vats of her delicious coronation chicken into the back of my Volvo, she happened to mention that her version of the dish invented by Constance Spry to mark the Queen's coronation in 1953 had been eaten by, of all people, the Queen.

It turned out that she had a regular gig catering a carriage-racing weekend in Cumbria, sometimes attended by the Queen and the Duke of Edinburgh. And a couple of years earlier, she told me, she had been obliged to take her baby son along, as he was still on breast milk. Having laid out a splendid buffet, she had retired to her Subaru to feed her son, but had trouble getting him to take her milk. He bawled. And while he was bawling and she was trying to manoeuvre her nipple into his mouth, she failed to notice an elderly woman in a headscarf walking purposefully towards the car. The woman stuck her head solicitously through the window.

'Everything all right?' said a clipped voice.

The caterer gave a start. 'Your Majesty,' she said. 'I'm, erm, just trying to get him to latch on.'

'Oh, I know,' said the Queen. 'It can be awfully difficult.'

In the paper I pondered this, cheekily wondering which one one had had problems with. And that was that, except that in a shop in our local town I was angrily harangued by a friend of the caterer's, a man who felt that I should never have committed the story to print. Whether she objected herself, I never found out. She hadn't asked me not to, and it seemed to me like a rather charming tale. But what had irked this guy the most, it transpired, was the use of the N-word: nipple. There is, of course, an N-word that rightly causes offence these days, but 'nipple' isn't it. It's no wonder that breastfeeding in public remains a contentious business in Britain, when grown men can get flustered even by a reference to it in a newspaper.

Anyway, at that Wednesday's ante-natal gathering, while England's footballers were shipping goals at Wembley, Jane cheerfully gave the class both my reasons for not being there. Jasmine made no attempt to hide her disapproval, and I didn't worm my way back into her good books until a few months later when I was half of a double-act, the Little to Jane's Large, or maybe she'd prefer the Wise to her Morecambe, with our own child-birth story to tell. It was a straightforward birth without pain relief, the kind of birth the NCT love.

2

It's A Little Baby, Rodney

Be assertive with your preferred name, otherwise the
baby might be named by the midwife.

Eleanor was born at St Mary's Hospital in west London,
shortly after midnight on Saturday 19 June 1993. We had
arrived shortly before midnight, having been instructed
not to go in until Jane's labour contractions were three
minutes apart. It was a frantically busy night on the St
Mary's maternity ward, so busy that one woman ended
up giving birth on a trolley in a corridor. Happily for us, it
wasn't Jane. But her bed might have been even more
makeshift than a hospital trolley. Had Eleanor arrived in
the world just half an hour sooner, she would have met her
instantly besotted parents on the back seat of a green
Morris Marina underneath the Marylebone flyover.

Jane had been in labour since mid-morning, and by 10 p.m., according to the kitchen clock, the contractions were coming every four minutes. Then, suddenly, they increased not from four minutes to three minutes apart, but to every two minutes. We were cutting it alarmingly fine.

I phoned our friends Doug and Rosie, contemporaries of mine from St Andrews University, who lived a mile away, and asked as collectedly as I could if they might drive us to the hospital. They arrived in their elderly Marina not quite like Starsky and Hutch of blessed memory, but half-mounting the pavement all the same, and off we accelerated through the mercifully quiet London streets, with the slight hitch that Doug at the wheel wasn't certain of the way to St Mary's, and nor was Rosie, and nor, less excusably, was I. So Jane, half-sitting and half-lying on the back seat, found herself, in the ninety seconds or so between violent contractions, navigating us round roundabouts and telling us all to calm down.

A small detour seems as timely here as it would not have seemed on that dramatic summer's evening. A generation earlier, on a December night in 1959, Jane's mother Anne had also given birth to her first child, Jane's older sister Jackie. It was two days before Christmas, more than a week before the baby was due, when Anne first felt a spasm while crossing the road in Barnsley. She was twenty-two, her husband Bob twenty-seven, and neither of them had so much as read a pamphlet about parenthood, still less been to ante-natal gatherings to learn how he might administer some soothing perineal massage.

It was two years since the formation of the NCT, but Grantly Dick-Read's theories about natural childbirth hadn't quite permeated the pit villages and towns of South Yorkshire. Nor did the National Health Service, itself still in its adolescence, offer much beyond a few exercise classes. Bob, who as it turned out would take to fatherhood like a miner to an old tin bath full of piping hot water, knew even less than his young wife about what was happening to her body, beyond the obvious fact that there was a baby about to emerge from it. He certainly hadn't been made aware that if only his blad-der had been powered by a muscle as strong as the uterus he would have been able to pee across the Thames, which incidentally was a river he had seen for the first time on his three-day honeymoon to London eighteen months earlier.

Bob had been married for just over a year when he told his mother and older sister Jose that Anne was expecting their first child. More than half a century later he still vividly remembered the exchange. 'I went round to their house and told them. Then two of our Jose's friends came in and it wasn't mentioned again. I walked out so deflated. My mother thought it was too soon, you see. And when Jackie and then Jane arrived, she never once came to babysit for us. "Tha's made tha bed, tha can lig on it," she said.'

This was the same Nellie who later happily philosophised that worst things 'appen at sea, on being informed that her granddaughter, Jane, was pregnant before being wed. The same Nellie, indeed, to whom in 2011 Jane dedicated her first novel, *Netherwood*, remembering a nurturing matriarch whose cooking had fed the soul as well as the body, and in that respect the model for *Netherwood*'s doughty heroine, Eve Williams. The years had mellowed Nellie by the time Jane sat at her table. But the message to Bob as he prepared for fatherhood was strikingly different from the message I would subsequently get from him, Anne and my mum: you're on your own, son.

It is sobering in other ways to compare Bob's experience in the late 1950s with mine in the early 1990s. They had no indoor toilet, no bathroom and no telephone in their little terraced house in Hoyland Common near Barnsley, and certainly no car, so when Anne felt that initial spasm on the pedestrian crossing she walked to her Auntie Dinah's house for a bath, and then she and

Bob traipsed half a mile to the bus stop and caught the bus home. It was packed with Christmas shoppers and they both spent the entire journey standing up, Anne wincing with every bump and jolt. That she was obviously in the late stages of pregnancy cut no ice with the people on the crowded bus; so much as we in Britain like to tut at the policy of racial segregation that prevailed on buses in parts of the southern United States at the same time, it's worth reminding ourselves that nobody on the Barnsley to Rotherham bus two days before Christmas in 1959 saw fit to offer their seat to a young woman in labour. The notion among those of a certain age that bad manners are a modern phenomenon, that young people today lack the civility that in their own youth they'd had drilled into them, is perhaps misplaced.

When they got home, Bob walked to the nearest phone box to call Beckett Hospital in Barnsley for advice. An ambulance was promptly despatched and off they both went to the hospital, but as soon as Anne had been made comfortable on the maternity ward Bob was told to leave. He caught the bus home, and then called to see how Anne was getting on. It hadn't occurred to him that he might already be a father, but a nurse conveyed the unexpected news that she'd not long since given birth, to a healthy baby girl, and Bob emerged from the phone box in a state of bewildered happiness just as his Uncle Wilf and Auntie Doris – who were deemed the posh part of the family, on account of owning their own car – were driving past. They slowed down to acknowledge him, and thus were the first people he told that he'd become a father.

'It's a little girl with platinum blonde hair,' he said, excitedly.

'It'll go dark,' responded Uncle Wilf, matter-of-factly, and that was that.

Sentimentality has never been abundant in South Yorkshire, and yet the first people I told that I'd become a father were Anne and Bob, who already had two grandchildren courtesy of Jackie and her husband Tony, but were utterly and tearfully thrilled to have a third. There were tears, indeed, at both ends of the phone. If my first challenge as a prospective dad had been to tell my mum, my inaugural challenge as a new dad was to convey the news of my first child's arrival in a reasonably self-possessed, dry-eyed state. That too was a challenge I flunked, as plenty of men quite understandably do. Ian, the friend of mine who was so naive in his expectations of fatherhood, tells me that half an hour after his first son Steven had been born in Hereford County Hospital, he calmly dialled his mother's number only to find, on hearing her voice, that he couldn't talk. Literally couldn't utter a word, so intense was his blubbing.

I wasn't as lachrymose as that, and by the time I'd made my third phone call – the first to Anne and Bob, the second to my mother and stepfather, and the third to Doug and Rosie, who knew how close we'd come to ditching our chosen names and selecting Morris for a boy and Marina for a girl – I was almost calm. After seeing Jane and Eleanor safely to the maternity ward I was then asked to leave, and remember flagging down a cab outside the hospital, and telling the driver that I'd just become a father.

'Congratulations, guvnor,' he said.

The fare was £3.20, and all I had was a £10 note. I handed it over and he hesitated, transparently hoping that, suffused with joy, I might invite him to keep all the change. I didn't.

'Erm, can you give me a fiver back,' I said. It was only right to let him share some of my elation, but five quid's worth seemed sufficient. I was on cloud nine, but not quite in cloud cuckoo land.

All the same, it is a curious, dazed kind of elation that engulfs a man shortly after the birth of his first child. Having spent twenty years of my career as a TV critic, I can tell you that the late, greatly lamented John Sullivan captured it beautifully in the episode of *Only Fools and Horses* in which Tessa Peake-Jones as Raquel gives birth, and David Jason's Del emerges, crying in disbelief, into the hospital corridor, where his brother Rodney and Uncle Albert are waiting.

'What is it, Del?' asks Rodney.

'It's a little baby, Rodney,' says Del.

'Is it a boy or a girl?'

Del hesitates. 'Oh, hang on . . .' he says, and rushes back to the bedside to find out.

Like all the greatest comedy writers, Sullivan knew how to squeeze laughs from poignancy and pathos, in a cleverer way than is credited even by some avowed *Fools and Horses* enthusiasts. On a message board discussing the best moments in the show's illustrious history, one fan remembers Rodney saying, 'What about the sex?' and Del replying, 'Give it time, Rodders, she's only just given birth!' But that was the fan's line, not Sullivan's, who didn't need any clunky wit to generate the comedy; all he needed was the moving spectacle of Del so intoxicated at becoming a father that with all the emotion of it he had entirely forgotten to find out the baby's gender.

It is actually one of the sweetest moments in sitcom history, comparable with gruff, boorish old Jim Royle ladling tender endearments on his baby grandson in *The Royle Family*, and all the more impressive for David Jason not yet being able to draw on personal experience. Obviously his skill as a fine actor stood him in perfectly good stead, but you'd have wagered that here was a performer, in his early fifties, tapping into memories of his own emotions on becoming a first-time parent. In fact it was not until ten years later that Jason became a father for the first time, at the advanced age of sixty-one, and in due course reported on Michael Parkinson's chat show that all the medical staff around the bed had quite clearly been hoping that he'd say, just once, just for their benefit, 'It's a little baby, Rodney.' He didn't oblige.

I'll come back to older dads later, in chapter 21, but it seems worth pondering here whether first-time fatherhood feels more special at sixty-one than it does at thirty-one, as I was. According to my friend Mike, who sired Ben in his early twenties, Mabel in his mid-forties, and three other children between, Mabel's arrival unleashed 'a greater sense of wonder at the enormity of it'.

This was partly because the two experiences were at opposite extremes, in the sense that Ben had been entirely unplanned, whereas Mabel was planned with more care than the launch of a NASA space shuttle. Mike had endured not one but two vasectomies after his first four children had been born (such was his fecundity that the first snip didn't work, they had to keep on snipping), but then he met and married Lou, who was childless and wanted more than anything to be a mum. He duly booked himself in for an operation to reverse his surgically induced infertility, the start of a saga that, like all the best sagas, contained hilarity, pain, despair and, ultimately, joy.

To begin with the hilarity, Mike remembers lying in a bed at Southport General Hospital carefully shaving off his own pubic hair in preparation for the op and, as he was apprehensive, taking a while to realise why the sound of the razor seemed somehow distant yet amplified. It was the man in the next bed buttering his toast, in unwitting but perfect synchrony.

And so to the pain. I too have had a vasectomy, carried out in the town of Llandrindod Wells in the heart of Welsh hill-farming country, much to the amusement of my friends who happily seized the opportunity to crack jokes about sheep shearing, so I know all about post-operative discomfort and wearing Y-fronts two sizes too small to keep your wounded tackle tightly packed. But a reversal, or vasovasostomy, to give it the correct terminology, by all accounts and in particular Mike's account involves a different level of suffering altogether.

He is a singer-songwriter, and it was his misfortune to be heading off shortly afterwards, the numerous stitches still fresh in his scrotum, on a tour to Nashville, Tennessee that was too lucrative to be cancelled. After the long, miserably uncomfortable transatlantic flight he was, almost inevitably, singled out for prolonged interrogation at New York's John F. Kennedy Airport, leaving him with only forty minutes before his connecting flight to Nashville. Mike's lyrical description of gingerly running, walking and wincing through the terminal hall at JFK, guitar case in hand, could almost be a country ballad in its own right, with the kind of downbeat ending that the Grand Ole Opry audience would appreciate, for the pain was all for naught. The reversal didn't work, and two hugely expensive but failed attempts at IVF followed over the course of several frustrating and emotionally fraught years, before a third and final fling in which a surgeon inserted a syringe into one of his testicles and withdrew the sperm that, at long last, and in the nick of time, lit the blue touchpaper. Mabel was born in October 2005, a lovely little girl and a living testament to the fact that in the process of becoming parents women do not have a monopoly on physical pain.

But let's get back to my parents-in-law, news of whose own first little baby had been greeted by some relatives, and not just Uncle Wilf and Auntie Doris, in decidedly lacklustre fashion. There was, by contrast, nothing at all lacklustre about their response to my phone call. Not long after first light, they were heading south down the M1, and along with my mother and stepfather would offer as much emotional, practical and financial support as we felt we needed. Times had changed radically, in one family at least. But so in almost thirty-four years had the NHS, and not entirely for the better. After Anne had given birth to Jackie, she was kept in hospital for a full fortnight, to her increasing annoyance. The inside of Beckett Hospital wasn't remotely her idea of a place to spend the last Christmas of the 1950s, let alone somewhere to see in a new decade, but her forced hospitalisation at least meant that she could become accustomed to her new role as a mother surrounded by nurses, with advice on tap and meals on wheels.

Her younger daughter, by contrast, would be shown the door at St Mary's less than nine hours after giving birth, on account of them needing the bed back. Eleanor was born at 12.23 a.m. and by 8 a.m. I was back at the hospital to bring them home. As we left nobody said good luck or even goodbye.

Getting home was not so speedy, however. Saturday 19 June, as well as the day of Eleanor's birth, also marked the third day of that summer's second Test match between England and Australia, at Lord's. We lived in a small flat on the ground floor of a mansion block just across the road from Lord's, and, by 9 a.m., people and vehicles were already converging on the famous cricket ground from all directions. I had hailed another black cab outside St Mary's – my second that day, quite an extravagance for a lowly paid newspaperman – and when eventually it pulled up outside our block of flats, I asked the driver to double-park while I proudly took a series of photographs of Jane climbing out of the cab, clutching baby Eleanor in a blanket. My responsibilities as a new father, it seemed to me, began with the obligation to chronicle the homecoming. It was a duty that I felt the whole world would understand and indeed applaud, but I didn't reckon on the impatient driver of a large luxury coach, whose vehicle was stuck behind the taxi while I fiddled with the focus on my camera. He began hooting the horn so insistently that I bolshily took even longer over my impromptu photo-shoot than I might otherwise have done. It was only when the cab finally drove off, my photographic zeal sated, that I realised the coach contained the Australian cricket team.

It was the first feather in Eleanor's cap, that at approximately nine hours old she had obstructed and frustrated Allan Border's pugnacious Aussies, which alas was more than Graham Gooch's England team managed as the day unfolded. Australia resumed that morning on a massive 592 for 4, and then declared before lunch without losing another wicket. By the afternoon's close of play, England's feeble reply had stuttered to 193 for 9. I was a cricket nut, and with England already 1–0 down in that 1993 Ashes series this was a carry-on that I would have found enormously depressing had it not been for the state of light-headed euphoria that, not five hundred yards from where eleven English cricketers were miserably capitulating, completely overwhelmed me.

The euphoria was a heady mixture of happiness and relief, and had gripped me more or less from the moment the no-nonsense midwife confirmed that the baby was healthy, with all limbs intact. What, she then asked me, as she carried this tiny creature to the weighing-scales, had we thought of calling her? Had Eleanor been a boy, Joseph was our unwavering choice of name. But for a girl we had given ourselves a number of options. 'We're not sure,' I said. 'We're thinking of maybe Eleanor, or possibly Amelia, or Alice, or . . .' The hard-pressed midwife had no time for any airy-fairy nonsense. 'Right then, Eleanor,' she said, placing the baby on the scales. 'Let's see how much you weigh, Eleanor.' And so it was that, after all the conversation, all the debate, all the leafing through all the books of baby names, all the chuckling at Marmaduke and Engelbert and Esmerelda, our firstborn was named by an Irish midwife.

3

Geronimo!

Names are for life, not just for babies.

Choosing a name for your unborn child is one of the first great pleasures and responsibilities of parent-hood, an opportunity for both partners to share the delightful duty of giving their offspring an identity, as in a more basic biological sense they have already done with their genes and chromosomes. However, it can also be a challenging business, igniting arguments, tears, rages and sulks, especially if the father uses it, if only subliminally, as a means of muscling in on what can sometimes seem like the mother's show. 'But all the firstborn boys in my family have the middle name Percy,' he might reason. 'Not in my family they don't,' she might counter; and yet, of course, she might not. I don't suppose, for example, that the various wives of the former world heavyweight boxing champion, George Foreman, got too much of a look-in when it came to naming his five sons.

Foreman's first four children were daughters, and the first three of them were called, respectively, Natalie, Michi and Leona. Nothing too unusual there. But he called the next one Freeda George, and with that seemed to get a taste for naming his progeny after himself, because then came George Edward Foreman Jnr, George Edward Foreman III, George Edward Foreman IV, George Edward Foreman V and George Edward Foreman VI. In 2002 I had the pleasure of interviewing him, and he told me that he'd given all his sons the same name on the basis that if he ever started forgetting things, having taken all those blows to the head, at least he'd stand a fair chance of remembering what his boys were called. We both chuckled, but I don't think he was kidding. And after all those sons, incidentally, came another daughter. It probably won't surprise you to learn that she was christened Georgetta.

I didn't put it to Foreman, because he was still alarmingly large despite his transformation from the mean crittur he used to be into a cherubically amiable grill salesman, but there is clearly something more than a little egotistical about this. It's not about the prospect of losing his marbles, not really, it's about creating life not only in his own image but even with his own name. An expression of self-love, if you like. And that, to a greater or lesser degree, influences a lot of men in the naming of their children. Why else would the former Chancellor of the Exchequer Nigel Lawson (the third ex-Chancellor I have cited already in this book, slightly weirdly) have wanted to call his daughter Nigella?

It would be interesting to carry out a poll of parents, to find how often the choice of a child's name is a 50–50 decision, or whether it's more often the woman's preference, or more often the man's. Maybe it depends on the baby's gender, with more expectant mums claiming the right to decide on a girl's name, and more dads choosing boys' names. Maybe that was even the case with baby Nigella Lawson. But I doubt it. It seems to me, even though I don't have any supporting statistics, that, on the whole, men like to dominate in the name game.

I know of one fellow, another friend of a friend, who had long been fascinated in the life and times of King Richard I of England, and chose to call his son, not Richard, but Lionheart. That could only be a man's choice of name. A woman would see the potential pitfalls, realising at once the danger of making the child a hostage to fortune, which at least in this case conferred a certain symmetry, since the real King Richard was actually held hostage for a fortune, in the twelfth century, by the Holy Roman Emperor. Nevertheless, how daft the name would seem if the boy grew up to be weedy and cowardly and scared of spiders. Yet if such pragmatic objections were raised they were overruled, and in due course little Lionheart joined the Jacks and Oscars and Alfies at playgroup.

Similarly, it is more usually on a whim of the father's, not the mother's, when babies are named after a favourite rock star or sportsperson or even an entire team. My friend Ali has a brother whose middle name is Lester, after the jockey Lester Piggott, and much as Piggott was nicknamed 'the housewives' favourite', the tribute was entirely at the suggestion of Ali's dad, who'd pocketed more than a few bob down the years by betting on whichever horse Piggott was riding. In January 2011, rather more dramatically, avid Burnley F.C. fans Stephen and Amanda Preston, from Colne in Lancashire, chose to call their little boy Brian Jensen Jay Alexander Bikey Carlisle Duff Elliot Fox Iwelumo Marney Mears Paterson Thompson Wallace Preston, after the Burnley players who had beaten Nottingham Forest in the first game of the season. Again, there's something of the Lionheart syndrome here. What if young Brian grows up hating football, or worse, supporting Blackburn

Rovers? Either way, I wouldn't mind betting that he owes his extraordinarily long string of names more to his dad than his mum.

Perhaps this assertion of dominance on the father's part has something to do with his traditional role of registering the child, which in some households gave him *carte blanche* to call it anything he liked. According to Sanderson family lore, after Jane's grandma, Nellie, had given birth to her first and only daughter in 1931, she didn't have any idea of what the child was going to be called until her husband Joseph had got home from the registry office.

'What's 'er name, then?' she said.

'Josephine, Josephine Mary,' came the reply. Nigel Lawson-style, he had named her after himself.

Even for a South Yorkshire miner and his wife, that was arguably taking a lack of sentimentality a little too far, yet Jane has another story about her schoolfriend Denis, whose father omitted the second N not in tribute to the great footballer Denis Law but because he was worried (as perhaps was Denis Law's father, an Aberdonian fisherman and hard-up father of seven) that he might have to pay the registrar by the letter. Jane's friend was lucky not to be called plain D. Moreover, even when both parents had jointly decided on a name, and the spelling of it, there was still bureaucracy to deal with. When Bob went to Barnsley to register his first-born as Jackie, the woman behind the desk said, 'I think you mean Jacqueline?' 'No, I mean Jackie,' he said, but that cut no ice with the pompous registrar.

Again, times have changed. If you think of the bizarre names registered these days, it's unimaginable that 'Jackie' would be deemed unacceptably *outré*. There are more than a few modern registrars who have experienced the full gamut of wacky names from Amadeus to Zebedee, especially if there's a rock star in the locality. The Blur bass guitarist Alex James named his sons Geronimo, Artemis and Galileo, and his daughters, almost prosaically by comparison, Sable and Beatrix. I know James slightly, I've met his wife Claire, and once more my theory about fathers holds up: it's my educated guess that Geronimo, Artemis and Galileo were his picks, not hers, just as I don't suppose that Angie Bowie came up with the name Zowie for the son she had with the rock legend born plain David Robert Jones.

Whatever, the problem with extravagant names is that they generate extravagant expectations. Surely it's better to go through life as a charismatic Trevor, exceeding expectations, than a dull Zebedee, failing to meet them. And I should think it's enough of a challenge being the offspring of a famous father without also having to live up to his name. Among the few who have managed to overcome this predicament are Nigella Lawson and Zowie Bowie, as it happens. But significantly, by the time Bowie junior started enjoying success as a film producer, he had long since declared his wish to be known as Duncan Jones.

Nonetheless, Bob might have reminded the bossy Barnsley registrar that there was actually a proud heritage in that area of unusual names. Those who populated the working pit villages of South Yorkshire might not have had much variety or sparkle in their lives, but by God they put some imagination into naming their nippers. On 8 June 1946, the day Bob started work at Wharncliffe Silkstone colliery, which also happened to be his fourteenth birthday, he was taken under the wing of a kindly older miner called Di Reckless. Later, he found out that Di was short for Diamond Jubilee, Di having been born in 1897, in the week of the sixtieth anniversary of Queen Victoria's accession to the throne. And there was also a Gadsby Reckless down the pit, Di's brother. Yet by the late 1950s, hardly anyone in Yorkshire was saddling their children with names like that. There, as elsewhere in the country, John, Mark, Peter, Andrew, Simon and Robert held sway as boys' names, with Susan, Carol, Helen, Alison, Gillian and Joanna the leading options for girls. And Jacqueline. But seemingly not Jackie.

Bob had less trouble, getting on for three years later, registering Jane. Neither child had a middle name, which was doubtless considered a bit of a frippery in the Barnsley area in those days, or maybe he didn't fancy extending his encounter with the unsympathetic registrar. Anyway, Anne had now given birth to two daughters, having herself been one of two sisters. And by the time Jane became pregnant for the first time, her older sister Jackie had also produced a pair of daughters. So although we didn't actually have a clue, up to and including the authoritative things we were told by self-styled gestation experts about the revealing shape of the bump (which in fact has everything to do with the woman's body shape and muscle tone, and nothing at all to do with the gender of what's inside), we felt pretty sure throughout Jane's pregnancy that the baby would be a girl. We gave the foetus a pet name, Dilberta, after a popular female elephant at London Zoo that I read about in the paper one day.

It sounds soppy to nickname one's unborn baby, but plenty of folk do it. The thumpingly successful thriller writer Lee Child – originally plain Jim Grant, from Coventry – tells a good story about falling into conversation, on a train in the United States, with a garrulous Texan. Delighted to be speaking to a European, this guy started rhapsodising about his new car, a Renault 5, which was marketed in America as 'Le Car'. But he pronounced the French word 'le' the Texan way – 'lee' – which so amused Jim Grant and his wife that it became an in-joke between them, and they began to substitute it for the definite article, as in 'shall we watch "lee" news.' or 'could you pass "lee" salt?'. So in due course, when they became expectant parents, the bump naturally became 'lee' child. And when Grant then embarked on a writing career and was looking for a *nom de plume*, there it was. So if a thriller writer called Dilberta Viner suddenly arrives on the literary scene, you'll know whence she came.

I can't remember it ever occurring to us to give our unborn child a male pet name, so sure were we that it would be a girl. In the event of the unexpected we both liked the name Joseph equally, and for Jane it had the added poignancy of having been the name of her grand-father, the very chap who in 1931 had taken the unilateral decision to call his daughter Josephine, and who eleven years after that had perished in an under-ground rock fall at Wharncliffe Silkstone. It is a cruel paradox that the most basic challenge for a father, to stay alive to provide for his children, is the very one over which he has no control. Joe Sanderson was the only man who died in that accident, and was buried on Bob's tenth birthday, four years to the day before Bob began his working life down the same mine that had killed his dad.

Next to mortality, a name seems like a frivolous detail in a person's life, and yet, if only superficially, nothing defines us more than our names. So it is best to have parental consensus on the subject, though of course not every couple reaches it. That Jane and I liked the name Joseph transcended its significance to her family, but to some people, the significance of a forename is more important than liking it, and in my experience men are generally less willing than women to concede ground in the matter.

This might be construed as plain greedy, since the child almost always gets his or her father's surname, but as an outsider it's best not to stray into such territory. Jane and I once did so unwittingly, at the home of our friends Nick and Nicky not long after Eleanor had been born. Nicky was about five months pregnant, and the conversation round the dinner table turned to names.

'A colleague of mine,' said Jane, chuckling, 'has gone and called her newborn son Arthur. What sort of name is that to give a child in the last decade of the twentieth century?'

I chuckled along in support. There was a fleeting but heavy silence. 'See!' said Nicky to Nick, pointedly.

She then explained, to our acute and ill-concealed

embarrassment, that every firstborn son in her husband's family, going back generations, had been christened Arthur. He himself was Arthur Nicholas, not that we'd ever had the slightest idea. That wonderful sketch series *The Fast Show* hadn't yet blessed the nation's television screens, but if it had, Jane would have identified with the hapless Mark Williams character who drops a terrible social clanger and then mutters, 'I'll get me coat.' In fact we did get our coats not long afterwards, doubtless leaving them to a proper barney over the washing-up. A battle between a man weighed down by family pressure, and a woman weighed down by an unborn baby, amounts to an awful lot of emotions, hormones and, possibly, dinner plates flying around. Happily, a compromise was reached. Alexander Arthur, rather than Arthur Alexander, was born four months later.

His arrival, I should add, was anything but straightforward. Nick and Nicky had been greatly encouraged by the story of Eleanor's speedy birth, naively if understandably thinking that it augured well for them. We had ourselves found, during Jane's pregnancy, that her swollen tummy seemed to give people licence to tell us stories of excruciating 48-hour labours and agonising forceps deliveries, and maybe Nicky and Nick had suffered the same grisly tales, making the account of Jane's experience blessedly welcome.

Unfortunately, Alexander's birth turned out to be horrendously prolonged, complicated and traumatic, and the memory of it never faded sufficiently for them to loosen their resolve never to have another child. Nick felt just as strongly about it as Nicky, if not more so.

'I can't face the possibility,' he once told me, 'of subjecting Nicky to such physical torture again, and myself to such emotional torment.'

Sitting in a quiet pub many months later, this seemed to me a pretty extreme response, but there it was. They insisted that Alexander would be their last baby as well as their first, and he was. They also clearly felt that we'd led them plumb up the garden path with all that talk of arriving at the hospital just half an hour before the baby was born, and mother and infant being happily, healthily, back at home later the same morning. We hadn't meant to, but maybe we had.

Of course, now that I'm a careworn, fifty-something father of three, I know that no two birth experiences are alike just as no two children are alike. And maybe there's some benefit in hearing all those horror stories, on the basis that it's best to be prepared for the worst. The NCT have the opposite philosophy, or at least did in 1993, when we subscribed, albeit less gullibly than some, to their vision if not of the immaculate conception then certainly of the perfect birth.

In some NCT classes, words such as 'pethidine' and 'epidural' were and perhaps still are treated as you might expect words such as 'America' and 'Zionist' to be received in an al-Qaeda training camp. But that only set up couples for a fall. When your teacher has been proselytising about birth plans and the touchy-feely joy of minimal pain relief, there is a very real danger that the woman will feel inadequate, when push comes to shove, or more aptly when push comes to push harder, for demanding as much pain relief as the medics can muster. I know a woman who endured a miserable bout of post-natal depression, and I remain firmly of the belief that it was ignited in part by her elevated expectations of herself and her body. She'd given birth to a healthy baby, but the stuff she'd heard in ante-natal classes convinced her that she hadn't come up to scratch, hadn't given her child the best possible start in life.

I should hasten to add that the NCT is a marvellous organisation in many respects, not least in the way it generates support networks for new mothers. But of the five women in our class, Jane was the only one whose experience of childbirth was uncomplicated, and we were the only couple who were invited back to talk to Jasmine's next class of *ingénues*. Even at the time that seemed disingenuous, although any reservations we might have felt were easily suppressed. Eleanor's arrival was a subject on which we could both talk the hind legs off any donkey, at least until one of the prospective dads asked us earnestly, over his mug of peppermint tea, whether we had thought of eating the placenta, as he and his partner intended to do. That was a show-stopper.

4

From Here To Paternity

Dads don't have to be present at the birth. In fact, it might be better for everyone if they're not.

We hadn't eaten the placenta. Nor had we buried it in the garden, as Jane's sister Jackie and our brother-in-law Tony had. Childbirth, in my view, was a profound enough experience without getting all New Agey about it. But hey, live and let live. Eat and let eat. And I was certainly enough of a new man to assert my right to paternity leave, which took some asserting, since even by 1993 it was by no means enshrined in my contract of employment. Instead, I asked my boss, Gerry Isaaman, the terrier-like editor of the *Hampstead & Highgate Express*, if I could take some time off, and he said yes. That's how the system worked. The exact duration of 'some time' was not discussed.

Isaaman was no doubt feeling indulgent because it was in his newsroom that I had first met Jane. She was the paper's deputy news editor when I arrived in 1989 as a cub reporter, and it's safe enough to say that in those few months, as I sat at her desk telling her what stories I had gathered from the previous night's meeting of Haringey Council's housing committee, neither of us expected that we'd end up making three children together. She didn't even like my housing stories very much. Still, after a few false starts our relationship flourished, especially once she had left the paper for the BBC, and the editor, who was rightly proud of the lofty professional heights scaled by quite a few of his former hacks, was now entitled to feel that his recruitment skills had brokered a baby. His indulgence, however, went only so far. On the Friday after Eleanor's birth, when I still hadn't returned to work, he phoned me and bluntly suggested that it was time to get back to my desk, and to Haringey Town Hall.

'Five days seems quite long enough,' he said. 'And I know Jane. She'll cope perfectly well with the babe on her own.'

If I were to father a child now, which is highly unlikely in light of what happened to me in Welsh sheep-shearing country, things would be different. I would get a statutory minimum of two weeks' paid leave and up to twenty-six weeks more if Jane had returned to work. But I didn't argue. It didn't seem unreasonable, and there wasn't much for me to do at home anyway, except gaze lovingly at Eleanor and burp her occasionally. Besides, Gerry was about the same age as my father-in-law Bob, a generation for whom paternity leave was still a slightly confusing novelty. Far from taking time off work when Jackie and Jane were born, Bob had volunteered for every available shift. Fifty or more years ago, fatherhood carried a responsibility to get out and maximise your income, not stay at home bonding with your newborn. And even that was an improvement on the lot of the previous generation of fathers, who had a war to fight. I don't know what paternity leave is like now in the armed forces, but I can guess what it was like in 1943.

Wartime complicated the fundamental requirements of fatherhood – to provide for your children and to protect them – but really those requirements haven't changed in 10,000 years. 'I cannot think of any need in childhood as strong as the need for a father's protection,' Sigmund Freud had written a few years earlier, which might have been pitching it a bit strong, as old Sigmund was wont to do, for what about the need of a mother's love? Nevertheless, that fatherly instinct to protect his children plainly connects us, in the twenty-first century, with Neolithic man. In other respects, though, things have changed dramatically even since 1993. Fatherhood has somehow become much more public in that time, with some of the highest-profile men in Britain wearing their status as dads almost as a badge of honour.

In 2009 and 2010, all three main party political leaders – David Cameron, Ed Miliband and Nick Clegg – took full paternity leave. If that had happened in 1993, it would have been remarkable, and not only because John Major, John Smith and Paddy Ashdown were all in their fifties. It would also have been remarkable because politicians then didn't draw attention to any time they might spend not working on behalf of the electorate. How things have changed in twenty years. Back then, Britain had only just emerged, blinking in the sunlight, from thirteen years under Margaret Thatcher, a workaholic who believed that only wimps needed more than four hours' sleep a night, and who, despite having given birth herself to twins Carol and Mark (such solid 1950s names), was surely too busy climbing the greasy political pole to give much time to the frivolities of motherhood. Indeed, the very thought of her mothering was disconcerting, as Caroline Aherne knew when, as the spoof chat-show host Mrs Merton, she welcomed the daughter of the former Prime Minister with a mock-guileless: 'So, Carol Thatcher, were you breastfed as a baby?' How we all laughed.

By contrast with his party's great she-wolf, in November 2010 Cameron welcomed Miliband back to the House of Commons after the Labour leader's fortnight-long paternity leave, not with a jibe about taking time off but with a positively fraternal joke. 'I very much know what it's like – the noise, the mess, the chaos and trying to get the children to shut up,' he said. 'I'm sure it was lovely to have two weeks away from it all.' How they all laughed.

As for Clegg, in early 2011 he unveiled plans to extend the rights of new fathers, enabling them to share twelve months of paid leave with the mother. The statutory two weeks of paternity leave, he said, patronised women and marginalised men. They were based on 'a view of life in which mothers stay at home and fathers are the only breadwinners. That's an Edwardian system that has no place in twenty-first-century Britain.' Moreover, he added, 'we know that where fathers are involved in their children's lives they develop better friendships, they learn to empathise, they have higher self-esteem, and they achieve better at school.'

The nation's dads gave a collective hurrah. Either that, or a collective gulp, for it seemed the onus was suddenly on us to produce happy, successful, well-adjusted children. And not everyone applauded Clegg's proposals. The British Chamber of Commerce called them a potential 'sledgehammer' to business, and employment lawyers talked ominously of a 'chilling' effect on recruitment, warning that employers would avoid hiring men with, so to speak, a twinkle in their eye. Of course, plenty of companies down the years had been reluctant to employ women of child-bearing age, but that wasn't at all the kind of equality Clegg was aiming for. Nor had he intended to conjure the irresistible image of gay men, old men and infertile men becoming, one might say at a stroke, the most desirable candidates for any job.

Still, whatever the rights and wrongs of the plans to extend paternity leave, at least they moved fatherhood to the heart of political debate.

It was also, in the first decade of the twenty-first century, not infrequently at the heart of sporting debate, as some of Britain's best-known sportsmen defiantly put daddying duties before boots, bats and balls.

In June 2004 the England cricket captain Michael Vaughan actually raced off the field of play, during a Test match at Headingley, when news arrived that down the M1 in Sheffield his wife, Nichola, had gone into labour with their first child. Before the match he had informed the opposing team, New Zealand, that he might get an emergency call, and asked for their under-standing in the event of him having to dash off. They were happy to oblige. It would never have happened in the days of W. G. Grace, or Len Hutton, or even Ian Botham, and nor had it happened when Vaughan himself was born. His father, Graham, was playing for Worsley Cricket Club in Manchester when in October 1974 someone in the clubhouse took a telephone call to say that Mrs Vaughan's waters had broken. He chose to play the match out, and then stayed for a celebratory drink before heading for the hospital with his team-mates to see his newborn son, little Michael, the future Ashes-winning captain of England.

Again, how times have changed. In recent years it seems that scarcely an overseas Test series has passed without at least one England cricketer – including no fewer than three other Test captains in Andrew Flintoff, Kevin Pietersen and Andrew Strauss – flying home to be present at the birth of a child. During the Ashes in 2010–11 the team's leading strike bowler James Anderson had barely finished taking six wickets to wrap up victory in the second Test match in Adelaide before he was on a long flight home to see his second child being born. A few days later he was airborne again, getting back to Australia in time to join the team for the third Test. It was hardly ideal preparation for one of the more gruelling challenges in the world of sport.

But it wasn't just cricketers who had entered a new

age as the twenty-first century got into its stride. In 2008 the newly appointed manager of the England rugby union team, Martin Johnson, missed what would have been his inaugural tour at the helm, to New Zealand, to stay at home with his pregnant wife Kay – a New Zealander, coincidentally. Even those who criticised the delivery-room cricketers as big wusses – and some did – could hardly level the same accusation at the mighty Johnno, who five years earlier had hoisted the World Cup and whose stature as an authentic English hero survived even England's catastrophic 2011 World Cup campaign.

It is estimated that some 90 per cent of fathers attend the births of their children in Britain these days, a statistic quite unthinkable around the time that I was born, in 1961. But just imagine if it weren't the case, and that an advertising campaign were launched to encourage men to get more in touch with their sensitive side, and to be with their partners while their kids are being born. The campaign could not hope to recruit a more influential pair of supporters than big Johnno and 'Freddie' Flintoff, the very definitions of brawny he-men. Endorsements from those two is the stuff of an ad man's dreams. And yet, while I wouldn't say it to their faces, which in any case I could only do by standing on a box, I wonder if the impulse to be there at the birth isn't fundamentally a selfish one, or at least based, if you'll pardon the pun, on a misconception? It's not as though the baby cares, and nor, according to the veteran French obstetrician Michel Odent, is it necessarily marvellous news for the mother, either.

Odent has forged a media career out of being controversial, but it's surely worth at least considering his view, as ventured to the *Observer* in 2009, that, 'The ideal birth environment involves no men.' He offered half a century of experience, in homes and hospitals in France, England and Africa, as back-up for his theory that, 'The best environment I know for an easy birth is when there is nobody around the woman in labour apart from a silent, low-profile and experienced midwife – and no doctor and no husband, nobody else. In this situation, more often than not, the birth is easier and faster than what happens when there are other people around, especially male figures – husbands and doctors.'

Odent's view that childbirth should ideally be a man-free zone – somewhat undermined by him being there to grumble about men being there, if we're going to be pedantic about it – puts me in mind of the advice once given to me by an acquaintance, who emailed me some years ago after I had written in my newspaper column that we had acquired some hens for our little orchard in Herefordshire, and were wondering whether to add a cockerel. She strongly advised me not to do so. In her experience the presence of a cockerel turned hens silly and squawky. 'It is for largely the same reason,' she added, splendidly, 'that we don't permit men to join our book club.'

But there is a world of difference between reading a book and giving birth, at least until you've grappled with the works of James Joyce. According to Odent, the presence of a man produces adrenaline in his partner, making her tense and slowing down her production of the hormone oxytocin, which is important in the birthing process, because oxytocin encourages effective contractions. Without it, labour becomes longer, more painful and more difficult, all as a consequence of what Odent called the masculinisation of the birth environment. This is a phenomenon he linked to the 'industrialisation' of childbirth, whereby the vast majority of women give birth in hospitals, not at home. Society's growing affluence and mobility as the twentieth century unfolded in Britain meant that women, for the first time, were having babies away from their mothers, sisters, grandmothers, aunts, one or all of whom would once have been at the bedside, sleeves rolled up and hot water on hand. In their stead came the husbands and the boyfriends, if not to muck in quite as literally, then at least to offer a comforting pat and an encouraging word.

This so-called industrialisation of childbirth also goes by the name of progress, yet I can see why the substitution of men for women at the bedside might be deemed a backward step. Could it in fact be that one of the newest challenges of fatherhood is not to force yourself to be at the birth, but to force yourself not to be? It is a challenge that is becoming harder and harder to overcome. On Chris Evans' Radio 2 show in September 2012, Robbie Williams admitted that, with his wife about to give birth but also a series of live concerts to perform around the UK, he felt that his overriding duty was to his fans – that if Mrs Williams happened to go into labour just before or during a show, he would finish it before dashing to his wife's bedside. The reaction to this, from Evans as well as listeners, including plenty who had tickets for his tour, could not have been more outraged if the singer had admitted to massacring baby seals. No, they spluttered; he could sing his songs any time, but would only have one chance to see his first child being born.

And yet, Odent's theories about men being unnecessary or even unwelcome spectators at the birth have been to some extent supported by the NCT, the very organisation that took a decidedly dim view of me watching a football match on the telly instead of going to that evening's breastfeeding class. In 2009 a spokeswoman agreed with him that cultural expectations put some men under considerable, sometimes intolerable, pressure. 'There's such a feeling among women that, "You got me into this, I have carried the baby for nine months and now I have to go through labour and birth, so the least you can do is be with me, and if you feel a bit squeamish, then tough,"' she said. 'I wouldn't go as far as Michel Odent in saying that men are always unhelpful in labour. But it's not men's right to be there. The most important thing is that the woman feels safe, secure and supported, so if she wants to have a woman around instead, that's fine.'

Fair enough, but where the blazes does that leave us men? We can't assert our right to be at the birth if it's not, in fact, our right. Should it really be, as it were, entirely the woman's shout? Whatever, Odent is also on record as insisting that the spectacle of childbirth can destroy the sexual attraction between a couple, leading ultimately to divorce. It takes proper Gallic gloom to find in what should be one of the greatest passages in any relationship the seeds of its destruction. But there you are, and he is supported by the American film director Tim Burton who, talking about the moment Helena Bonham-Carter produced their son, declared that, 'Birth is the most shocking thing that can happen to anybody. I've seen plenty of horror movies, but this about tops it.'

I can understand how, if you see it that way, it might

freak you out to the point of undermining the relationship. The macho chef Gordon Ramsay once admitted as much, justifying his resolve not to be at his wife Tana's side. 'We have a very active sex life and we both contemplated over a bottle of wine that it wasn't good for our sexual relationship for me to be at the childbirth,' he said. 'I'd feel squeamish seeing that level of mess. It's like sending twenty-five vegans into a kitchen with meat in the blender.'

Ramsay was wrong; it's really not like that at all. All the same, we don't hear much about the vulnerability of fathers during childbirth, apart from the jokey cliché of the man passing out and the woman worrying about his well-being rather than her own, and maybe we should.

Michel Odent claimed for years, without too much academic evidence to back him up, that there is a male equivalent of post-natal depression into which some men plunge. Eventually, the academic endorsement arrived: a study by the Medical Research Council suggested that a form of post-natal depression affects as many as one father in five, and further research at Oxford University showed that these depressed fathers, not surprisingly, spend less time than other new dads talking and playing with their babies. In *The Times*, in April 2012, a journalist called Rufus Purdy bravely admitted to being a sufferer of post-natal depression himself.

'I love my children with all my heart,' he wrote, 'but increasingly I feel unable to cope with them.' He confessed to dreading the responsibility of childcare, and being downright terrified by the very thought of Fridays, the day when his wife was at work and he had sole charge of his kids. Accompanying his candid feature in *The Times* was an article by a clinical psychologist, the exotically named Dr Cecilia D'Felice, who explained that, emotionally, many men are inadequately prepared for fatherhood. 'Holding his newborn for the first time may not bring the expected rush of love so often talked about,' she wrote. 'His partner's hormonally induced state has been designed by nature to focus all her energy and attention on the baby, leaving the father feeling superfluous.'

It is that feeling of superfluousness, too, according to Michel Odent, that makes other men turn to 'golf or computer games' to avoid the new reality of their lives, or simply walk out and never come back. Oh, and becoming fathers apparently sends a few of them schizophrenic or lands them with other mental disorders.

So, if you're reading this book as a first-time expectant father, you could be forgiven for wondering what kind of unholy mess you've got yourself into. You might also have resolved to do childbirth the 1960s way and stay in the pub, or at the very least pace anxiously up and down the hospital corridor, avoiding the business end of the operation until it's all over. By way of further guidance, all I can offer is my own experience, which is that I feel hugely honoured to have seen two of my three children being born (the other having been delivered by Caesarian section, to which I wasn't invited). It didn't undermine the sexual attraction I felt for my wife, and I didn't disappear to the golf course, or take up computer games, or become schizophrenic. Maybe I was simply one of the lucky ones.

When I sought Jane's input on the subject, she expressed the view that it would have been 'annoying' if I'd been waiting in the pub while she gave birth. 'If the father's not there, it's impossible to impress on him the extent of the ordeal it can be,' she said, which was fair enough. On the other hand, she also sympathised with the view that the father's presence can be inhibiting, although she was good enough not to remind me that, when she quite understandably let out a short, sharp fart while in labour with our third child, I let out, fleetingly and involuntarily, but nevertheless unmistakably, a snort of laughter. It was instantly and bitterly regretted, I hasten to add. All the same, I was grateful that our old NCT teacher Jasmine wasn't there. She would have smothered me with a bean bag.

5

Four Weddings And A Birth

If you're the father, don't pretend you're not.

In a way, the arguments for and against the father's presence at the birth are a distraction. As, in another way, in the whole scheme of fatherhood, is the birth itself. I wouldn't want to arm-wrestle Freddie Flintoff or any other England cricketer over the matter, still less big Martin Johnson, but this business of doing whatever it takes to be there for the birth is not remotely, or maybe only remotely, what fathering is about.

It's more about doing whatever it takes for the next eighteen, twenty-one, twenty-five years, and equipping your children with all the confidence and self-esteem they need for their own trip into adulthood. The Ottoman philosopher-poet Khalil Gibran phrased it nicely, when he wrote that parents are the bows from which children as living arrows are sent forth. The stronger the bow, the further and straighter they fly.

Unarguably, the legacies of good – and bad – fathering stay with people well into their dotage, and at every stage along the way. As a schoolgirl my mother wanted to go to university to read chemistry, but her father hadn't heard of chemistry, so rejected the idea out of hand. That was more than seventy years ago. She's almost ninety now, and still talks about it with regret. Conversely, I once read a magazine interview with the stand-up comedian Sarah Millican, in which she spoke about her dad who like my own father-in-law was an electrical engineer at a colliery, in this case in South Shields. 'Laziness was the one thing he couldn't tolerate in people,' she said. 'I think that's where I used to get my positivity from, and my drive. He always used to say, "There's no such thing as can't. The only thing you can't do is stick your bum out the window, run downstairs and throw stones at it. You can do anything apart from that."'

Now, I've come across some good lines about the wisdom of fathers, not least a famous one attributed to Mark Twain, who is supposed to have said that when he was a fourteen-year-old boy his father was so ignorant that he could hardly stand to have the old man around, but when he got to twenty-one he was astonished how much his father had learnt in seven years. All fathers with grumpy teenage sons should learn that one by heart, even if it perhaps owes less to Twain than to the poetic licence of *Reader's Digest*, where the quotation first appeared in the 1930s. Inconveniently, Twain had been only eleven when his father died of pneumonia.

By contrast, I think we can assume that Sarah Millican was quoting her dad accurately, and if so I feel he deserves his own entry in a dictionary of quotations. Quite how or why he stumbled on running downstairs and throwing stones at your own bum as the only thing in life that can't be achieved I don't know, but it does show that, for powerful imagery, ordinary working-class English folk can match Ottoman philosopher-poets any day of the week.

As for that emotive word 'paternity', in recent times it has acquired almost a pejorative sense. Not so its sister word 'maternity'. If 'maternity' had ever cropped up on the TV game show *Family Fortunes*, the 100 people polled would doubtless think first of maternity wear, or maternity ward, or perhaps maternity leave. But what word springs immediately to mind to go with paternity? It is surely 'suit'. And of course a paternity suit is quite different from a maternity dress.

The growing sophistication of DNA testing has made all the difference to paternity suits. Before, a blood test was the only scientific means of investigating paternity, and not very helpfully it could never prove that a man conclusively was the father of a child, only that he categorically wasn't.

Such was the case with Charlie Chaplin, who in 1943 was identified by actress Joan Barry, with whom he'd had a brief relationship, as the father of her newborn daughter, Carol Ann. Chaplin insisted that the dates didn't add up; that their affair had been over long before the child was conceived. However, Californian law at the time gave the woman the entire benefit of the doubt; incredibly, the mere allegation of paternity was enough to force a man to support both woman and child until the suit had been settled. So Barry agreed to submit herself and the child to blood tests, and Chaplin was compelled to pay $500 a month in maintenance. The tests then showed that his blood type was O, Barry's was B and the baby's was A, so whoever was the father, it wasn't Chaplin. And yet, with the press monitoring every twist and turn – no less slaveringly than they would now – the unequivocal evidence of the blood tests was disregarded. In 1943 only ten US states recognised blood testing in paternity cases, and California wasn't among them. Chaplin was forced to pay $75 per week to a child that wasn't his until her twenty-first birthday.

So, it's not only fatherhood that can be expensive for a

chap, but non-fatherhood too. The hugely rich and famous Charlie Chaplin could easily bear the financial hit, of course, but the cost to his reputation was enormous. An examination of the actual trial shows why. The septuagenarian prosecuting attorney Joseph Scott was, as David Robinson put it in his magisterial 1985 biography of Chaplin, 'a craggy-faced old lawyer of the all-stops-out histrionic school'. Even experienced court reporters were shocked by the floweriness of Scott's invective.

It is true that Chaplin was known almost as well for his libido as for his Little Tramp. By 1944 he had embarked on his fourth marriage, to eighteen-year-old Oona O'Neill, and so it was easy enough to present him as a lascivious old goat. All the same, Scott might have exercised a bit more subtlety. Laying flamboyant claim to the moral high ground, and without any censure from the judge, he called Chaplin 'a grey-headed old buzzard', a 'cheap Cockney cad', a 'lecherous hound' and 'a reptile' who had looked upon Barry 'as so much carrion'. He boomed at the jury that, 'Wives and mothers all over the country are watching to see you stop him dead in his tracks.' In the event, the jurors failed to reach a verdict. But at the retrial in 1945, Scott became even more grandiloquent in his denunciations, and this time the jury swallowed them whole. Chaplin was solemnly pronounced the father of the child, even though he wasn't.

With DNA, there can be no such miscarriage of justice. Indeed, with DNA, paternity tests can even take place posthumously. In 1998 the body of the actor and singer Yves Montand was exhumed, seven years after his death, to determine whether a 22-year-old woman called Aurore Drossart was, as she claimed, his daughter. Montand had had affairs with Marilyn Monroe and Shirley MacLaine, among many others, during his long marriage to Simone Signoret. He was certainly no angel. But nor, in this case, was he the father.

Angel, coincidentally, is also the name of the daughter of Melanie Brown, once of the Spice Girls. Angel's daddy is Beverly Hills' favourite cop Eddie Murphy, not that the rotter admitted it until she forced a paternity test on him, in 2007. That'll teach him for messing with Scary Spice. Among other reluctant dads to have been nailed by DNA are Boris Becker and Mick Jagger. Yet in the autumn of 2011, 51-year-old Hugh Grant was only too happy to admit paternity during a flurry of publicity about him fathering a daughter with a Chinese woman almost twenty years his junior called Tinglan Hong, who was described as an actress even though nobody could find evidence of any film or play she'd acted in.

I wouldn't want to sound snide myself, however, since there was quite enough of that at the time, one newspaper reporting with ill-concealed disapproval that Grant, whose first child it was, 'is not believed to have been at the birth but he is said to have spent around half an hour with her the following day before heading to Scotland to play in a golf tournament'. This wasn't quite disappearing off to the golf course as the obstetrician Michel Odent meant it, as part of a fatherhood-induced panic attack, yet some chose to present it as an abhorrent dereliction of duty, and Grant's unmistakable delight at becoming a dad bizarrely got the blogosphere even more steamed up than it might have been had he denied, in the more usual style of male celebrities, that the baby was anything to do with him.

'When everyone starts asking why there are so many single Mums in the UK look no further than the behaviour of feckless Hugh Grant,' went one message-boarder. Another bewailed 'yet another child brought into the world, the victim of a free relationship where adults have put either a lack of planning or their own selfish wants ahead of what is best for the child'.

We are all, to some extent, occasionally guilty of the presumption that we know better than a child's own parents what is best for it. And sometimes that presumption is supported by all the available evidence, as when kids of eight or nine are allowed to roam the streets after dark. On other occasions, however, there's something more than a little distasteful about this outraged, ill-tempered stomp towards the moral high ground. 'There is no spectacle so ridiculous as the British public in one of its periodic fits of morality,' wrote the historian Lord Macaulay in the mid-nineteenth century. It is no less ridiculous now.

It was the *Daily Mail* columnist Amanda Platell who led the spluttering condemnation of Grant, furiously lambasting him in language that Charlie Chaplin's nemesis Joseph Scott would have recognised, for accidentally fathering a child during an 'apparently loveless, insignificant liaison' and generally behaving reprehensibly 'even by the sleazy standards of this oleaginous, womanising lounge-lizard'. And yet the lounge-lizard not so oleaginously declared his intention to cherish and support the child, setting up her and her mother in a comfortable home and declaring that they would never want for material comforts, an arrangement that appears to have been more than acceptable to Tinglan Hong, who still seemed genuinely fond of Grant even though their brief romance – or loveless liaison, as Platell preferred it – was over.

In the *Independent*, Tim Lott struck an entirely different note, pointing out that Grant would only see his child when he wanted to, which isn't such a bad thing. 'After all, when I don't want to see my kids, either because I'm tired or irritable, I'm usually horrible to them,' he wrote. 'Separating from the mother before the child has even gone the first trimester turns out to be an excellent solution to future discontents. I bet there are plenty of couples who wished they'd thought of it themselves. The bonds of familiarity that keep so many unhappy couples together haven't had time to forge themselves. Everybody wins.'

What was striking about this newspaper talk, and plenty more of it not repeated here, was not so much the range of opinions as the aggregate number of column inches reporting and reflecting on Hugh Grant becoming a father. Military coups in small African countries have received less coverage. In the *Guardian*, columnist Hugo Schwyzer (a very *Guardian* byline) even used it to draw some conclusions about the evolving nature of fatherhood itself.

Modern men expect babies to change their lives in a way that their fathers and grandfathers never did, he reasoned, and ascribed it partly to first-time fathers being, on average, much older than ever before. In America and Europe, more than 50 per cent of first-time fathers are now over thirty, which in Schwyzer's view increases their emotional awareness of what is happening to them. 'They are more likely to have wondered if they ever would become parents,' he wrote, and 'more likely to have considered the possibility that it might not happen. They are also less likely to be self-absorbed and still finding themselves.'

For most men, whatever their age, the onset of fatherhood at least brings a realisation that the most important creature in his life is no longer himself. Hugh Grant recognised that equation some years before he impregnated Tinglan Hong. 'As much as I adore myself,' he once wryly told *Vogue* magazine, when the subject of prospective parenthood came up in an interview, 'I'm quite keen to find someone else to care about more.'

New mums undergo the same transformation, of course, except that it is usually ignited by pregnancy rather than birth. In the 2007 film *Juno*, an engaging comedy set in Minnesota about a sixteen-year-old girl's unplanned pregnancy, a character blithely observes that whereas women become mothers when they get pregnant, men don't become fathers until they see their baby. There's something in that. I know I've already observed that it tends to be the man, not the woman, who goes ga-ga over the first ultrasound photograph, whipping it out of his wallet at the slightest provocation and speculating on whether a small indistinct blob might or might not be a willy, but in general it's only at or just after the birth that a chap feels the mighty rush of emotion that for months has been coursing on a hormonal tide around his partner's body.

In general. It doesn't always work like that. A writer called Jim Keeble admitted in the *Guardian* in May 2012 that having thrown himself into the role of expectant father with textbook zeal, he then felt entirely alienated by the birth itself. 'From feeling intrinsically connected to my wife, part of a two-person team about to ascend Everest, I felt suddenly and overwhelmingly alone, cast out on a rock face without a rope,' he wrote. In the days and weeks following the birth of his son, Milo, he felt only emptiness where he knew there should have been a surge of love.

'In public, I was cooing and attentive to the baby,' he recalled. 'I told my wife how much I loved him. But I didn't own the emotion. I was, in many ways, going through the motions, seeing myself in a movie in which I was playing the doting dad . . . But in the depths of the east London night, as I paced with this small, sleepless – often screaming – homunculus, unable to figure out what he needed, and suspecting it was simply his mother, I found myself finally in tears . . . What did it mean being a father, if I didn't feel close to my little boy at all?'

Ernest Hemingway had one answer. 'To be a successful father, there's one absolute rule,' he once wrote. 'When you have a kid, don't look at it for the first two years.'

In Keeble's case, however, the powerful, unstoppable rush of love finally came when his son started smiling and gurgling at him. Maybe the problem lay in that textbook zeal he wrote about; that he had invested so much emotion in being an expectant dad that the reality seemed like a let-down.

Many expectant fathers are emotional, of course, but for some of them those emotions are wrapped up with performance anxiety: will they feel the immediate devotion to their child that they're expected to feel, and that Jim Keeble didn't? Will they be up to the job? And will they be able to change that lifetime's habit of putting themselves first? That was what troubled me before Eleanor was born. I had been in full employment for six years or so, and pretty much everything I earned had gone towards my own upkeep, my own holidays, my own nights on the town, my own indulgences. I remember being genuinely perturbed – not that I confided in anyone, least of all Jane – by the prospect of being a provider. It wasn't meanness, either with money or of spirit, that got me thinking that way. I just didn't know whether it would come naturally.

I should have had more faith in my Stone Age antecedents. Even before I made the Australian cricket team wait in their coach, while I took photographs of Jane and Eleanor emerging from the taxi outside Lord's, my primitive hunter-gatherer instincts had overwhelmed any lingering doubts in myself as a provider. I didn't quite wear a leopard-skin loin-cloth when I strode out the next morning to buy disposable nappies, but I might as well have done.

6

Has She Done A Poo Yet?

No man should ever refuse to change a nappy. It's
unmanly.

Eleanor's first birthday one year later also happened to
be Father's Day, which seemed a good excuse to write a
column in a national newspaper about my first year of
daddying. Out of the blue I had been offered a job by the
Mail on Sunday when Eleanor was just a few months old,
a decidedly serendipitous turn of events, for it meant
that my modest local newspaperman's salary doubled
more or less overnight. At a stroke, hunter-gathering
became a little easier.

In the piece I wrote, I included the surprising and
worrying statistic that 60 per cent of couples experience problems with their relationship within the first

year of parenthood. My feeling, and Jane's, was that ours had grown stronger, although we recognised that parenthood had done nothing for our range of conversation. It wasn't as though, even as journalists, and even though she worked for the Radio 4 news programmes *The World at One* and *PM*, that we had ever really had deep and meaningful discussions about global affairs, but it was still a shock to the system to realise that a fairly typical conversational overture now was, 'Has she done a poo yet?'

This is one of the paradoxes of the early stages of parenting, that your intellectual life contracts as your emotional life becomes richer. But the trade-off seemed worthwhile in every way, and I'm sure most fathers would agree. That hard-knock actor Sean Penn once said, sweetly if a little soppily: 'I'm not going to have a better day, a more magical moment, than the first time I heard my daughter giggle.' I might once have said the same, with a pint or two inside me to stir my emotions. But it didn't seem to matter that I stopped going to the pub quite so often to talk football and swap jokes; our new little family unit threw up situations far more comical than any story about an Englishman, an Irishman and a Scotsman on a desert island.

When Eleanor was seven months old we took her for her first weekend by the seaside, staying for two nights at The Swan, a handsome old inn in the genteel Suffolk town of Southwold. Just before bathtime on the first night we removed her nappy to get some air to her bottom, an exercise that to first-time parents assumes roughly the same strategic importance as any pincer movement ever did to a Second World War general, but as she romped around on the floor of the hotel bedroom we noticed a single sausage-shaped poo on the carpet: what the babycare guru Penelope Leach would have described as 'a large solid stool'. We leapt into action, and yet as so often in those early stages of parenting, the mother's leap was marginally more urgent and athletic than the father's, and so I arrived at the scene a crucial split-second behind Jane, who gingerly scooped it up with a handy room-service menu and flushed it down the loo. Relieved, we turned back to baby Eleanor, only to find that she had another, even bigger poo in her little hand, and was waving it around triumphantly, rather as a winning captain might show off the FA Cup.

Poos and pooing: I hadn't realised, before I became a father, just how large they would loom in my new life. An acquaintance of mine and a fine, humorous writer, Marcus Berkmann, records in his 2005 book about becoming a new father, *Fatherhood: The Truth*, that of all the men he talked to during his research, 89 per cent agreed with the statement: 'Changing nappies was the thing I most feared before I became a father.' And his 89 per cent thought that the other 11 per cent were lying. And yet, as I have recorded, while there were plenty of aspects of fatherhood that worried me, nappy-changing wasn't one of them.

On the contrary, I actually recall looking forward to a full shift (note to typesetters: please don't inadvertently miss out the 'f') on the nappy-changing front. I didn't want to be a father who left that sort of thing to the mother, not that there was the slightest bloody chance of Jane permitting me to be, I might add. Besides, as Berkmann also observes, 'New fathers anxious to impress friends and family, not to mention social workers, will take any opportunity to change a nappy in public.' It could, he astutely notes, be the most visible rite of passage that new fatherhood offers. 'It is also, to be frank, a piece of cake. Changing nappies is so much less appalling than you think it's going to be that, in a strange sort of way, you almost end up enjoying it. Were it not for the enormous quantities of excrement involved, you could nearly call it a hobby.'

I certainly remember the sense of satisfaction that came with changing a really explosive nappy, restoring order and talc to an area where shortly before there had been chaos and poo. It is a feeling that Gordon Ramsay, last encountered in this book explaining why he avoided his children's births like vegans might avoid an offal counter, has never experienced. A father of four, he likes to boast that he has never changed a nappy in his life. This is a boast one sometimes hears from men who became fathers in the 1950s and 1960s, but these days it is something a bloke should keep between himself and his wife, like a propensity for cross-dressing in the bedroom. Ramsay has also boasted of having a penis the size of a baby's arm, and he clearly believes that the no-nappy thing is consistent with being immensely well-hung, a demonstration of alpha-masculinity. But at some point in the last couple of decades it became down-right manly to tackle those dirty nappies, and properly wimpish to avoid them. When Ramsay grinningly owned up on a TV chat show to never, ever changing a nappy, he was roundly booed. And by the men in the audience as well as the women, I shouldn't wonder.

What I would say, though, is that while fatherhood equips most men with all the resources they need to deal with their child's poo, it fails to equip them with the resources to deal with somebody else's child's poo. It's a remarkably rum thing, but the unconditional love you feel for your own infant must trigger some mental impulse, which in turn sends messages to your eyes and in particular your nose, so that whatever kind of mess you're dealing with, and however pungent the smell, you can get it dealt with. Yet in instances when that unconditional love is absent – and I'm relieved even now to say that I only ever had to change two or three non-family nappies – it's a different matter entirely, a matter of gurning uncontrollably to stop yourself throwing up. I don't think women experience this phenomenon, or at least not to the same extent. When they become mothers they become, by definition, motherly. It's different for fathers.

But for both first-time parents, life becomes elemental, reduced to a series of single-syllable obsessions: poo, wee, sick, sleep. As it happens, Eleanor was pretty good at sleeping. It wasn't until after 1995, when we had our next child, Joseph, that we came to understand the real meaning of sleep deprivation, and the semi-madness that engulfs you when, again and again through the night, just as you are sinking into the deep unconsciousness to which you feel so richly entitled, the cries and shouts propel you upright again. Upright, unhinged and resentful, and in our case it lasted for the best part of five years, pretty much until Joseph started school.

In more than fifty years on the planet, nothing else that has ever happened to me, including the very different but shattering traumas of sudden bereavement and unexpected redundancy, has led me to feel that a few intensive sessions of group therapy might have made life easier to bear. At times of personal tribulation, I have generally taken the view that I would be better off tackling the situation on my own, and that things would inexorably get better. But I could have done then with the psychological comfort of knowing that other people were in the same boat.

Much later, the American novelist Adam Mansbach wrote a collection of sweet rhymes with X-rated endings. One of them went: 'The windows are dark in the town, child/ The whales are huddled down in the deep/ I'll read one very last book if you swear/ You'll go the fuck to sleep.' The book was boldly titled *Go the Fuck to Sleep*, and as I read it, chortling, I reflected that trying to compose appropriate lullabies might have brought a wisp of entertainment to the seemingly endless nocturnal trudging back and forth to Joseph's bedroom. I wish I'd had the idea before Mansbach did; it would have done me good to sing, even under my breath: 'The spiders and beetles are sleeping, Joe/ The cows are too tired to moo/ The mice in our cellar are sleeping, Joe/ So why the fuck aren't you?'

Of course, it's a long time now since I've been a father to babies or toddlers, and on the whole the challenges from that phase of my life are akin to toothache: I know they were difficult at the time, but now that they're behind me I can't really remember the pain. The years of sleep deprivation, however, are different. I can recall exactly how sapped we were not only of physical but also emotional energy, and when I see young parents suffering now my heart goes out to them. One winter's morning in early 2012 I had some firewood delivered by a chap in a pick-up truck, who'd brought his baby son with him to allow the child's mother to get some desperately needed kip. They were first-time parents and the baby, he said, was already very demanding.

'Please tell me it gets easier,' he implored, as I helped him load the wood into our log shed.

'It does,' I said, at which point, as if on cue, the baby, who was sitting next to us on the gravel still strapped into his car seat, began to bawl.

'How old is he?' I asked.

'He's four months,' said the wood man, tenderly rocking the car seat. The crying stopped.

'And what's his name?' I said.

The man stopped rocking and looked up at me, ashen-faced. 'Do you know,' he said, in his broad Herefordshire accent, 'my mind's gone blank.' He gazed silently at me for three or four more seconds. 'Fred,' he said finally. 'It's Fred.'

I suppose that little memory lapse might have seemed shocking to someone who wasn't a father, or had never had to deal with persistent lack of sleep, but I understood completely what it was like to feel so drained that your only child's name might slip your mind.

My own first year as a father was a period of upheaval in more ways than one because we moved out of our small mansion-block flat near Lord's to a terraced house in the more child-friendly north London suburb of Crouch End. Since we weren't quite able to coordinate both sale and purchase, however, we had to bridge the move by lodging with my mother and stepfather, setting up home for several months in their basement.

It was a stressful time, and although baby Eleanor slept like a top compared with her future little brother, she was still demanding feeds every few hours through the night. After four months of breastfeeding, Jane decided to move her onto the bottle, applying the fierce diligence that had characterised her work at the BBC, from which she was taking six months' maternity leave, to matters such as sterilising rubber teats.

This seems like a suitable juncture to confess another of my ante-natal anxieties: one of the characteristics I had found so appealing about Jane in the first place was her professional expertise, even if it did mean her rubbishing my news stories about Haringey Council. When she then landed a coveted place on a BBC scheme to train up newspaper journalists for jobs in broadcasting, I took at least as much pride in her achievement as she did. And so I was worried that when she stopped work to focus on mothering, something of what had so attracted me to her might be lost. What I hadn't anticipated, hopelessly naive though it now seems, was that her competence in the workplace would overnight seem less important to both of us than her competence as a mother.

In my defence, I know from having spoken to other fathers that, whether perceived or real, this is a common concern. You fall in love with a childless woman, perhaps whose ambitious careerism you greatly admire, and then a baby arrives to move the goalposts. Will motherhood change her? Will maternity leave make her less stimulating company, or less fun, than she was when you were meeting at a wine bar after work and going on to a cinema or theatre, or pleasing nobody but yourselves on a lazy Sunday morning? Will it alter her demands of you? I know these are questions that might be considered irredeemably sexist, but to an apprehensive expectant father that makes them no less valid. And they raise issues that are doubtless sometimes responsible for the first-year friction experienced by 60 per cent of new parents. But I should think that the main cause of that friction is plain tiredness. And so back to rubber teats.

Jane, with a first-time mother's obsessive zeal for

keeping the things regularly sterilised, had put eight of them in a small saucepan to boil. Unfortunately, exhausted after a string of disrupted nights and a little discombobulated by lodging with the in-laws, she had clean forgotten about them until they were a welded mass of stinking rubber, the copper-bottomed pan a write-off, the kitchen walls and ceiling blackened, and the entire house filled with acrid smoke. Eleanor had to be evacuated and all windows opened for twenty-four hours. We apologised profusely, almost tearfully, to my mother and stepfather. Kindly, they told us not to worry.

The following evening, with noxious remnants of the horrible smell still wafting around the house, Jane put the precious three remaining teats on to boil. My job was to remind her about them five minutes later. But I was tired too, and there was a particularly distracting Sunday-night drama on the telly. It was forty-five minutes later when the same poisonous stink of carbonised rubber hit us like a truck, and I yelled a word that should never be uttered within earshot of one's children, or one's parents, let alone both.

The baby had to be evacuated again, all the windows opened for a further twenty-four hours. My mother, confronting a freshly re-blackened kitchen ceiling and another destroyed saucepan, again told us not to worry, with almost as much sincerity as before, and laughed off

Jane's laments that she was clearly unfit for motherhood. So did I, but neither of us were able to stop Jane from driving into the night in search of a teat shop. It was my first real taste of that leonine distinction that is part of the parental experience: the lioness getting tremendously agitated on behalf of her cub, and the lion looking on, if not always yawning, then certainly not prey to quite the same primal emotions. It's fair to say that the indomitable yachtswoman Ellen MacArthur would later set off round the world in her trimaran with a less ferocious, less single-minded sense of purpose than propelled Jane round London in search of new rubber teats that Sunday night. She eventually found them in an all-night pharmacy on a bleak stretch of the Edgware Road, and from then on, night after night after night, we sat and watched the damn things boil.

You learn all sorts of things about yourself, both practical and psychological, during that first year of parenthood. And underpinning them all, proving that we are actually far more complicated than lions and lionesses, is the extraordinary intensity of your feelings for this new little creature, the more overwhelming for being wholly unprecedented and unfamiliar. After all, to what can a first-time father compare his feelings for a newborn child? Perhaps only in his own babyhood, which he can't remember anyway, has he looked upon another human being with the same unconditional adoration with which he now regards his own child. And that adoration of a baby for its mother, frankly, is actually more like that of a dog towards its owner: why wouldn't you gaze lovingly at a person who smiles at you, strokes you, feeds you, cleans up your poo?

As life wears on, however, it becomes clearer and clearer that the love of a child for a parent is not like that of a parent for a child. There's a deeply affecting scene addressing just this emotive topic in the marvellous 1967 film *Guess Who's Coming to Dinner?*, which tackled the subject of interracial marriage at a time when it remained illegal in no fewer than seventeen US states, most of them in the South.

Sidney Poitier's character, Dr John Prentice, having announced his intention to marry Joanna Drayton (Katharine Houghton) just ten days after meeting her, has just had a broadside from his father (Roy Glenn), a retired mailman who can't come to terms with the idea of his son marrying 'above his station' into a white family so fantastically well-bred that Joanna's parents are Katharine Hepburn and Spencer Tracy. John Prentice has been married before, to a black woman, but his wife and son both died in a road accident. He has no qualms about marrying again, nor about marrying a white girl. But his old dad tells him now that he didn't carry that mailbag for all those years, and make all those sacrifices to put him through medical school, to sit back and watch him make such a foolish mistake. In short, that the son owes the father a duty to do the right thing.

'I owe you nothing,' replies Prentice, with that quivering, barely suppressed moral outrage that Poitier did so well in practically every film he ever made. 'If you carried that bag a million miles, you did what you were supposed to do, because you brought me into this world, and from that day you owe me everything you could ever do for me, like I will owe my son if I ever have another . . .'

The last time I watched that scene, I felt like applauding. But I didn't, because my three teenage children were watching it with me, late one Sunday afternoon, and I didn't want them to think that they could get out of doing the washing-up that evening, on the assumption that I owed them everything in terms of tackling the roasting pan, and they owed me nothing. Of course, that wasn't quite what Poitier, or William Rose's Academy Award-winning script, was getting at. The point, upon which the character continued to expand, was that a son should love, respect and honour his father but not feel in any way morally or materially beholden to him.

That seems to me about right, and yet in terms of our relationships we all live by different codes of behaviour. Whether out of simple filial love or a feeling of obligation, or a combination of the two, some adult children end up doing at the end of the relationship cycle what their parents did for them at the beginning: feeding them, helping them to walk, taking them to the toilet. Conversely, some fathers fall a very long way short of doing what Poitier said they were supposed to do, having brought their children into the world.

It was force of circumstance and the times in which he lived that brought Jane's maternal grandfather Colin, my mother-in-law Anne's father, into this category. Anne's mother died when Anne was three, and her sister Janet eighteen months. Colin was a miner; nobody expected him to bring up two little girls between demanding shifts down the pit. So the sisters went to live with their father's mother, but then she died too, after which they were raised by their mother's sister Dinah – the woman whose home Anne went to for a bath when, in December 1959, she first felt labour pains crossing the road in Barnsley.

I never met Dinah, but she was clearly a woman of substance, sharing not only her home with her mother-less little nieces, but even her bed. And she held down two jobs to pay for their upkeep, working in a school canteen by day and cleaning the public lavatories in Barnsley bus station by night. Even in the 1940s, I don't suppose that jobs got much more menial than cleaning

Barnsley bus station toilets, yet by all accounts Dinah did it uncomplainingly, only occasionally sending Anne to ask her father for money. That was usually a hopeless task. And it wasn't as though there was any appealing to the Child Support Agency, which was not set up until 1993. The CSA isn't much use now, but it was even less use fifty years before it existed.

Colin, despite living only a couple of miles away, visited his daughters no more than once a month. When in due course both daughters became mothers, he was much more attentive, dropping in to see Jackie and Jane every Sunday morning when they were small. I never knew Colin, either – he died just as I came on the Sanderson family scene – but I knew the affection Jane had for him. Clearly, he was considerably more dutiful as a granddad than he had ever been as a dad. He bought Anne a bike as a present for passing her 11-plus in 1947, but on the whole he was scarcely more engaged with Anne and Janet than if he had disappeared from their lives altogether. Yet in much later life, he took full credit for their achievements. Janet ended up running Barnsley social services, and Anne, who went on to have a distinguished career as an educationalist, remembers taking Colin to a local clinic where the nurse told him he'd done a marvellous job bringing up his two girls. 'Aye,' he said proudly and without irony, 'I 'ave.'

THE GOOD, THE DAD AND THE UGLY

And, in a hands-off sense, maybe he had. There are more ways than one for a father to bring up his children successfully. Sometimes, the biggest favour he can do for them is leaving the job to somebody else.

7

A Juvenile Herring Gull
In Summer Plumage

*There's nothing emasculating about being a
house-husband.*

The uterus might be more powerful than any muscle in
the male body but if ever someone works out a way of
harnessing the power of a father's pride, we could all
push boulders to the top of Mount Kilimanjaro.

It was fatherly pride, and the conviction that
Eleanor was a bonnier baby than most, that prompted
me to enter her in a nationwide competition when she
was but nine months old. This was the Boots Baby of
the Year contest, the entry form obtained, aptly
enough, from the very same branch where Jane had
bought the pregnancy testing kit that alerted us to our
entrant's existence in the first place. All we had to do

was send in a photograph, with our address and telephone number.

We were still staying with my mother and stepfather,
so it was my mother who took the call from the branch
manager to say that on the basis of her excellent photo
Eleanor had won the first heat, finishing top out of thirty-
eight babies. I was in the room with my mum when she
answered the phone. There was no excitement, still less
an expression of surprise. 'Of course Eleanor won,' she
told the manager, as if it had always been more a question of when, not whether, he would call. Eleanor's prize
was a teddy bear and a supply of nappies, but disappointingly she wasn't one of the five finalists, who were
invited with their parents to stay at the Ritz hotel in
London for the weekend. My mother assumed that this
was because they had lost the photo. I wondered how the
local Boots manager had handled the other thirty-seven
mothers and grandmothers.

Proud as I was of my pretty little girl, and for all that it
had been me who had brought home the entry form and
sent in Eleanor's photo, I soon realised that this fiercely
competitive instinct was more of a womanly trait. Male
pride in a young child is, I think, more straightforward
than female pride, which is laced with rivalry. For us the
first hint of it had come at the ante-natal classes, when
that one mother-to-be had proclaimed her intention to

play her newborn some Chopin as soon as she got home from the hospital. And at the post-natal groups to which Jane started taking Eleanor, some of the mums could not conceal their smugness that their baby was sitting up straighter than the next, or in due course crawling, talking or walking sooner.

The father's challenge later on the same day is to placate the mother, who feels wounded either because her child is lagging in the race to sit up straight, crawl, walk or talk; or – as in the case of my own child's mother – because she resents being made to feel like a sports coach, the NCT's answer to Alex Ferguson or Arsene Wenger, nurturing her protégé into bigger, better performances than the rest. 'They're so bloody competitive,' she complained, after practically every mother-and-baby session. 'It's not as though our babies aren't all going to crawl. Why does it need to be a race?'

Manifestly, it is at mother-and-baby groups that this competition really begins. Jane and I had assumed that it was a north London thing, north London being the global capital of competitive parenting, but we assumed wrong. Years later, after we had moved to Herefordshire and made dear friends of a couple called Jane and James, we compared notes and Jane told us that exactly the same had happened to them in Birmingham. She had taken her son Jack to an NCT post-natal group and

almost from the start there was ferocious one-upman-
ship, which did not especially favour Jack, who was slow
to both walk and talk.

But Jane kept going along, and she and James have
understandably fond memories of a birthday party in
Bourneville for a little red-haired boy called Toby, whose
parents had arranged for a man to show his birds of prey.
Toby was three years old, barely old enough to enjoy
pass-the-parcel, let alone the beady-eyed presence of an
eagle owl, but his mother and father were adamant that
Toby was extremely interested in wildlife. More interested, they implied, than anyone else's child.

Boy, were they mistaken. For some reason that Jane
and James still can't explain, Jack had formed an obsessive, possessive attachment to a battered old book of
his grandfather's, called *A Field Guide to the Birds of
Britain and Europe*, published in 1958. As I write, Jack
is sixteen, and still jolly bright but really not the slightest bit interested in the birdlife of Britain and Europe.
At three, however, he could have given both Bill Oddie
and David Attenborough a run for their money. He
looked at the book endlessly, and, a remarkably early
reader, even made sense of some of the words. Those
that he couldn't understand, he asked to be explained
to him. But Jane and James, lacking a competitive
streak, had kept this to themselves. To the other mums,

Jack was labelled as the late-talker, a serious, unde-
monstrative little boy whom they would have expected,
if they had thought about it at all, to sit quietly when
the birdman lifted a large feathered creature out of his
basket and said to the fifteen assembled kiddies, 'Hands
up if anybody who knows what this is.' His tone
suggested, not unreasonably, that nobody would. Only
he too was wrong. Jack, sitting cross-legged at the back,
stuck his hand up immediately.

'It's a peregrine falcon,' he said.

The man was visibly shocked. 'Well yes, that's right,'
he said, and then, recovering his composure, added, 'But
I bet nobody here knows what he eats.'

'Sausages,' came a cry from the front.

Almost wearily, in the presence of such ignorance,
three-year-old Jack stuck up his hand again. 'They like
voles but prefer carrion,' he said.

It wasn't to be the last time that little Jack used his
detailed knowledge of *A Field Guide to the Birds of
Britain and Europe* to explosive public effect. A few
months later, James was wheeling him in his pushchair
along the seafront at Great Yarmouth. When they
stopped to look at a gull just in front of them on the pavement, Jack leaning forward in his seat and scrutinising it
carefully, a female passer-by smiled down at him and
said, 'Isn't it a nice birdie?' He shot her a fleeting,

pitying glance. 'It's a juvenile herring gull in summer plumage,' he said. The woman gave a start, and hurried on, while James offered thanks that he had been in on a moment that would clearly go down in family lore.

Traditionally, fathers are not as involved as mothers in the walking, talking stage of a child's development. On the other hand, society has moved beyond the conventional constraints of family life as colourfully represented by Judith Kerr's classic 1968 children's book *The Tiger Who Came to Tea*, in which Mummy and Sophie tell Daddy, who has just arrived home from work and is already sitting in his armchair, about the unexpected arrival of a hungry, thirsty tiger, who ate all the food in the house and even drank all Daddy's beer. Like a true paterfamilias, Daddy then solves the problem by taking Mummy and Sophie out to a café for their supper, where they eat sausage, chips and ice-cream.

I like to cite *The Tiger Who Came to Tea*, partly because it was written when I was about the same age as Sophie, and I recognise my own 1960s small-town childhood in Kerr's illustrations, but also because it so charmingly evokes an era when the notion of a house-husband scarcely existed in Britain, and even the notion of both parents being out at work all day was still in its infancy. If the story were rewritten for the twenty-first century, Sophie would be a latch-key kid or, at the very least, in the care of a stay-at-home daddy while mummy (or perhaps a second daddy), goes out to work.

It is plain wrong, however, to see the house-husband as wholly a modern phenomenon. The very word husband stems from the medieval spelling of house – 'hus' – and the 'band' refers to the strength of the bond between the man and his home. Before the Industrial Revolution, mothers and fathers had clearly delineated household tasks. The mother's might have been the hand that rocked the cradle, but the father's was the hand that built the cradle. In 1795, a traveller visiting an English village chronicled how a long winter's evening might unfold in an ordinary household, observing that 'the husband cobbles shoes and attends the children while the wife spins'. More than two hundred years later, it would be more usual to find the wife cobbling shoes, attending the children and spinning, while the husband watches a Champions League match on ITV.

But in centuries gone by, men were very often thrust into the role of primary carers simply because so many mothers died in childbirth. It is estimated that in Britain today, one in twelve single-parent households is run by a man. Between about 1600 and 1800, however, it was more like one in four.

In the *Guardian* in early 2012, a house-husband called Roman Krznaric (another very *Guardian* byline) addressed just this issue. 'Let's not pretend that pre-industrial man was a domestic goddess,' he wrote. 'Women were typically still at the heart of the home and frequently couldn't drag their men out of the ale-house. But the modern hands-on father clearly has his predecessors.'

For Krznaric, the really intriguing question was how women came to shoulder the main burden of childcare. The answer was largely that the Industrial Revolution had created a patriarchal society, whereby the men went to the factory while the mothers stayed at home. But Krznaric also recognised that men were 'deskilled' by new industrial technology, diminishing their usefulness in the home. So they didn't, couldn't, cobble shoes any more. Yet there had been no clever gadgets invented to nurse sick children. That was still done by mothers, while fathers went out to work.

'Nobody is taught this history at school,' he wrote. 'But when I discovered it, one of the most powerful myths of our time exploded before my eyes. Despite decades of women's liberation, it is still widely seen as "natural" for women to be in charge of the home, while men charge off to the office. History has forced me to admit that, while women might breastfeed, there is no special female gene for sterilising bottles or cleaning the bathroom. This is what inspired me to join the proud – if forgotten – tradition of the house-husband.'

I applaud him for doing so, and yet, notwithstanding the new paternity-leave legislation, it is still mothers, or child-carers, who are likelier than fathers to hear the first word, see the first step. Nature's way of compensating for this is by making 'dadda' most commonly the earliest word. A national survey in 2010 showed that 'dadda' or variations thereof was the first fully formed utterance of 15 per cent of children, with 'mamma' or something similar registered by a mere 10 per cent. Of course, this may be because a D is easier to form than an M. It's also worth noting that 'beer' and 'Hoover' featured on the first-word list, and perhaps a few rather ruder offerings.

The expression 'out of the mouths of babes' comes from the New Testament, so it seems a little blasphemous to quote it in relation to expletives and other vulgarities, but here goes anyway. I can't recall which actress it was who not so long ago told a marvellous story on a chat show, about her angelic-looking daughter who was sitting in a high-chair when her grandmother, the actress's mother, came into the kitchen one tea-time. The child looked up sweetly from her mashed bananas and custard, shook her blonde ringlets, and said, 'What the fuck are you doing here?' All hell broke loose, with the grandmother accusing the actress of swearing in front of the child, the actress accusing her mother of over-reacting, and the child doubtless making a mental note of what it takes to cause such a stir.

Of course, a child can also be a source of embarrassment *before* it learns to talk. Eleanor had only just reached the crawling stage when we took her to the flat of some childless friends, Glenn and Linda, and there let her explore, secure in the knowledge that there were no stairs for her to fall down, and only realising that we needed to keep a closer eye on her when she crawled back into the living room from their bedroom clutching a pack of Linda's contraceptive tablets obtained from a bedside drawer. It might have been worse – a vibrating sex toy, for instance – but it was still an awkward moment, relieved only when we started wondering what might have happened if she'd managed to open the packet and eat one. Would she have disappeared?

I was, as it happened, already used to the embarrassments that can befall an adoring father. When Eleanor was but six weeks old, I carried her, fast asleep in her car seat, into the men's toilets at a service station on the M1. I only needed to pee but it didn't seem right to park her by the urinals, so we went into a cubicle, where I sat down looking forward to studying the sports pages in that day's newspaper. Scarcely had I started on the football reports, however, than baby Eleanor opened her eyes.

'Hello, little sausage,' I cooed softly. 'Have you woken up?'

It was only when I heard a man hurriedly finishing his business in the adjacent cubicle, and making a hasty exit, that I realised that my words, and in particular the sausage reference, had through the flimsy cubicle wall been open to misinterpretation. In fact, my use of 'sausage' as an endearment would be misunderstood again. When Joseph was a toddler he once sat at the top of a playground slide in Muswell Hill, north London, adamantly refusing to come down, and oblivious to the build-up of children behind him. 'Come on, sausage,' I repeatedly encouraged him from the bottom, but he continued to sit tight, shaking his head, whereupon the frustrated infant directly behind him shouted exasperatedly to his own father: 'Daddy! Sausage won't go down the slide!'

Those years between two and about six are fraught with potential embarrassment for parents. And in north London it is a particular middle-class variety of embarrassment. I'm told that it was in Waitrose on Crouch End Broadway that a little boy was heard earnestly saying to his father: 'Daddy, does Lego have a T at the end, like Merlot?' It's a story that reminds me of my friend Steve's daughter Olivia – also raised in north London – whose grandmother asked her, when she was very small, whether she had ever been to Bath? 'No,' she replied solemnly, 'but I've been to Barthelona.'

As for Joseph, the obstruction he caused at the top of a playground slide was a blessed problem to have compared with what we'd anticipated when Jane was pregnant with him, at least during a challenging couple of weeks which followed an alarming telephone call from the Whittington Hospital in Archway one Saturday morning.

The call was to report the results of a routine blood test, called a triple test, which had thrown up an extremely high probability of a chromosomal imbalance in the baby. We were given a one-in-eight chance of our second child being born with Down's syndrome. Once we had absorbed the shock we stayed up late into the night, and many nights thereafter, discussing the implications. Would we, could we, have a pregnancy terminated if we knew the baby wasn't going to be 'normal'? Should we opt for an amniocentesis, a diagnostic procedure requiring the insertion of an improbably large needle through the abdominal wall and into the amniotic sac, which would tell us for sure whether the baby had Down's syndrome but which itself carried a one in two hundred chance of causing a miscarriage?

Never exactly a mathematics whizz in my schooldays, these different sets of probabilities reminded me uncomfortably of Venn diagrams, and headache-inducing multiplications involving fractions. What was one in eight multiplied by one in two hundred? Or did it in fact need long division? For a while even my dreams became bogged down with random variables and variable randoms. When I confided in my boss at the *Mail on Sunday*, a horse-racing enthusiast, he offered me encouragement by likening the situation to the 2.45 at Uttoxeter. Nobody in their right mind would put their shirt on an 8/1 shot, he said. After all, in plain terms, it means that something is seven times more likely not to happen than to happen.

At the BBC, where Jane was by now working as a producer on *Woman's Hour*, her boss Sally Feldman, the programme's editor, tried similarly to offer solace, though her choice of analogy could have been better. 'If you were one of eight people applying for a job,' she told Jane, 'you wouldn't expect to get it, would you?' If nothing else, that at least had the effect of distracting Jane from the possibility that she was carrying a Down's syndrome baby. 'What does she mean, I wouldn't get the sodding job?' she thought, indignantly.

Away from work, friends and acquaintances kept telling us that the same thing had happened to them: that they'd been given a one in thirty-five chance, or one in sixty, or one in 250, and everything had turned out wonderfully. But nobody reported anything as high as one in eight, and of course all these examples of happy endings made Jane in particular, whose glass was resolutely half-empty while I tried to keep mine half-full, feel sure that the balance of probabilities was weighted even more heavily against us.

In the end, we decided that we would have the 'amnio'. When you start casually abbreviating words for medical procedures, you know that your life is taking a new turn. And while we waited for the hospital appointment, and in the days afterwards while we waited for the results, we continued to feel oppressed by this grim game of probabilities. Meanwhile, practically overnight, we started encountering people with Down's syndrome everywhere: seemingly on every bus, train and pavement; in every shop, bank and queue. One day, when a minibus stopped alongside me on an otherwise empty London street, it disgorged no fewer than nine teenagers with Down's syndrome. We mentioned this to Jane's community midwife, a jolly Irishwoman called Sandra, then determinedly changed the subject.

'Are you planning on getting away for Christmas, Sandra?'

'Yes, I'm going to stay with my sister and her family in . . .' – with an 'oh no' she clapped both hands to her ruddy cheeks – '. . . County Down.'

We took all this as a sure sign that our baby had

Down's, yet would that really be such a terrible thing? I phoned the Down's Syndrome Society to get more information, and of course they told me that children with Down's are invariably a happy and rewarding presence in a family. I also called a friend whose much-loved older brother had Down's (and who told me, rather shockingly, that her parents had once admitted that if they had their time again, and had been presented with the choice, they would have terminated the pregnancy). In the event, the amnio showed that my boss had got it right with his horse-racing analogy: if I'd backed this particular 8/1 chance, I would have lost. There was no chromosomal abnormality; the baby was fine. Joseph was born at the Whittington on 19 April 1995, by emergency Caesarian section.

8

Son Of My Father

When your firstborn goes to school, brace yourself
for some unexpected emotions.

It wasn't meant to be a Caesarian. Jane had desperately wanted a home delivery, which for me had always meant lamb pasanda, pilau rice and a peshwari naan, itself a messy enough business, although childbirth in the upstairs bathroom promised to be even messier.

Home births weren't hard to arrange in the London Borough of Haringey in the mid-1990s: anything to relieve the barely tolerable pressure on the area's NHS hospitals. Jane's decision was why she had been assigned Sandra as a midwife. Sandra specialised in home midwifery, and so effectively doubled as a health visitor both before and after the birth. However, when a scan revealed a placenta praevia, a complication whereby the placenta attaches itself to the uterine wall covering the cervix, we were summoned to see the consultant obstetrician at the Whittington, Miss Henson, who informed us matter-of-factly that the baby would need to be delivered in hospital by Caesarian section.

Jane, having set her heart on giving birth under her own roof with as little medical intervention as possible, burst into tears at the prospect of the ultimate kind of medical intervention. Miss Henson, a no-nonsense sort as I suppose one would hope a consultant obstetrician to be, bluntly told her not to be silly, pointing out that not so many years earlier, before ultrasound, a woman with placenta praevia would likely have bled to death during childbirth. Ours would overnight have become a single-parent family, with me the single parent. Jane, normally a no-nonsense woman herself, took the point and pulled herself together. I kept quiet, but ventured a quip when we got back to our street in Crouch End, and found a vehicle blocking next-door's drive, stopping their car getting out. How apt, I noted, that it was a Toyota Previa. It was my first obstetrics-related gag, and, we both agreed, quite a good one. Indeed it felt like a small rite of passage, as though I had finally come of age in terms of understanding at least some of the myriad mysteries of a woman's insides.

A date was made for the Caesarian. It felt weird determining our second child's birthday in advance, but as it happened Joseph had other ideas. On 19 April, a Wednesday, and still a week or so away from the scheduled operation, I got home from the Associated Newspapers offices in Kensington to find a note pinned to the front door (older readers will remember the era of notes pinned to front doors, those halcyon days when we knew Blackberry and Apple only as pie fillings). The note said that Jane had gone into labour and our next-door neighbour, Bridget, had driven her to the Whittington. Eleanor, aged twenty-two months, had been deposited with other neighbours, next door but one. I dashed to the hospital, just in time to see Jane before she was wheeled in for her emergency Caesarian. And forty-five minutes or so later, with her still unconscious under general anaesthetic, a red-haired nurse emerged from the operating theatre and delivered a 7 lb 8 oz baby into my arms, with the unvarnished but memorable words: 'Congratulations, you have a son.'

We were united in wanting to call him Joseph, which would have been Eleanor's name had she been a boy. Joe Viner sounded to us like a good name, a solid name, a name with integrity. What we didn't consider, I still think excusably, was that his peer group at secondary school fifteen years or so later would transpose his initials

118

and call him Voe Jiner, squeezing maximum mirth from its similarity to 'vagina'.

Already in this book I've had some gentle fun at the expense of rock stars and actors who seem to think that a birth certificate is a place for flights of whimsy, without much thought as to whether a gawky teenager or a middle-aged parent or indeed a feeble old person in a nursing home will enjoy being lumbered with a daft name. But in a way we too were guilty of not thinking it through, and if I have any tips for parents-to-be, it's to bear fully in mind that a name is for life, not just for infancy but for adolescence and beyond.

None of which entered my head, of course, as I sat outside the operating theatre pondering the significance of having a son. Was it any more significant than having a daughter? Of course not. I couldn't have been any more euphoric when our firstborn turned out to be a girl, just as I would have been thrilled to have a second daughter (and not only as an opportunity to use up one of the names that the St Mary's midwife had discarded). Nevertheless, there was something profoundly, viscerally meaningful about becoming the father of a son.

It wasn't that I held him in the hospital looking forward to going to our first football match together, or buying him his first pint of bitter, or any of that corny male-bonding stuff. But it still had something to do with the same-gender dimension. As a babe in arms myself I had been adopted, and still, at the time of Joseph's arrival, didn't know anything about my biological father. We met for the first time three or four years later, but in 1995 nobody had ever told me that I looked the image of my dad, and perhaps for that reason, and also slightly narcissistically, I liked the prospect of Joseph one day being told that he looked just like his old man.

That said, anyone whose first record purchase was Chicory Tip's number one hit 'Son of My Father', as mine had been in February 1972 at the impressionable age of ten, would surely have to be aware that raising a child in your own image is the great no-no of fatherhood. 'Son of my father,' it goes, 'Changing, rearranging into someone new/ Son of my father/ Collecting and selecting independent views.'

Now, it has to be said that most of Chicory Tip's lyrics in that song don't really stand up to close scrutiny; indeed, God bless the internet, because after just a few minutes of idly Googling around I found an entire debate on their meaning, conducted online in January 2009. It is truly one of the wonders of the age, that you can find an earnest discussion on an internet forum concerning the words of Chicory Tip's 'Son of My Father' almost thirty-seven years after it climbed to number one. Anyway, the consensus seemed to be that the words didn't make much sense, but the overall message remains clear enough: that the son in the song was constricted and controlled by his father until he broke free and became his own man.

Still, in Joseph's case, it was clear from the start that he would be his own man. His arrival a week before the scheduled Caesarian had been an early indication that he would do things on his own terms, and if his strength of character was evident long before he started teething, the arrival of teeth allowed him to assert it even more; albeit in a particularly regrettable way, by sinking them into other children. He wasn't motivated by malice, more by frustration. He didn't hit or push other kids when there was a proprietorial issue over a toy; he bit them. It went on sporadically for four or five months, until he was about two years old, and during that time we did our best to police it, going so far as to withdraw him and his occasional anti-social tendencies from the morning playgroup sessions in a nearby church hall.

When it did happen it was invariably more upsetting for us than for the parents of the children he had bitten. However, Jane went one lunchtime to pick him up from a friend's house, and arrived to find a terrible ballyhoo, with another mother quite hysterical.

'Joseph has bitten Archie's nose,' she cried, gesturing

at a bawling little boy, while Joseph stood in the corner of the room, his expression a mixture of pride and worry.

There was certainly no questioning it, not with a perfect circle of teeth marks at the end of the child's throbbing proboscis, and Jane was duly appalled, if also taken aback by a reaction that could hardly have been more histrionic if a baying pack of rabid dingoes had burst into the front room. It wasn't as though blood had been drawn. Still, Joseph was swiftly removed from the crime scene, and of course the sternest of bollockings was administered on the way home.

That evening, we took a phone call. It was the young victim's father, a man neither of us had ever met.

'Can you please tell me what action has been taken?' he said, pompously.

Clearly, the child's mother had still been distressed when her husband got home from work, so here he was, gravely implying that the matter was now out of the realm of silly, sensitive women, and in the firm, capable hands of the male of the species. For that reason he'd probably have preferred me at the other end of the line, but he got Jane. She apologised profusely, again, and assured him that Joseph had been given an almighty telling-off, accompanied by all sorts of dark warnings of what would happen in the event of another such episode.

'Frankly,' he said, 'I think that's the very least you should do.'

The conversation reached a brusque conclusion soon afterwards, and he didn't get as much chance as he might have liked to elaborate, but plainly he thought that child behavioural experts should be brought in, if not the Metropolitan Police, and that we had on our hands a tiny version of Hannibal Lecter, whose graduation to full-blown cannibalism was only a matter of time. Our anxiety about Joseph's unfortunate habit gave way, practically at a stroke, to defensive indignation. How dare this supercilious prick take such a high moral tone with us? Who did he think he was? To which the answer, I knew even at the time, was that he simply thought he was being a dutiful father, behaving as he thought a father should.

To an extent, that is the best any father can do, though of course there are about as many interpretations of the role of a father as there are fathers. Oblivious to this fact, however, in 2002 the Equal Opportunities Commission commissioned a study called 'Dads on Dads', which examined working fathers' perceptions of their roles within the family. It identified just four distinct types: the 'Enforcer Dad', the 'Entertainer Dad', the 'Useful Dad' and the 'Fully Involved Dad'.

The Enforcer was defined as a man not involved at all

with the day-to-day care of his kids. In fact he barely qualifies as a dad, being very much a father, if not a 'sir'. He sees it as his job to instil discipline, to impose a moral code, to give his children a backbone. His spiritual alter ego is the forbidding Victorian paterfamilias so familiar to us from nineteenth-century literature and endless TV and film adaptations, and it is hard to believe that he exists in sufficient numbers these days to represent a type, but, according to the EOC, he does.

The Entertainer, by stark contrast, plays hide-and-seek and indoor cricket with the children, also wrestling with them and giving them fireman's lifts, very often while the mother is busy with housework and cleaning, these being jobs at which he is wholly useless. Most other dads are not quite sure whether to look on him with envy or pity. Most kids think he's a hoot, although there's every chance that, as they grow older, his own will begin to consider him a bit of a pillock.

Then there is Useful Dad, who obligingly mucks in around the house, but usually only when the mother tells him what needs doing.

Finally, the Fully Involved Dad shares housework and childcare responsibilities equally, rendering the roles of mother and father more or less interchangeable. 'Dads in this category are more likely to need the kind of flexibility at work that is more closely associated with working mothers,' concluded the EOC report, approvingly.

I don't know how much expense and time was invested in carrying out this study, but in asserting that 'most fathers fall into the middle two categories, playing a supporting role in the household', and that 'fewer are Enforcers or Fully Involved dads', it hardly revealed anything that most of us couldn't have worked out in the pub. It was absurdly simplistic. How many fathers in the twenty-first century fall fully into one of these categories, or even straddle only two of them? Rather, there are divisions, and sub-divisions, and divisions of sub-divisions, and even then you can't really generalise about fathers as a homogenous group. There are no neat categories.

In my own case, I recognise characteristics of Entertainer, Useful, Fully Involved, and, yes, stern Enforcer too, plus hundreds of other traits not even vaguely alluded to in the EOC report. For example, what about Little-Boy Dad, for whom, disconcertingly and sometimes downright unnervingly, the responsibilities of fatherhood bring on the emotions of boyhood?

Let me offer an example. When Eleanor was approaching school age, there was one state primary school in our part of north London to which we wanted her to go with all our hearts. This, I have to confess, is a peculiar and unhealthy phenomenon more prevalent among middle-class London dwellers than anywhere else in Britain, and quite possibly anywhere else in the world. If I had a pound for every angst-ridden conversation about schooling options between middle-class London parents, I would be able to buy Chelsea from Roman Abramovich, with change left over for his super-yacht. And although it is mostly a Mum Thing, dads are inexorably sucked in too.

This was one of the reasons I wanted to leave London in 2002, because I couldn't bear any more earnest dinner-party discussions about schools. At some of the north London dinner parties we went to, if you'd also prohibited any references to property prices and vasectomies, there would have been nothing left, except, 'Please could you pass the salt and pepper?'

It was for this reason that a year or two earlier Jane and I, with our good friends Kim and Will, had cooked up a dastardly plan, whereby we would all start casually dropping into conversation the name of an excellent yet entirely fictitious state secondary school that was soaring up the league tables and sending increasing numbers of sixth-formers to Oxford and Cambridge. We called it Dame Sally Allen's, located it indeterminately and a little rudely somewhere between 'Clissold Park and the Arsenal', and revelled sadistically in the expressions of alarm on the faces of parents who wondered how such a go-getting educational establishment could possibly have slipped off their radar.

Even more gratifyingly, it wasn't long before people began mentioning it back to us, saying things like, 'We're thinking of sending her to Dame Sally Allen's' or, 'Have you heard that a team from Dame Sally Allen's won the world under-eighteens debating championships in Copenhagen last week?, which was a fiction that we had started. Naturally, we feigned interest, and at social gatherings continued to laud the achievements of a non-existent school. All that was more than ten years ago, yet I wouldn't be surprised if even now there are people in Crouch End and Muswell Hill wondering about sixth-form availability at Dame Sally Allen's. At any rate, with a bit of imagination, there was no end of fun available at the expense of anxiously aspirational parents, although we only knew it because that's what we had been, too.

The infants school to which we longed to send Eleanor was called St Mary's, confusingly the same name as the hospital in which she'd been born. It owed its fine local reputation in large part to a famously redoubtable headteacher called Mrs Morgan, and Jane and I made an appointment to see her, taking Eleanor with us. Significantly, it was my first time in a primary school since my own primary schooldays, and the rows of shiny wooden lockers containing little black plimsolls, the wall bars in the hall, the smells, the noise, immediately in a Proustian or possibly Pavlovian way, or maybe both, brought out the short-trousered child in me.

Compounding this was Mrs Morgan's immaculately coiffed imperiousness; think Margaret Thatcher *circa* 1983. It was all I could do, on entering her office, not to settle down cross-legged on the floor and break into 'All Things Bright and Beautiful'. And so when she wrote down Eleanor's name on a form, and then looked at me and barked 'parents' names?' without any hesitation I yelped the names of my own mother and stepfather. Jane looked at me askance. Even Eleanor looked puzzled. 'Actually,' said Jane, 'parents' names are Jane and Brian.' Mrs Morgan glared at me over her half-moon spectacles, and reached for the Tipp-Ex. Somehow, I managed not to cry, or worse, wet myself.

9

Useless Twat Dad

If your partner wants a home birth, make sure you
at least know how to operate the washing-machine.

From my extensive research, I know that I am not the
only father to experience this kind of disorientation
when a child starts school. I'm certain that fathers are
more prone than mothers, anyway, probably because it
is usually mums who very quickly absorb the school run,
and school life generally, into their daily routines. I did
plenty of school runs myself to and from the gates of St
Mary's, yet I was never fully at ease there, not in the way
that Jane was.

'Hello Cath, hello Frankie, hello Nicola,' I would hear
her call to other mums, on the few occasions we picked
up the kids together. 'Hello Louise, hello Sandy, hello

Deborah, hello Yvonne, hello Greta, hello Carolyn . . .'
And to their children: "Hello Sam, hello Albie, hello
Sinead, hello Maddie, hello Casper, hello Binka . . .'

I cut short this litany of hellos only because I don't
want to overface you. At the time they seemed to go on
almost for ever. I was lost in admiration. How did she
know all those names? It seemed to be part of that maternal, nurturing impulse. It certainly eluded most of the
fathers I knew, even those who were regulars at the
school gates.

Heaven knows that in this age of house-husbands
and Fully Involved Dads, I shouldn't really make
gender comparisons, but I think it's fair to say that
many fathers, unlike most mothers, have to overcome a
degree of self-consciousness at the school gates, or even
when picking up their toddlers from nursery. The
comedian Michael McIntyre has a very funny routine
about this, explaining just how much of an outsider he
felt when he first went to collect his son from playgroup. At first he was roundly ignored, but when a
generous-spirited mother finally did attempt to engage
him in conversation, asking which child was his, he
tried misguidedly to crack a joke. 'None of them,' he
said. Nervously, she backed away.

Still, there was something about Eleanor starting
school that felt like a rite of passage for me almost as

much as it clearly was for her, launching me into a world of PTA fundraisers, parents' evenings, sports days, concerts and nativity plays that had previously been entirely untrodden territory, like parts of Africa to Victorian explorers, who knew they were there but not what they contained.

It certainly felt momentous to see her, aged four, in her school uniform for the first time. Four years old is surely too young for a child to start school; indeed I once heard the TV writer Kay Mellor on the radio, recalling that when she'd started school, also aged four, she had still been so attached to her dummy, and so aghast at being separated from it, that her mother came every lunchtime and surreptitiously stuck it through the fence so that she could have a reassuring, restorative suck.

Eleanor had never had a dummy. Jane and I were united in our dislike of the things. Nor did she rely on a comfort blanket in the form of a piece of cloth, normally silk or velvet, as some of her little friends did. And she seemed to set off for school each day with something approaching a spring in her step. Nevertheless, after she had been in reception class for about a month, I dropped her off one morning, but on a sudden impulse waited outside the school fence – risking arrest, now that I think about it – to watch her in the playground.

I hoped to see her at the heart of a lively group of

children, skipping and chattering and laughing, but feared that I might instead see her with only herself for company. Almost inevitably, heart-rendingly, it was the latter. She sat alone on a bench making a great perform-ance of playing with a doll, but occasionally looking up hopefully, as if willing somebody to join her. After a while, I wandered away, a little troubled, for it was the first time that I had felt powerless to improve my child's day. But I also realised that this was an important step forward for both of us; that at a very basic level she was learning to cope, independently, with the world, and I was learning to let her. It's a lesson that fathers find easier to absorb than mothers, in my experience. Jane to this day will do everything in her ever-diminishing power to ensure that her children's lives at school or university are as happy as they can possibly be. Whereas I, on the whole, take the view that they're better off resolving their difficulties themselves.

On a very few occasions those difficulties have related to friendship groups. What I never anticipated on becom-ing the father of a school-age child was that it would throw up friendship-group issues for me, too, for the first time since my own schooldays. No sooner had Eleanor started at St Mary's than I found myself plunged into a kind of fathers' hierarchy, whereby the dads of older children, who'd long been a fixture at PTA events, looked down on newcomers like seasoned officers on newly promoted lance-bombardiers, barely even acknowledging their existence.

Some of them did, anyway. Eager to throw myself into the fundraising fray, and always happy to lark about in the name of a good cause, I volunteered during Eleanor's first summer at St Mary's to be part of a human fruit machine at the school fête. This entailed me and two other dads wandering around dressed like clowns and, on being paid twenty pence, whirling round three times before producing a lemon, a plum or a banana from a bag. If we all brandished the same piece of fruit, we paid out.

It was a nice day and I enjoyed myself. Eleanor and three-year-old Joseph were hugely tickled to see their daddy looking and behaving like a fool, and we certainly added to the general air of merriment while raising a few quid for the school. It helped that one of the other dads was already a good mate. The other was a guy called Mark, who had older children than ours and, aptly enough, was one of the PTA's big bananas. He'd always seemed a trifle stand-offish to me, but, like the forbidding Mrs Morgan sitting imperiously behind her desk, PTA politics made me feel like a child again. I wanted him to be my friend.

Accordingly, I took childlike pleasure in the fact that

Mark and I got along famously that day. We were turning synchronised circles, wearing red noses and making
silly fruit machine noises, so it was hard for him to be
stand-offish, but he seemed to have enjoyed my company
and as I walked home with the children at the end of a
jolly afternoon I felt as though I'd been inducted into the
best and biggest gang. I knew it was pathetic of me, but
that was how it was. And the next time I saw Mark, at
another PTA event, I nodded a friendly hello. He
blanked me. And continued to blank me at all subsequent fêtes, quiz nights, barbecues or whatever. Which
even at the time I realised was more his problem than
mine – in plain terms, he was being a dickhead – but that
didn't stop indignation welling up inside me. It didn't
reach my tear ducts, thank God.

Meanwhile, with Eleanor's reception year behind her
and less than a month before she started Year 1, the
family unit expanded again, with the birth, on 14 August
1998, of Jacob. That was a rite of passage, too, in the
sense that I now felt that our unit was complete.

Some parents deem the family complete with one
child, some with two, but for us the magic number was
three. We'd always wanted three kids, and once we had
them, we never wanted any more. And better yet, Jane
finally got the home birth she'd yearned for second time
around, expelling Jacob in a spectacular, gooey slither in

our en-suite bathroom. In most parts of the country, we were told, there would have been no chance of a home birth when the previous birth had required an emergency Caesarian, but in the London Borough of Haringey, if it meant one more free bed at the Whittington, no questions were asked. This information worried me, and I was also slightly disappointed that we wouldn't be going back to the Whittington, where, while visiting Jane the day after Joseph's arrival, I had seen a woman in the maternity ward with a guard on either side of the bed. That wasn't a spectacle you see every day. She was a heavily pregnant inmate of nearby Holloway Prison.

Whatever my reservations, a woman surely deserves the last say in where she is to give birth, so the upstairs bathroom it was. Again, Sandra was the midwife assigned to us, but she happened to be away when Jane went into labour. Instead, a matronly West Indian woman called Margaret arrived on the doorstep.

We'd heard about Margaret, who had delivered the babies of several of our friends and was considered rather fabulous. She was certainly a character, with the most improbably deep, fruitily posh voice I'd heard since Brian Blessed had last appeared on a television chat show, and without anything like his amount of facial hair. She also had a grown-up daughter, Mel, who shortly afterwards became, with 'Nasty' Nick, the most written-about participant in the first series of Channel 4's *Big Brother*. If you can remember when *Big Brother* seemed fresh and innovative, rather than the stale, exploitative bore-fest it became, then you might also recall just how it obsessed the tabloids in particular (at the Leveson Inquiry in early 2012, the former editor of the *Daily Star* actually declared his pride at having led no fewer than twenty-eight consecutive issues of his paper with *Big Brother* stories) and in 2000 they briefly turned Mel into the woman the nation loved to hate. I wondered whether I could interest the *Star* or the *Sun* in a story about having had her mother as a midwife: 'Mel's Mum Saw Wife's Bum'.

Actually, I didn't. It would have been shameful to exploit our home birth experience for financial gain, and in any case, there had been shame enough in not knowing what to do when Margaret bundled up the towels on which Jane had knelt while giving birth and dumped them into my arms.

'Can you go and put these in the washing-machine?' she said, fruitily.

I nodded, uncertainly. I knew where the washing-machine was, of course, but not how it worked. It was the only practical task I was charged with carrying out that night, and it was beyond me. Other than that, I was entirely surplus to requirements, while Jane and Margaret got on with the important business of bringing our third child into the world. Fatherhood is like that sometimes, and not only during childbirth.

Not so long ago, incidentally, a woman clearly at the end of her domestic tether posted the following on the parenting website Mumsnet. 'It has just dawned on me that my husband has absolutely no idea how hard I work looking after three kids under four whilst running my own business. I want to punch the useless twat!' There were scores, if not hundreds, of sympathetic responses, and it occurs to me now that Useless Twat Dad really should have been one of the categories unveiled by the Equal Opportunities Commission survey. I'd prefer not to think of myself in those terms, but it was certainly rather uselessly twattish of me not to know which buttons to press on the Zanussi.

At this point, I'd better not name the friend of ours, a mother of three, whose husband takes a fortnight-long holiday with his mates every year. During one of these extended breaks Jane asked her whether she missed him. 'Not really,' she said. 'In fact, if I could find a vibrator that puts the bins out, I really wouldn't mind if he was gone for longer.' She would be the first to defend him from charges of being a Useless Twat Dad, but I suppose it's salutary for us fathers to bear in mind that not being useless doesn't mean being indispensable.

THE GOOD, THE DAD AND THE UGLY

I suppose, too, that it would be interesting to know in which countries, which societies, Useless Twat Dad is most prevalent. Or least prevalent, come to that. The latter distinction probably belongs to the Aka pygmies of the western Congo Basin. According to an anthropologist called Barry Hewlett, who devoted the best part of twenty years studying them, the Aka men have an extraordinarily keen sense of fatherly responsibilities, most likely as a consequence of the subsistence hunting which occupies so much of their lives, and in which entire families traditionally take part. It is the father's job on hunting trips to carry the children, often over long distances, and Hewlett reckons that the carrying duties attach them emotionally as well as physically to their children, to such an extent that they cheerfully take on other burdens of childcare, too. I don't suppose washing-machines are especially common in the western Congo Basin, but if they were, you can be sure that every adult male in the Aka tribe would know exactly how to operate them.

Some distance north-west of the Congo, in Crouch End, Jacob had been born shortly after midnight, with Eleanor and Joseph soundly asleep and oblivious. It was typical of Joseph that he should sleep through all that commotion, yet wake us at regular intervals through all the nights of peace and quiet. Still, we valued the opportunity to lie on our bed with newborn Jacob between us, and nobody in the world except us and Margaret the midwife even aware of his existence.

In the morning I went to tell the other two that they had a new little brother. Eleanor rushed up the stairs to our bedroom as fast as possible. If her little legs could have cleared three steps at a time they would have done. But Joseph, aged three years and four months, tarried.

'Joseph, aren't you coming to say hello?' I called.

'I'm just looking at the weather,' he replied, noncommittally, and sure enough he was standing on our half-landing gazing fixedly out of the window, clearly determined to treat the newcomer with cool circumspection.

It was an early exhibition of sibling politics, and by all accounts not uncommon. A hundred yards down the road, just five weeks earlier, our friend Ali had given birth to her third child. For weeks she had prepared her younger daughter, two-year-old Rosie, for the arrival, and when Rosie was summoned to meet Jake for the first time, all the textbook briefings appeared to have paid off.

'Ahh, it's really cute,' said Rosie, gazing at the baby from a few paces away.

Ali congratulated herself: Rosie didn't seem at all disconcerted by the sight of a baby in her precious mother's arms.

Rosie moved in closer. 'Who's its mummy?' she asked, guilelessly. Clearly, there was still work to do.

In our house, once Joseph became accustomed to having a younger rival for his mummy's attention, the only shadow was cast by Jacob's tongue. That was the whole point; it was big enough to cast a shadow. I'd noticed just moments after the birth that his little mouth didn't seem able to contain his tongue, and in the days and weeks that followed it became clear that our third child had an unusual whopper of a tongue, which was also clearly asymmetrical, with an off-centre tip some distance from where we might have expected it to be. In all other respects little Jacob was perfect, but we couldn't help wondering whether his tongue signified some other problem.

We went to see our GP, who conceded that he had never seen a tongue quite like it, and referred us to an Ears, Nose and Throat consultant at the Whittington. He too was flummoxed, and passed us on to someone illustrious at the Royal Free Hospital in Hampstead, who similarly wasn't sure how worried to be about Jacob's tongue, and recommended that we take him to the maxillofacial unit at the world-famous Great Ormond Street Hospital for children.

By this time Jacob was six months old, a demonstrably happy, active, alert baby, and although his tongue was still very much in evidence, Jane was pretty certain that there wasn't, in fact, anything to worry about. I was less sure, but mothers, maybe even in the Aka tribe, generally have more reliable instincts than fathers in these matters. And in the waiting room at Great Ormond Street, even I began to wonder what we'd been concerned about. Sitting opposite us was a couple with an inert young child who looked severely disfigured. They must have looked across at Jacob gurgling on my knee and wondered what the hell we were doing there. Sure enough, when we got in to see the consultant, he checked Jacob up and down and then said: 'You have a beautiful baby. He has a slightly unusual tongue, that's all. Take him home and enjoy him.' So we did, and of course revelled, as Jacob grew, in his party-piece of being able to lick the end of his nose.

We also, as he grew, had to adjust to the fact that we were now outnumbered by our children. Which brings me to the BBC sitcom about two bright, likeable but stressed south London parents struggling with the demands of raising their three kids. It would have been a welcome addition to the TV schedules whatever name the writers, Guy Jenkin and Andy Hamilton, had given it, but it was a particular masterstroke to call it *Outnumbered*. Television had for years been delivering up sitcoms about middle-class mums and dads grappling with the responsibilities and challenges of parenting, so in that sense *Outnumbered* was simply ploughing the same extensively churned furrow as *My Family*, *2point4 Children*, *Butterflies*, *Bless This House*, *And Mother Makes Three* and loads of others back practically to the beginning of the medium. But there was never a simpler or better title.

I can quite understand why some parents call a halt to reproduction before this adults–children ratio tips, see-saw like, in favour of the kids. But, as already chronicled, three seemed to us like the right number, not just emotionally and instinctively but also pragmatically: with four offspring we felt we'd need a bigger house and a bigger car, not to mention all the other complications that would arise from being outnumbered two to one. Even being outnumbered three to two had its difficulties, however, not least on the day when I was sitting in my little office at home talking to the DJ Johnnie Walker live on Radio 2.

At the time I was the *Mail on Sunday*'s TV critic, and had a regular Tuesday slot on the Johnnie Walker Show, in which I would share with the Great British Public my suggestion of the best programmes to watch on telly that evening. The day's producer would phone me at home at a pre-appointed time, I'd chat for four or five minutes to Johnnie, and that was that. Easy. Except that on one particular Tuesday the pre-appointed time coincided with Jane breastfeeding Jacob in our bedroom, and Joseph going to the toilet directly outside my office.

Normally, I would have reminded Jane about my broadcasting commitment, and for those few minutes with me on the radio she would make sure that the children were safely corralled out of earshot, but on that Tuesday, I forgot. So just as Johnnie introduced me to the nation, or whatever portion of the nation was listening to Radio 2, I heard Joseph go into the loo just the other side of the wall, and prayed, while trying to talk knowledgeably about television, that I would finish my job before he finished his. I didn't.

'Mummy, can you wipe my bottom?' he yelled.

From our bedroom came a distant, ominous shout: 'I'm busy, ask Daddy.'

There followed a three-year-old's irritated hurrumph, and then, with added volume: 'DADDY, CAN YOU WIPE MY BOTTOM?'

There was no pretending that this stentorian if high-pitched plea hadn't carried across the airwaves. 'I think you might be needed elsewhere, Brian,' said a chuckling Johnnie Walker, while I mentally wrote an obituary for my short-lived broadcasting career, and a friend of mine, driving on the A565 near Liverpool, almost swerved off the road because he was laughing so much.

He clipped the kerb so hard that a hubcap was dislodged, apparently, but not even that was enough to arrest his helpless mirth.

I had known after less than nine hours of fatherhood, when I unwittingly held up the entire Australian cricket team while I snapped Jane and Eleanor climbing out of the back of a London cab, that it would propel me into many unexpected situations. But I never thought it would make me a national laughing-stock.

10

All Joints On The Table Will Be Carved

Enforcing table manners is important – but possibly not at the expense of everybody's happiness.

Not all fathers get to become a national laughing-stock, but I should think that most of them, at one stage or another, and whether they know it or not, become a domestic laughing-stock. It is one of our roles in life, to be laughed at by our families, and it is a role I have fulfilled diligently if often unwittingly over the years, not least through my efforts to institute good table manners.

Significantly, this was something that my own father, too, took very much to heart. When I was fourteen, before he died, he was the one who policed the family meal table, and I don't think 'policed' is the wrong verb, for if he'd had a truncheon, he would have wielded it.

Certainly, just as the local bobby on his beat looked out for youths climbing on bus shelters, so – at 58 Lynton Road, Southport, a three-bedroomed semi backing on to the Southport–Liverpool railway line – my dad looked out for milk bottles on the table, which he considered unspeakably vulgar. It was also a no-no to start eating before my mother – always the cook in our house – had sat down to join us. We would sit patiently at the table, my dad and I, with plates of food in front of us but cutlery untouched, until my mum came through from our tiny kitchen into what we grandly called the breakfast room, even though it was where we ate all our meals.

It was unthinkable, by the way, to eat in the lounge in front of the television, which of course was rented, like everybody's telly in those days. I was deeply envious of friends who were allowed to do so on trays, or on those little nests of tables that everyone had back then. What ever happened to nests of tables? Were they all swooped up in the dead of night by some kind of 1970s furniture hit squad, along with drinks cabinets masquerading as eighteenth-century globes? I think they must have been.

The friends I envied most were those who had a television within sight of the meal table. To be able to sit and eat in comfort while watching *The Generation Game* seemed like living about as high on the hog as was possible, at least in 1970s' Southport. In our house, television-viewing and mealtimes were kept strictly separate, and given that it was also an era before video recorders, I can vividly remember the near-physical agony of being called through for dinner just as the opening credits rolled on *The Virginian* or, more agonising still, *The Persuaders!*. No quarter was asked or given. Our evening meal did not always start at the same time, but depended entirely on when my parents got home from work, so I never knew how much of my favourite TV programmes I would manage to watch before being summoned to the table.

It was doubtless because I was an only child that I always ate with my mum and dad, and eating alone with my parents meant that my table manners were subject, from an early age, to close scrutiny. Until my father's death in 1976 I always had to ask for permission to leave the table, and before doing so was also expected to thank my mother. After he died the formality eased a little. I think my mum and I might even, on occasion, have sullied the table with a half-full milk bottle, and felt liberation and guilt in equal measure.

I'm still not sure where my dad's preoccupation with table manners came from. It wasn't as though he came from a gentrified background. The family business in Liverpool had been fishmongery. Indeed, the *Daily*

Telegraph's veteran radio critic Gillian Reynolds once wrote to me asking if I was anything to do with Viners' fish shop in Smithdown Road, Liverpool, where she and her family had been customers in the 1950s. I was able to say that I was, and there ensued an unlikely but enjoyable correspondence about Finnan haddock.

Wherever it came from, my dad's insistence on rectitude at the table, it wormed its way, twenty years and more after his death, into my expectations of my own children. It wasn't that I wanted to be lord and master at mealtimes. In any case, the writer Hunter Davies spotted years before I became a parent that fathers were no longer accorded the deference at the table that had once been theirs by virtue of their status as head of the household, a title that now sounds as quaintly old-fashioned as bob-a-job week. When he was a child, he recorded in his Father's Day column in *Punch* in the 1980s, 'All dads, even humble little clerks, not only got instant attention, they got endless respect. And they got the biggest helpings.'

Those days had ended by the time his kids were teenagers, are long vanished now, and I wouldn't want them back. Nor have I ever minded the principle of Jane calling the shots in terms of how her cooking was consumed. Her own fondest childhood memories of food were of wolfing the meals cooked by her paternal grandmother, the matriarchal miner's widow Nellie, who enjoyed no spectacle more than her granddaughters lifting up their plates and licking them clean. I could see why Jane would want her own children to have similarly warm, food-related memories.

However, I wouldn't want to present her childhood mealtimes in Yorkshire as carefree and joyous and mine on the other side of the Pennines as stultifying and repressed. As long as I stayed within the constraints of my father's rulebook, which I almost always did, conversation flowed happily. And yet, it was undoubtedly the influence of our respective childhoods that made table manners the one child-rearing subject on which Jane and I did not agree. Consequently, the meal table, when the kids were little, sometimes became a battleground.

It was invariably over Sunday lunch that the battle raged most fiercely. With Jane having toiled for hours in the kitchen, I felt, as my own dad would have done, that the children should respect her efforts by eating correctly. Meaning no knives in mouths, no gravy dabbed with fingers, no slouching. She, however, took precisely the opposite view; that all those transgressions simply radiated an appreciation of her food, which was all she wanted. And what she least wanted was me getting cross and the kids getting upset. That, to her, showed far more disrespect for her cooking than eating peas with a knife or custard with a serving spoon.

The biggest battle was fought over one Sunday lunch in October 2001, when for the umpteenth time six-year-old Joseph grabbed a roast potato from his plate, and started dipping it in gravy.

'HOW MANY TIMES DO YOU NEED TELLING? DO NOT USE YOUR FINGERS!' I bellowed at him.

He fled from the table, crying. Jane then stormed out after him.

'DO YOU KNOW WHAT?' she yelled as she went. 'I'M NEVER COOKING SUNDAY LUNCH AGAIN. I CAN'T BEAR THIS. IT'S NOT FAIR!'

At this Eleanor left the table, sobbing. And then Jacob, aged only three and also beginning to whimper, clambered down too. Which left me, tucking into roast lamb, potatoes, carrots and minted peas on my own, using my knife and fork impeccably, of course, elbows off the table, and unable to shake the conviction that I had been absolutely right to make a stand. As I worked my solitary way through the rest of my meal, I felt like the Martin Luther King of table manners, bravely suffering the consequences of my high-minded principles.

Nevertheless, that day marked the start of my retreat from the battleground, albeit with the battle far from won. A couple of months later I watched Joseph eat his

Christmas dinner standing on his chair and wearing only his pants, and astonished myself by enjoying the spectacle. Jane's parents normally joined us for Christmas dinner but that year they were away in a Cornish hotel, and much as we all missed them, it seemed gloriously anarchic to do things of which they would have so heartily disapproved.

At Christmas, especially, there's no escaping the feeling that your own parents – or parents-in-law – are casting a judgemental eye over your parenting skills. Every year, Anne and Bob manifestly felt that the children got too many presents, and every year, Jane, who'd lovingly done all the buying and wrapping, took it as a personal rebuke. I inclined to Anne and Bob's side of the (usually silent) argument, but also understood that my wife's lavishness with the children was indivisible from the extravagance of her catering, from which we all benefited and about which nobody complained. It was her generosity of spirit that stuffed the children's stockings full to overflowing, and the same generosity of spirit that stuffed us all full of excellent food. As a husband as well as a father, you have to pick your battles. And compromise is always easier on a full stomach.

With knife-and-fork rules, though, compromise was painful. After all, I knew that my dad would be looking

down from the celestial breakfast room, smiling indul-
gently at the grandchildren he'd never known, then
wincing as they mopped their plates with their fingers.

So, retreating from the battleground did not mean
laying down arms altogether. Five years to the very
month after the Battle of the Roast Potato, we took the
children to New York for half-term. We were able to
stay in a friend's apartment, making the trip just about
affordable, but it was my forty-fifth birthday while
we were there, and to celebrate it I suggested a family
breakfast somewhere swanky. I chose the Mandarin
Oriental Hotel at Columbus Circle, where the dining
room is thirty-five storeys up, affording fantastic
views over Central Park and the Manhattan skyline.
But, as we whooshed up in the fancy elevator, I recited
the old mantra.

'Guys, this is a very smart hotel, and people pay a lot
of money to stay here. So I don't want you to disrupt
anyone else's breakfast by being noisy, or in any way
misbehaving. OK?'

They nodded.

We were shown to a table in the centre of the room,
and set about ordering all those magnificently over-the-
top dishes that the Americans treat as breakfast staples:
apple-pecan French toast (when did you ever see that in
France?); poached eggs drowning in hollandaise sauce

on English muffins (when did you ever see those in England?). To drink, Jane and I ordered coffee, and the children asked for hot chocolate. As the birthday boy, rather than as paterfamilias, I sat at the head of the table.

The drinks arrived, regrettably just as Eleanor was embarking on a story that for some reason involved a flamboyant sweep of her right arm. Her hand caught her cup of still-steaming hot chocolate, which flew upwards towards me, sitting next to her. Sharply, instinctively, I moved back, but as I did so my chair tipped and I fell backwards onto the lush carpet, booting the table several inches off the floor as I went. Cutlery, crockery, coffee and hot chocolate flew in all directions. The crash seemed to last for about a minute, and made a noise like the entire brass section of the New York Philharmonic Orchestra collectively falling down a flight of stairs. Everybody in the room stared. Startled waiters came running. I could not have attracted more attention had I started singing 'Yankee Doodle' through a loudhailer. For my wife and three children, it was an episode to be instantly and enduringly cherished, and of course to be invoked on all future occasions when I asked for decorum at the meal table.

But still the crusade went on, albeit less stridently, and it continues to this day. I take heart, as so often on this voyage of fatherhood, from the empathy of my fellow-travellers. In particular, my friend Will, who is convinced that this preoccupation with table manners is a Dad Thing. He has three children too, and a wife, Kim, who like Jane is much more *laissez-faire* about the children's eating habits. There have been some ferocious battles fought at their dinner table, as at ours.

'I'm actually quite fascistic about it,' Will admitted to me when, during the writing of this book, I phoned to quiz him on the extent of his magnificent obsession. 'I've told them I will never take them to eat in a smart restaurant, ever.'

For Will, the biggest, least forgivable misdemeanour is licking the knife. But it's not just his kids who get monitored for knife-licking *faux pas*. 'If I'm ever thinking of offering someone a job, I always take them out for dinner beforehand, and if their table manners aren't up to scratch then no matter how bright they are they don't get the job,' he told me. I loved that. All the professional promise in the world, undermined by a swift lick of your knife. He was speaking my language.

With family, though, there's no escape for him. And ultimately, that's the hold that children have over fathers. They know you're stuck with them. As the American comedian Jerry Seinfeld once said about his own lacklustre approach to cutting the lawn during his teenage years: 'There was nothing they could do. My father couldn't go, "Listen son. You're not really cutting the mustard out there on that lawn. Now I know you've been in the family for about fifteen years, but I'm afraid we're going to have to let you go. Don't feel too bad about it. We're making cutbacks all over the house. The dog's only coming in three days a week."'

Will told me that once his older two kids had left home, leaving him and Kim on their own with their youngest – who let me swiftly add is a lovely boy, justifiably the source of much parental pride – he had to agree to the TV being switched on during mealtimes, purely so that his scrutiny of mouth, cutlery and plate, and the interaction between the three, didn't become too intense.

Like me, Will traces his own powerful sense of mealtime decorum to his father's unrelentingly high standards, and recalled a childhood incident when the youngest of his three sisters, Jane, committed some outrage or other and was ordered to get down from the table and leave the room. The meal then continued in silence, Will's dad still with a face like thunder and everyone else keeping their heads down, only for the tense hush to be interrupted ten minutes or so later by a tap-tap-tapping at the window. They all looked up, to see a small wicker basket being dangled on a long string from an upstairs window with a note inside it saying 'Can I come back yet?' There was an outburst of laughter, the eruption all the greater for having broken such a stony silence. But Will's dad, unlike me in the Mandarin Oriental, refused to see the funny side.

Will is sure that it's a trait, this mealtime intransigence, that has been paternalistically handed down for generations. He never knew his father's father, who was born in the 1880s, but the surviving photographs of him, wearing a linen suit and a high collar, strongly suggest a man who would brook no behavioural lapses at the table.

Those were the real olden days, but until not so very long ago my children would refer even to my childhood as 'the olden days'. They weren't being facetious, either. Maybe I brought it on myself, inducing wide-eyed disbelief in them by describing a sepia-tinted era of only three television channels and no mobile phones.

Those were also the days – the late 1960s and early 1970s – when even some teachers would take an interest not just in what you ate in the school canteen, but also how you ate it. I'd forgotten this until Will recalled that at his junior school in Hampshire there was a teacher who would swoop on any child seen shovelling his or her peas with the fork tines-up. 'We're not Americans,' he would say, with maximum contempt.

Another friend of mine re-confirms the theory that fathers more than mothers are the arbiters and enforcers of table manners. He has some frankly hair-raising tales from his childhood, although they are understandable when you know the circumstances.

His father was a Polish Jew, who was in his late teens when he managed to escape from the Warsaw Ghetto, an area little bigger than a single square mile, into which the Nazis had crammed more than 400,000 people. He made his way to France, where he joined the French Resistance, and then on to England, where he enlisted with the Free Polish Army. Back in Britain after the war he married a classic English rose, a former debutante, no less, and promptly fathered six children in seven years, urgently creating a new family to replace his old one, for his parents and siblings had all died at Auschwitz.

If that tragedy explained his desire for lots of children, so his experiences in the Warsaw Ghetto, watching people die of starvation, explained his attitude towards family mealtimes. He was to die young, only just reaching his fifties, but having settled in England he hardly ever talked about his experiences in Nazi-occupied Poland; the rest of his life was all about forging a successful future, not dwelling on a traumatic past. Nonetheless, his children all knew, literally, where he was coming from when he insisted that you ate what you were given, and never complained. If any of them did leave food on the plate, it was re-presented at the next meal, and the next, until it was consumed.

'We were all brilliant at dividing things by six,' recalls my friend now (I'll call him Bill), 'because the rule was that whoever had the knife got their piece last, so slices of a cake or tart were exact practically to the millimetre.' The regime sounds like the Von Trapp household before Julie Andrews got her lovely hands on it. A gong was sounded exactly five minutes before every family meal began, and then again immediately prior to eating. 'If you weren't sitting down by the time the gong rang for a second time, you didn't eat,' Bill says.

Bill's mother and sisters were always served first and slouching was forbidden. Every child had to sit perfectly upright, and elbows on tables incurred instant wrath, as coincidentally they did during the childhood of Bill's partner, whom I'll call Sue. 'All joints on the table will be carved,' was the ritual warning from Sue's father, and there was no great certainty that he was bluffing.

By comparison, my own dad was a soft touch. He certainly never addressed my unsatisfactory posture by making me eat with a stair rod across my back and tucked into the crooks of my elbows, as Bill's father did at one memorable family meal. But Bill knows now, even if he didn't then, that the rulebook was intended to smooth rather than complicate his own passage through life. And, unsurprisingly, with Sue having also been raised with a stern emphasis on table manners, he is downright uncompromising himself with his own children. The younger two are still only little, and yet it is not entirely melodramatic to say that more than seven decades after the event they eat in the faint but long shadow of the Warsaw Ghetto.

11

Fun And Games

Competitive Dads are Losers.

Fatherhood is meant to be enjoyable. That's easily forgotten when you're in the grip of one or more of the many other conditions that come with the package: fear, anxiety, distress, anger, irritation, exhaustion and financial gloom all spring effortlessly to mind, not to mention public embarrassment. But if it's not also pleasurable, then what's the point? Then it's just about carrying out and seeing through a biological urge, making us little different from slugs and snails.

In January 2012, a magazine questionnaire featured the actor Benedict Cumberbatch, who was asked what had been his life's biggest disappointment. 'Not being a dad by the age of thirty-two,' was his response. And just four questions later, invited to declare his greatest achievement, he replied, plaintively: 'I wish I could say children.'

Even P. G. Wodehouse's immortal creation Bertie Wooster knew those yearnings. 'Jeeves, I wish I had a daughter,' he said in *Carry On, Jeeves*, first published in 1925. 'I wonder what the procedure is?'

Bertie never did have children, although I fervently hope that by the time this book is published, Cumberbatch is elbow-deep in soft toys and nappies. But at the time of writing, he exemplified the truth that intense broodiness is not just confined to women, and one can only hope that he hadn't read a newspaper interview with his fellow actor Philip Glenister only a week or so earlier. 'I don't see how having children isn't the defining thing of anyone's life,' enthused Glenister, who also talked about his approach to fathering: 'Because we've got two girls, I'm a big soft dad and they wrap me round their little fingers, to be uncurled by mum.' So much for his image in the hit TV series *Life on Mars* as the unreconstructed 1970s detective Gene Hunt. Anyone who'd called DCI Gene Hunt big and soft would have been chucked headfirst through a pub window.

As for the fun of being a dad, I'd like to think that it has remained more or less constant since the beginning of the human race, that Stone Age cave-dwellers played hide-and-seek behind boulders and generally enjoyed wonderful larks with their kids, and so on through the ages. I'd like to think so, but I'm not sure.

It is a dispiriting thought that twenty-first-century dads, at least in the more technologically advanced cultures, are not as creative in having fun with their children as their forebears were required to be. We are told that pleasure is more accessible now than it has ever been, just the touch of a button or click of a mouse away, but actually that's precisely the problem. Never in the history of humankind have children been less dependent on their fathers, or for that matter any other human beings, for fun. At home, dads have been marginalised by the microchip and, even away from the home, the message to our kids from the time they can walk is that all they need to have the time of their lives is an indoor maze and a ball pool.

All those kiddie fun palaces, the Wacky Warehouses and Fun Factories and Clown Towns that started to spring up in the 1980s on every ring-road in every town and city, are populated every Saturday and Sunday morning with fathers drinking insipid coffee and occasionally peering out from behind their newspapers to try to get a fix on the whereabouts of little Oscar or Olivia. Sometimes, a particularly game dad will go galumphing through the ball pool himself, but it's rarely a good idea, and when he accidentally sits on somebody else's child and breaks her glasses he realises that he's in the wrong place and skulks back to his motoring supplement.

Hand in hand with all this, of course, is the unmistakable truth that there has never been more social and cultural pressure to keep Britain's children entertained. In the 1960s and 1970s, when I was a child, such pressure was negligible. We were sent outside to make our own fun. And if it happened to be raining, we stayed indoors and read about the Famous Five and the Secret Seven going outside to make their own fun. There was no daytime telly, still less DVDs, game consoles, Facebook and all those myriad other sources of modern entertainment, and nobody expected dads to take up the slack. After all, we didn't even recognise it as slack. Except in the most enlightened households, nobody acknowledged that children needed stimulation just as much as, perhaps even more than, their elders. For the most part, kids either made their own fun, or they didn't have any.

It's remarkable how utterly things have changed in a generation. My friend Ali, who worked so hard to prepare two-year-old Rosie for the arrival of a new baby lest she feel any sense of displacement, remembers her dad locking her and her siblings in the car with a bag of crisps most Sunday lunchtimes, while he spent a couple of hours in the pub. These days, that would count as abuse. Yet he was a decent, intelligent man, and a loving, engaged father. Back then, it was simply how Sundays were distinguished from Saturdays.

Every parent of my generation can draw a similarly vivid contrast between then and now. Of course, parenting now is driven partly by paranoia: the widespread belief that every wood hides a flasher, that a rapist stalks every quiet alley, that every bicycle ride is a dice with death under the wheels of a lorry. Society's answer is to create safe play zones at the expense of initiative and adventure. I think that's sad.

As part of the same equation, we spend almost infinitely more time addressing the wants and needs of our kids than our own parents did, and they were probably considered excessively indulgent by their parents. I'll come later in this book to holidaying as a father, but a story I told in my last book, about the British on their hols, seems worth repeating here. It was told to me by another friend, Becky, who recalled interminable summer car journeys to French campsites, spending endless hours in a dense fug formed by her mother's cigarette smoke mixing with the fumes of her Rive Gauche perfume. Yet the children on the back seat were expected to sit uncomplainingly for the entire journey, and if one of them so much as wound a window down an inch, their dad at the wheel would raise hell.

These days, children would throw themselves on the mercy of the social services rather than endure such a journey. But they wouldn't have to, because on long car journeys now they have iPads to look at, iPods to listen to, mobile phones to play with; indeed, their travel needs, in more families than not, are deemed more of a priority than those of their parents. It's called progress, but to me it seems dangerously regressive. I wouldn't go so far as to suggest that boredom and discomfort breed character, but instant gratification, surely, is the greater curse. That said, I can't honestly pretend that I didn't, when the children were small, spend ages rigging up a DVD player in the back of the car before we set off on family holidays, to stop them squabbling with each other.

Meanwhile, for divorced and separated fathers, who perhaps only get access to their children at weekends, it must be harder than it is for the rest of us to find themselves supplanted as a source of enjoyment by the DVD player or Xbox or Nintendo Wii. When we lived in London I knew a couple of so-called Weekend Dads who in the late 1990s, like me, were reluctant Sunday morning regulars at Clown Town just behind an enormous Tesco on the North Circular Road. It hardly counted as quality time with their kids, and yet it was what little Oscar or Olivia devoutly wanted to do.

Maybe, come to think of it, the reason why those Fathers 4 Justice campaigners dream up such high jinks to publicise themselves, is that not only are they denied as much access as they would like to their kids, but kids themselves aren't as much fun as they used to be. Whatever, I remember talking before the 2012 Olympic Games to one of the policemen in charge of security arrangements at the sailing venue. He admitted to me that his main security concern was not that al-Qaeda might spirit a boat into Weymouth Harbour packed to the gunwales with explosives, but that a lone Fathers 4 Justice activist might suddenly lurch into the television picture riding a pedalo, and dressed as Batman.

Happily, I've never known what it feels like to have access to my own children restricted or denied. From time to time, really dreadful stories hit the headlines about fathers who are so tormented by the thought of being separated from their kids that they kill them, more often than not before killing themselves. Such incidents are rare, and yet not nearly rare enough. When in October 2012 ex-soldier Michael Pedersen ended his two children's lives and then his own, it was less than three months after a man called Ceri Fuller had committed suicide at a beauty spot not far from where we live, after killing all three of his kids. Both men were described as having been 'loving' fathers. What kind of madness engulfed them?

Of course, there have always been fathers who should have their access to their children restricted, and for that matter fathers who restrict their children's access to them. Take the great novelist Evelyn Waugh, a father of six, who in 1954 wrote: 'Of children as of procreation – the pleasure momentary, the posture ridiculous, the expense damnable.'

Waugh didn't mind who knew about his low regard for children generally and his own children in particular, once telling Lady Diana Cooper: 'I abhor their company because I can only regard children as defective adults, hate their physical ineptitude, find their jokes flat and monotonous . . . I do not see them until luncheon, as I have my breakfast alone in the library, and they are in fact well trained to avoid my part of the house; but I am aware of them from the moment I wake. Luncheon is very painful.'

He wasn't joking. His son Auberon, in his 1991 auto-biography, related that just after the Second World War, Clement Attlee's Labour government decided that every child in the country should be given a banana, which had been unobtainable during the war years. Special coupons were issued, and when the first magical consignment reached Britain, Auberon's mother, Laura, got hold of three bananas, for her son and two daughters. This was considered a hugely exotic and exciting treat, yet when she took them home, Evelyn, in front of the children and with tremendous ceremony, peeled them, cut them up, covered them with cream and sugar, and ate them all.

Have you ever heard a story of fatherly nastiness quite as shocking as that? On reflection, you probably have: the case of Josef Fritzl, the Austrian electrician who held his daughter captive in his basement for twenty-four years, raped her repeatedly and fathered seven children with her. But for casual emotional cruelty, the banana story takes some beating. 'It would be absurd to say that I never forgave him,' wrote Auberon, 'but he was permanently marked down in my estimation.'

Clearly, the author of *Brideshead Revisited* would have had no truck with my notion that fatherhood should be fun, though I dare say that the old curmudgeon derived some sporadic pleasure from his children, even if he would rather have died than admit it. Fun, of course, comes in many forms, and what a father considers fun – in Waugh's case, scoffing those three bananas – might not remotely tally with his offspring's interpretation. The good-parenting trick is in finding the common ground. At any rate, the most fun I've given my kids has been when I was enjoying myself as much as they were

– in my experience, however young they are, they tend to know when you're not – and while I can't speak for anybody's family but my own, that has usually involved running, throwing, kicking, hitting or catching.

In 2010, the cricket writer Christopher Martin-Jenkins composed a characteristically elegant essay following the death of the illustrious, South Africa-born former England batsman Basil D'Oliveira. 'His passion for cricket was engendered, as more often than not it is throughout the world, by a keen father,' Martin-Jenkins wrote, and for cricket read any kind of sport. It was Earl Woods who assiduously, some would say manically, turned his son Tiger into the greatest golfer of his age, a project that began when the boy was but three years old. Mike Agassi, an Armenian immigrant to the United States, was similarly ambitious for his son Andre, taping table-tennis bats to the boy's hands when Andre was a toddler, so he would start to think of them as mere extensions of his arms.

There are countless comparable examples in tennis alone. The stage mum might be a cliché of pushiness, but so is the tennis dad. Significantly, Andre Agassi is reportedly the very opposite of pushy with his own children, whose mother happens to be Steffi Graf. If there were such a thing as a genetically engineered future Wimbledon men's champion, then it would surely be

Jaden Gil Agassi, born in 2001. Yet both Agassi and Graf have enthusiastically steered their kids away from tennis – 'It's lonely, no-one to talk to, no-one to pass the ball to,' Agassi has said, from doubtless bitter boyhood experience – and towards other sports.

Of course, there is another reason why a high-achieving sportsman might not want his offspring to follow him into the same sport, fearing that the youngster will be saddled with endless comparisons. I once fell rather seriously foul of this precise situation, when in the mid-1990s I went to interview Ian Botham, for the *Mail on Sunday*, at Edgbaston Cricket Ground.

England's greatest all-rounder was the first globally famous sportsman I had interviewed, and of course his mighty reputation preceded him, blowing a loud trumpet and banging a timpani drum. I was, not to put too fine a point on it, decidedly nervous, the more so when he failed to remove his wraparound glasses. It's hard to interview someone without eye contact.

There was a Test match in progress, and he told me he wanted to sit in the stand, so that he could keep an eye – through the ever-present sunglasses – on proceedings out in the middle. As we lowered ourselves into adjacent seats, however, the great man somehow contrived to sit on the flap of my sports jacket, and I was basically too intimidated either to ask him to lift his sizeable posterior, or to wrench my jacket free. It wasn't really the texture of his backside that had earned him the name Iron Bottom on the sub-continent, but that day it might as well have been. My jacket flap was well and truly trapped, and thus I conducted the interview not only disconcertingly close to him, but listing slightly towards him.

All of which might not have been too much of a problem, had I not asked a question that Botham deeply resented. At the time, his nineteen-year-old son Liam was plying his trade as a cricketer, trying to break into the Hampshire first team. How much, I asked, did the teenage Liam remind him of himself at the same age, on the field of play? Botham snorted, in much the same way that an angry bull snorts. For the first time in the interview he half-turned towards me, which had the effect of making me list even more towards him, as more of my jacket was tugged underneath him. 'How is that lad ever going to make his way in cricket with pricks like you asking stupid questions like that?' was the essence of his response, and, shocked into silence, I silently contemplated the folly of my question with my head all but resting on his shoulder.

A few years later, I interviewed Botham again, three or four times in fact, and dared to remind him of my Edgbaston *faux pas*. 'Oh yeah, I was a bit sensitive about

Liam's cricket in those days,' he said cheerfully. By then, Liam had given up cricket for a career first in rugby union and then rugby league, so there was no longer a call for any comparison. And by then, too, I had enough experience as a father to understand better why he had reacted as explosively as he had.

Significantly, the great champions rarely become the pushiest fathers on the boundary or touchline. It is more often dads who had only a modest degree of sporting success themselves, or none at all, who drive their kids ever upwards, sometimes imperilling their own emotional health, or that of the child, or both. Tiger Woods never saw his father as anything other than a positive influence, and Venus and Serena Williams seem enduringly fond of their father Richard, yet the road to sporting success is littered with fractured relationships between an overbearing and demanding father, and a high-achieving but resentful child.

For sports-loving fathers who are not hell-bent on turning their kids into champions, of which I am one, and, seemingly, Andre Agassi another, simply chucking or kicking a ball around is a wonderful way of bonding, however. And if, in the process, you help to equip your children with physical skills that might eventually become a social asset, then so much the better.

In 2002, when Eleanor was nine, Joseph seven and

Jacob almost four, we left London and moved to Herefordshire. From the time Eleanor could walk I had been teaching her to catch and throw, but there was no netball team at St Mary's. At her primary school in Herefordshire there was, however, and she was a promising little player by the time she moved on to secondary school, where netball was taken with deadly seriousness by several games mistresses of varying formidableness. The arrival of the teen years is really the subject of a later chapter, but if I might just scoot forward, by the age of fourteen Eleanor was not only first-choice goal attack for the county under-16s team – the Wayne Rooney, if you will – but had also been selected for the 'elite' under-17s national training squad. Citing all the hours we'd spent practising ball skills in the back garden, I grabbed as much credit as I safely could, while Jane pointed out sweetly but meaningfully that she'd been a pretty good schoolgirl netballer herself, and that nature rather than nurture might have formed Eleanor's talent as a goal-shooter.

Whatever, as I progressed through my forties I surprised myself by becoming a netball enthusiast. It is another of the unexpected pleasures of fatherhood, that you often find yourself embracing your children's interests, interests that earlier in your life you could never have anticipated. Indeed, I started getting quite indignant on netball's behalf that it was persistently overlooked by the International Olympic Committee. Surely, it's exactly the sort of sport that should be in the Olympics – one which would benefit hugely from the exposure, and in which a set of Olympic medals would represent the absolute peak of attainment. Which cannot be said, whichever way you look at it, for tennis or the new Olympic sport of golf.

In my newspaper columns I sporadically tried to redress, in my own small way, the injustice of one of the nation's most popular participation sports occupying roughly the same space as mountain unicycling in the back pages of Britain's national newspapers. I knew why, of course. Sports pages are on the whole run and for that matter read by men, and men traditionally think of netball, if they think of it at all, as a bit, dare I say, girly. I had subscribed to that view myself, and yet the more netball I watched, the more I became convinced that coaches across a range of sports could learn a good deal from it. After all, one of the principal skills is running into space, anticipating passes and giving options to the person in possession, who is not permitted to carry the ball. Footballers, in particular, would benefit from studying netball. Gary and Phil Neville should know that better than anyone, with a former international netballer – Phil's twin, Tracey – in the family.

I digress. Eleanor's selection for the national

training squad meant an hour's drive first thing every third Sunday morning to the University of Wolverhampton's sports complex in Walsall. Despite the pleasure I took in her progress, this felt like a bit of a sacrifice – Sunday mornings are precious, after all – but I reminded myself that at Wimbledon one year I had sat close to a hyperventilating Yuri Sharapov during a match involving his daughter, Maria Sharapova. Sacrificing one Sunday morning in three hardly compared with what he had done: emigrating from Russia to Florida where, despite speaking no English, he washed dishes late into the night and worked double shifts on building sites to pay her coaching fees. Yuri had once been described by the celebrated tennis coach Nick Bollettieri as the most difficult tennis parent he had ever encountered – and, Heaven knows, old Bolly must have had plenty to choose from – but even so, some respect was due.

Happily, there were no pushy, pugnacious Yuri Sharapov types at Eleanor's netball matches. But on Sunday mornings when I wasn't driving her to Walsall, I would take Joseph to play for his under-13s football team. There was more aggression on the touchline than in your average dockside pub on a Friday night, and that was just the mums. The dads were worse. One Sunday, Joe was skipping down the wing when an opposition dad cried 'Fucking get him!' so furiously that I was relieved there weren't a couple of pit bulls to let off the leash.

There are two kinds of Competitive Dad: the one who turns his ferocious will to win against his own children, and the one who harnesses it in support of his own children. Of these two types, the former is the more laughable but the latter the more anti-social. A pal of mine recalls watching his son playing full-back in a school rugby match, and when a high up-and-under was hoisted by the opposing team towards his boy, one of the other team's dads, a respectable enough looking fellow in a waxed jacket and sturdy brogues, bellowed, 'DROP IT!' The idea that parents might want to set their children positive examples of sporting behaviour seems positively quaint these days, though at least we can console ourselves with the knowledge that touchline rage is not a uniquely British phenomenon. A British friend living in Chicago, Roger, told me a few years ago that parental misbehaviour at his ten-year-old daughter's soccer matches had got so bad that all parents had been forced to sign a deposition at the start of every season, promising among other things to cheer good play by the opposition.

I could easily fill the rest of this book with hair-raising instances of fathers behaving badly at their kids' sporting events, but let me offer just one more: in Wiltshire, not so long ago, one dad was so incensed by some refereeing in an under-11s football match that he drove his Range Rover onto the field and parked in the centre circle, refusing to move unless the ref rescinded his decision. The game was abandoned.

All of which adds up to another reason why I came to enjoy watching Eleanor playing netball: the girls were supported in a civilised fashion, and, anyway, you can't get a Range Rover into a sports hall. As for my conviction that netball set a good example to other sports on as well as off the court, I once talked to the Wales rugby union coach, Warren Gatland, about outside influences on his coaching philosophy. He confirmed that he had introduced some strategies from Gaelic and Aussie rules football, and, entirely unbidden by me, added that he'd also studied netball. 'It's not like basketball where you can bounce the ball and move forward,' he said. 'The ball is off the ground all the time, and the handling skills are very good. Rugby players can take a lot of skill sets out of netball.'

Plainly, if not even rugby union was too macho to draw inspiration from netball, football should consider it too. I also threatened to challenge Gatland to send out his Wales backs against Herefordshire's under-16 netballers. I wish now that I had. They would undoubtedly have got spanked.

12

Wait Till Your Father Gets Home

*Demand high standards of behaviour when your
children are small. You can always relax them when
they get older, but the process doesn't work in reverse.*

That word and its variations – spanked, spank, spanking
– has acquired several connotations. One sports team
can be said to have spanked another. A car can be brand
spanking new. But the original meaning, unless I'm
greatly mistaken, relates to one person administering
blows to another's buttocks, and another three cheers for
the internet, because Yahoo! Answers tells me, in answer
to the question 'Why is it common to spank or be
spanked on the butt?' that in ancient times, spanking by
pagan priests was considered to be a way of encouraging
fertility in women assumed to be barren.

That was the line taken by the pagan priests, anyway. Imagine how disappointed they must have been when pretty women got pregnant without giving them the opportunity to take them over their knees. A few centuries later, Catholic priests got round that particular problem, by spreading the word that spanking was an effective way of purging adult women of their sins.

What, though, of spanking, or smacking, as a form of parental discipline? Every few years, as sure as the Waitrose deli counter sells hummus, the British middle classes share a big heave of collective angst over this issue, and in late 2011 the Labour MP for Tottenham, David Lammy, stirred it up again with his book *Out of the Ashes*, asserting that the previous summer's urban riots had been partly provoked by the 2004 Labour Government's tightening of laws relating to smacking.

Admitting to having smacked his own two young sons, aged three and five, Lammy insisted that plenty of parents in his constituency would have been better able to stop their kids joining gangs, and becoming involved in knife crime, and indeed rioting, had they felt able to dish out some moderate corporal punishment without the fear that 'social workers will get involved and take their children away'.

Re-examining the 2004 Children's Act, he also rather shockingly pointed out that as legislation it was inherently

179

racist, because what it banned was 'unreasonable physical chastisement', defining 'unreasonable' as anything that caused more than 'a temporary reddening' of the skin. Erm, but black skin doesn't redden, explained Lammy, who is himself black, the son of Guyanese parents. Nobody needed to point out the inescapable irony of a Labour government trying hard to do the right thing, yet inadvertently overlooking the matter of skin colour.

Anyway, over the basic issue of smacking all hell broke loose, or at least that liberal form of hell that involves the *Today* programme on Radio 4 and trenchant articles in the *Guardian*. Unsurprisingly, nobody was quite daring enough to point out that, on the whole, the kind of people who habitually strike their children probably don't listen much to John Humphrys or read Polly Toynbee. In other words, it was a classic middle-class debate about how the working-classes should live, which Lammy was getting at when he identified a 'Muswell Hill/ Crouch End attitude' to the business of parenting: the belief that the key tactics, when confronted with a misbehaving, recalcitrant child, are negotiation and discussion. Which is all very well, he implied, when you don't have social services breathing down your neck. Not to mention the myriad other social and economic pressures rather more common in Tottenham than Muswell Hill.

The debate raged quite fiercely for a week or so. In a magazine questionnaire, the actress Samantha Morton, when asked which living person she most despised, ventured David Lammy, which to me seemed more than a little harsh (not Robert Mugabe? Ratko Mladić? Rosemary West?) but was obviously heartfelt. And on *BBC Breakfast* a professor of paediatrics, Terence Stephenson, opined that the very question of parents smacking their kids will seem absurd in fifty years time, and as an analogy suggested that fifty years ago plenty of people would have defended the right of a man to hit his wife.

Meanwhile, the emails, texts and tweets rained in, not a few of them adhering to the familiar view that 'I was smacked as a child, and it didn't do me any harm' or 'I spanked my son regularly, and now he's a pillar of society, in fact secretary of the local Rotary Club' (as if Rotary Club secretaries can't be maladjusted). Professor Stephenson, however, maintained firmly that 'smacking is generally a very ineffective deterrent' to bad behaviour. And as paediatricians, he added, with the grave and unimpeachable authority of a highly regarded professional, 'We see all too often today's smack become tomorrow's punch.'

I'm sure that's true, but what about all those households in which there is no chance whatever of today's smack becoming tomorrow's punch? Wasn't he rather stigmatising the parent who might on rare occasions issue a single sharp smack out of a firm belief that it would help a much-loved child to distinguish right from wrong, or safety from danger? I suspect that the professor's response to that would be that they deserve the stigma. It was certainly part of his argument that children should receive the same protection as adults against any form of physical assault, and when you think of it in those terms, it's hard to disagree.

Moreover, that was precisely the argument presented to me by a man with even more moral authority: Dr Rowan Williams, then the Archbishop of Wales. I interviewed him for a magazine, over lunch in an Italian restaurant in Newport, shortly before he became Archbishop of Canterbury in 2003. I liked him. He was passionate and eloquent, and also brave, for it took some nerve with a beard as full as his to order a large plate of pasta. He tucked in with gusto, and it was impossible to sit there and not feel inspired by his keen intellect, not to mention his manifest goodness, while the slight dab of *vongole* sauce on his grey whiskers seemed like an admirable sign of mortal frailty.

As for my line of questioning, I fear there may have been a whiff of the sixth form – had he ever broken one of the Ten Commandments? Been guilty of one of the

Seven Deadly Sins? Smacked his children? To this last question he confessed that he had once smacked his daughter, although he deeply regretted it, and had since resolved, like Professor Stephenson, that the right of a child not to be subjected to physical violence should be no less than that of an adult. Still, he said that he understood from personal experience how the pressure on a stressed parent could build and build to the point where a smack seemed the proper course of action.

When the article appeared, the press wove a substantial news story out of the Archbishop's admission, and a Lambeth Palace spokesman issued a statement, insisting that the Archbishop had been speaking off the record about smacking his daughter. This implied that I had behaved unethically by reporting his comments, which was untrue. There was never a suggestion that he wanted anything he said to be off the record, and I had a tape of our conversation to prove it. But I wasn't named in the story, and there seemed no point in making a fuss. I didn't fancy taking on the full force of the Anglican Church.

Nevertheless, I recall the episode now not because it showed that even the head of the worldwide Anglican Communion, or at any rate his official spokesman, was prepared to tell a fib to wriggle out of an embarrassing situation (although it did), but because it showed how extraordinarily emotive was, and is, the issue of smacking.

I had honestly thought that if the daily press made anything of that interview, it would arise from what Dr Williams said to me about being quite unperturbed by what back then was the highly contentious prospect of the Prince of Wales marrying Camilla Parker Bowles. But no. The story was 'Archbishop admits to smacking daughter', even though it had happened only once, and even though it was an incident he bitterly regretted. It wasn't as if he had owned up to a one-off, deeply regrettable incident with a lap-dancer, or voting for the British National Party, yet it was more or less presented as such.

A year or so later, writing about that episode in the *Independent*, I confessed that, like the Archbishop, I too was a reformed smacker. A little like the alcoholic who wakes up in the street one morning covered in vomit, and resolves never to drink again, or the compulsive gambler who finally realises the error of his ways when he is forced to sell his house to pay off his bookmaker, I'd had an epiphanic moment.

Joseph was four years old, and despite living in Crouch End, the global capital along with neighbouring Muswell Hill of parental reasoning and negotiation, I had smacked him on perhaps three or four previous occasions for various acts of epic (yet now long-forgotten) naughtiness.

But after another terrible misdemeanour one particular day, as I prepared to smack him, I suddenly saw not a naughty child, but a scared child, cowering from me, his expression a mask of fear. I realised at that moment that this anger/fear dynamic wasn't what I wanted out of my relationship with my beloved firstborn son, no matter how infrequently it might arise, and no matter what the circumstances. I promised myself that I would never do it again, either to him or to his siblings, and I never did.

Now, to some of you reading this book, this will seem like the parenting strategy of a wishy-washy liberal. Others will be dismayed and affronted that I ever found it necessary to strike my child. It is a subject on which everyone has an opinion, especially those of us who grew up in an era when corporal punishment really seemed like no big deal. I went to an old-fashioned boys' grammar school in the 1970s, and can still recall the modes of chastisement favoured by certain teachers. Mr Platford hauled us from our chairs by our sideburns; Mr Ashworth belted us round the head with anything that came to hand; Mr Stitchbury whacked our backsides with a gym shoe. Perhaps significantly for the parenting debate, however, the most effective disciplinarians tended to be the teachers who never lifted a finger to us, except of course to chuck the occasional wooden board rubber. In the 1970s, as far as I'm aware, board rubber throwing was on the syllabus at teacher training colleges, with top marks for a direct hit on the temple.

I suppose the point is that a society in which children were hit at school was perfectly at ease with them being hit at home. But that's no longer the society in which we live. Now that the slightest physical contact between teacher and pupil ends in a disciplinary hearing, if not page three of the *Daily Mail* – heck, now that nobody even hurls board rubbers any more – we are culturally disinclined to endorse smacking in the home. And that equation works the other way round, too. If we don't physically chastise our children at home, we don't want teachers doing so at school.

I'm slightly uneasy, however, with the idea of formal anti-smacking legislation. Like the Archbishop of Canterbury, I can see why a smack might sometimes seem like the right course of action to a stressed parent, and like David Lammy, I can understand why it might even, on rare occasions, be the right course of action. But stress alone on the part of the parent is never justification for striking a child. Besides, what is the definition of stress? For one man, stress might be created by jobless-ness, by yet another rejection letter in the same post as a raft of bills, compounded by ill-health, a disabled mother, a dying dog, a leak in the roof and anti-social neighbours. Another man might feel equally stressed because his annual bonus was smaller than expected, because summer lettings are slow on the second home in Tuscany, the Burgundy's run out and some bugger has scratched the Merc. And a third man might confuse stress simply with being in a bad mood. In all of these cases, a badly behaved child might feel like the last straw.

In the final analysis, no amount of legislation can determine how people raise and discipline their children, and if we're not going to sterilise all those considered likely to become unfit parents, then there has to be some level of trust between state and society, even though there will be frequent betrayals on both sides. Jane once outraged a friend of ours, a lawyer who deals with child neglect cases, by saying that it surprised her not that so many people hit their children, but that more don't. She wasn't trying to be funny, or provocative; she just honestly felt that most parents, when feeling under pressure, do pretty well to rein in their anger and frustration, or at least not let it spill into a slap on the legs or a clout round the head. I agree.

There was a time, of course, when in plenty of families just the threat of physical chastisement was enough to bring children into line. In some families, it doubtless still is. That isn't right, either. *Wait Till Your Father Gets Home* was an early 1970s Hanna-Barbera cartoon, and as a child I was inordinately fond of it. Yet the title would never pass muster with NBC or BBC executives today – not so much because it implies an imbalance in the authority of a mother and a father, and the assumption, as in *The Tiger Who Came to Tea*, that dads go out to work while mums stay at home – but because it no longer has much currency.

Indeed, it would be interesting to know how often that threat, 'Wait till your father gets home,' is issued today, compared with thirty or forty years ago. A tenth as often? A hundredth? A thousandth? The domestic role of the father as a hybrid of policeman, prosecuting lawyer, judge, jury and executioner has greatly diminished, and thank Heavens for it. Although, of course, this too varies from household to household.

Our own children certainly didn't grow up waiting in trepidation until their father got home, largely because Jane felt that, as principal carer, discipline was more her job than mine. In fact, like my strictures at the meal table, it created some tension between us. I would get home from the Associated Newspapers offices thrilled to see the kids, but if I then got cross with them after half an hour or so, her feeling was that I hadn't earned the right. She had been with them all day, dealing with all the mini-crises that arise when there are three infants about the place. Crossness was therefore her prerogative, not mine. It is another of the many paradoxes of parenthood, that couples have children as a manifestation of their love for one another, yet nothing tests their relationship like having children.

The issue of discipline is one of the major elements of that test, and broadly speaking, Jane and I have always agreed on the behavioural parameters we should set our children, and how we should impose them. Which sounds, now that I read it back, more than a little pompous. But then a dollop of pomposity is no bad thing in a father. Nor is it a bad thing to demand high standards of behaviour when your children are small, an approach which can always be relaxed as they get older. It's hellishly hard to operate that strategy in reverse: to clamp down more on bad behaviour as the years pass. That, at any rate, is how I justify an episode that Joseph, now an even-tempered, well-adjusted teenager and generally quite lovely to have around the place, still cites as one of his most vivid memories of being in trouble.

We were on holiday in the south of Spain, staying in a big resort-hotel where there were stage shows most nights. He was six years old, and as he recalls it, indignant even now, I wouldn't allow him to go to see that night's show – a medley of songs from *The Lion King* – because he didn't finish an apple!

Many of us, if pushed, can remember a telling-off in our childhoods that still seems like a dreadful injustice.

Psychoanalysts are doubtless quite used to the topic. In that particular instance, which of course I remember only dimly, while he recalls every detail, there must have been a steady build-up of small acts of naughtiness on his part, and his refusal to eat the whole apple tipped the scales of justice. He certainly had a habit at the time of taking only two or three bites out of an apple before throwing it away, which wound me up, and I suppose I must have issued an ultimatum: finish that apple or you won't go to tonight's show. That didn't, and doesn't, seem unreasonable to me as a dad. It also, rather handily, got me out of having to sit through amateur singers performing the *Lion King* medley. To Joseph aged six, however, and indeed to Joseph aged sixteen, the punishment did not remotely fit the crime. Of countless such episodes, and of course much else besides, is childhood, and parenthood, constructed.

Jane was always better, when the children were small, at matching punishment to crime. Crucially, because she spent so much time with them, she knew what all their favourite treats were, and also what constituted their most grievous disappointments.

In July 2003, when Jacob was nearly five, we had a house-warming party in our garden in Herefordshire, and hired a marquee in case the elements conspired against us after a week or so of unbroken sultry heat that, as of the time of writing, has yet to be repeated in the Welsh Marches. The marquee was erected the day before, but once it was up the man in charge walked into our kitchen wearing a thunderous expression.

'Somebody,' he snapped, 'has cut every piece of ornamental rope inside the marquee.'

It didn't need Miss Marple to find the culprit. The cuts were all at four-year-old Jacob's elbow height, and we found the scissors in his bedroom.

His act of vandalism cost us £200, which was punishment enough, but only for us. How should we impart the message that he must never do anything like that again? That burning question reminds me of a man I know who once told his three sons, when they were aged twelve, ten and eight, that he'd booked a family holiday to Disney World in Florida. The boys were beside themselves with excitement – it was their dearest wish to go to Disney World – and yet their father was lying to them: no such holiday had been booked.

The boys constantly ran their parents ragged and despairing of ways in which to keep them in line, this fellow had decided to invent a Disney World holiday – even going so far as to show them their accommodation online – so that he could use the threat of cancelling it to control their behaviour. It worked for a while, but he knew for certain that eventually there would be some outrage committed which would enable him to carry out his threat and 'cancel' the holiday he hadn't booked in the first place. Sure enough, that's just what happened, and they went to the north coast of Devon for a fortnight, as the man had planned all along. It's interesting how people gasp when I tell them that tale; far more than they might if I told them that all three boys had been spanked. The premeditated deceit of it seems shocking, but then not all of us have had three unruly sons to drag us to the ends of our tether. One naughty four-year-old with a pair of scissors was bad enough.

There was no longer any question of smacking bottoms, but I was all for some dramatic gesture – telling him that we wouldn't ever go to Disney World, perhaps? Instead, Jane said that on their visit to the cinema a few days later, he wouldn't be allowed any Pick 'n' Mix. 'That's not nearly severe enough,' I protested. 'Believe me, he will be distraught,' she said, and she was right. While Eleanor and Joseph chose their sweeties, Jacob had to stand and watch, firmly aware that he'd done wrong and that this was the consequence. It was the very opposite of 'Wait till your father gets home,' because father was home, and he was overruled. But, as he still readily acknowledges, it was good parenting.

13

It Takes A Man To Be A Father

*Learn from the ways other dads do it – they might
just be right. And if they're wrong, learn from
that, too.*

Good parenting. It is the holy grail of child-rearing
because to fulfil its requirements, all the time and on
every level, is, frankly, nigh-on impossible. Most of us
do the best job we can according to our temperaments,
our children's temperaments, and the circumstances of
any given situation. Experience helps too, but however
many kids you have, and however old the eldest is,
you've never had a child older than that. Which might
sound like something of a riddle, but I'm sure you get
the gist. When your eldest is twelve, you've got twelve
useful years of fathering behind you, and yet you've

never been the father of a teenager before. To an extent, therefore, fathering is about making it up as you along.

It also helps enormously, over the entire eighteen years or so from, you might say, the cradle to the rave, to keep an eye on how others do it. Mostly, it is a judgemental eye. Sometimes it is an admiring eye. Very occasionally it is an outraged eye, as when another parent rebukes your own children inappropriately or unfairly. The Australian writer Christos Tsiolkas recognised the dramatic potential of just that situation when he wrote a novel, which became a bestseller and in due course a TV series too, about the far-reaching consequences arising from a father slapping another man's son at a suburban barbecue. He called it, simply and effectively, *The Slap*.

Something vaguely similar happened to us once on a holiday with another family, when the other dad shouted at Joseph and Jacob in a restaurant. He would certainly never have raised his hand to them, and it's true that they were having a niggly tiff with one another, but I felt that it was my place to shout at them, not his; while he clearly felt, like the bloke in *The Slap*, that if I wasn't going to take action, he should. Whatever, my rising irritation with my sons was instantly redirected, unspoken, towards my friend. Like Jane when the children were very young, I felt that crossness was my prerogative, not his. His anger seemed like an implicit criticism of my parenting methods.

Certainly, the parenting methods of friends, relatives, and for that matter perfect strangers, are not only fascinating to most of us, but also, very often, wrong. Actually the process starts even before we become parents. It did in our case, anyway. Never, we resolved sniffily, would we do as our friends Cathy and Pete did, and plonk any toddler of ours in front of the telly to buy some peace and quiet. Yet as soon as we had toddlers of our own that's precisely what we did, issuing a silent apology to Cathy and Pete as we left the room, and years later we rolled our eyes when another good friend, who'd had two children in her forties, rationed their TV-watching habits with what seemed to us excessive zeal. Rolling your eyes at other people's rules is, to be sure, one of the great pleasures of parenthood.

It isn't just judgementalism entirely for its own sake, however. Most of us need reassurance that we're making a decent fist of this parenting lark, and measuring ourselves against others, whether consciously or not, is one of the ways we find it. I suppose it makes sense that this process of comparison is at its most intense when our children are small, when we're finding our feet as parents and also in more regular contact with other parents. For many dads, it is the park playground on a Sunday morning that affords an early opportunity to see how we measure up against others. As in the local Fun

Factory or Clown Town, there are fathers at both ends of the spectrum of engagement, from those who barely look up from their newspapers, to those who get at least as much fun as little Albie out of the see-saw, and strongly encourage him to visualise the climbing-frame as a pirate ship, even if a spray-painted skull and crossbones is the nearest it gets to the high seas.

My own game of make-believe with the children, when they were little, required them to get from one piece of playground equipment to the next without stepping on the wood-shavings, which in our imagination were shark-infested waters. But there were plenty of occasions, I should truthfully add, when I kept my nose in the *Sunday Times* sports pages. Either way, I don't doubt that there were other fathers making snap judgements of me as not engaged enough or too engaged by far.

Certainly, in the late 1980s and early 1990s, when I and many of my friends became fathers for the first time, there was increasing pressure from popular culture to be paragons of jollity. I can remember watching the film *Parenthood* and wondering whether, if and when the time came, I would be anything like as much of a hoot to my children as Steve Martin's character was to his. A few years later, along came Robin Williams as another jolly father, albeit one who had to dress up as a woman to get access to his children, in *Mrs Doubtfire*. And a few years after that came Eddie Murphy in *Daddy Day Care*.

It was no coincidence that these high-profile big-screen dads were played by comedians. Hollywood had dispensed many interpretations of fatherhood over the years, but it had invariably been a job given to serious actors: heavyweights such as Spencer Tracy in *Guess Who's Coming to Dinner* and *Father of the Bride*, Dustin Hoffman in *Kramer vs. Kramer*, Gregory Peck in *To Kill a Mockingbird*. Yet when *Father of the Bride* was remade in 1991, who got the gig but that man Steve Martin again. The message might not have been wholly intentional but it was nevertheless entirely clear: not only is fatherhood supposed to be enjoyable, but dads are meant to be fun.

At the same time, popular culture drove home even more strongly the message that fathers were meant above all to be responsible parents. In the early 1990s, a TV commercial showed a real He-Man, a proper alpha male, resisting pressure from his friends to play football, preferring to stay at home and look after his young son. 'Anybody can make a baby but it takes a man to be a father,' said a solemn voiceover at the end.

Unsurprisingly, the voice was American and it was American football that the man eschewed. He was also black, and I suppose the ad might have been prompted by the reported prevalence in the United States of young black males who get women pregnant but don't follow through with their fatherly responsibilities. When I lived in Atlanta, Georgia, in the mid-1980s, I often used to take visitors to the Ebenezer Baptist Church, close to where Martin Luther King is buried, and this was a common theme of Ebenezer Baptist's hugely charismatic (African-American) preacher, Pastor Joseph L. Roberts. Many of his powerful sermons, memorable even now, addressed the fecklessness of young African-American fathers.

On the other hand, that slogan, about anyone being able to father a child but it taking a man to be a father, plainly has universal relevance, even if such unfettered moralising would never have found a place in a British commercial break, between the Sunblest and Fairy Liquid ads. Still, it wasn't just television in the early 1990s that peddled the idea of wholehearted fathering; the movies did it too. *Sleepless in Seattle*, the veritable weep-fest starring Tom Hanks, showed just what the consequences might be for a lovely, loving dad who also happened to be a grieving widower: he would end up shagging Meg Ryan.

At any rate, if popular culture had ever been lacking in behavioural guidelines for new fathers, it certainly wasn't by the time I joined the club in the same year that *Sleepless in Seattle* was released. And that in turn encouraged us to look across at how the other bloke was doing. Mums are even more inclined to clock how other mums do things. But more than anything it seems to be a couples thing, this sneaky sideways glance of approval or, far more frequently, disapproval. I might even go so far as to suggest that it is part of the bonding process between men and women once they have parented a child.

After all, as already explored in this book, there are plenty of ways in which the arrival and raising of children can impart stress on a relationship. Not least, it has to be said, in the bedroom, where, as a very general rule, and to put it as politely as I can, the sexual desires of the man greatly exceed those of his partner, especially if she's the one clapped-out after a day's childcare. I can't remember which of our children once told an infant school teacher that 'mummy and daddy have lots of dressing-up clothes in their bedroom' but I do remember the teacher looking at us and raising a quizzically amused eyebrow. If I didn't actually mutter that the chance would be a fine thing, I certainly thought it. They were dressing-up clothes for children, needless to add, which we just happened to keep in a trunk by our bed. Show me the parents of young children who still have the energy for some adult roleplay at bedtime, and, well, I'll take my tri-cornered hat off to them.

Anyway, while some enthusiastic bitching about someone else's parenting methods might not be much of a stand-in for sex, I do think it's healthy in a relationship. However, you sometimes have to hold your hands up and concede that you deserve the criticism of others, and perhaps, on occasion, full-blown scorn. My own most scorn-worthy moment concerns an episode that I have mentioned in two previous books, which shows what an enduring effect it had on me. It featured in my last book, about the British on holiday, as an illustration of how – like Kate and Gerry McCann, the parents of poor, vanished Madeleine – we all sometimes take our eye off the ball when we're relaxing under a warm foreign sun. But I repeat it here for different reasons, because it also shows what it feels like when a father fails to discharge that most basic, primeval of duties: to keep his children safe.

Where my own children's safety was concerned, heights had worried me long before we went for lunch at the El Pirata restaurant at Cape Trafalgar on Spain's Costa de la Luz – the same holiday during which Joseph was punished for not finishing an apple – in July 2001.

Even before I was a father, I was never particularly happy with heights, and recall with a blush an episode in France when I was about twenty-five, and spending Christmas with my then-girlfriend and her family. We walked one day across the top of the Pont du Gard, the amazing Roman aqueduct near Nimes, and about half-way across, having made the mistake of focusing on the River Gard almost a thousand feet below, I lost my bottle and decided – the shame! – that I was going to have to crawl. I don't think you can walk across the highest extremity of the Pont du Gard now – even the French have deemed it a health and safety risk, which is saying something – but in those days you could. The top of Marcus Vipsanius Agrippa's millennia-old masterpiece of construction and engineering was maybe three yards wide, so safe enough to walk along if you kept to the middle, but there was no railing or barrier to protect strange people like me who at the top of bridges and towers are possessed by that disconcerting, groin-tingling urge to hurl ourselves off. So while my girlfriend, her sister, her mum, dad, aunt, uncle and two little cousins strolled insouciantly across, I brought up the rear, slowly and humiliatingly, on my hands and knees.

In due course, I directed this anxiety about heights at my children. Every time we checked into a hotel, I made straight for the balcony to see whether there was any chance of them toppling off it, and removed any chairs or tables that might have facilitated a terrible accident. I'd done the same in the hotel on the Costa de la Luz, and yet, at El Pirata, it simply didn't occur to me to see any danger in an open window, which overlooked a sheer drop of forty feet or so down to a rocky platform, and beyond it a beach.

Jacob was not yet three years old, but we were all going to be sitting at a table several yards from the window. The usual warning bells that clanged loudly in my head whenever I saw the potential for a child falling from a great height stayed silent.

It would have been inconceivable to find a comparable danger in a restaurant in Britain, but this was Spain, where we should have been more wary about custom and practice. The previous Easter we had holidayed on the Costa del Sol, and in the small town of Mijas saw posters outside the bullring advertising a show that afternoon, featuring horses and bulls. 'No blood,' declared the posters, in English. '*Sin sangre*,' added the woman at the booking office, as if to bury any lingering doubt. So, with three impressionable children under seven, should we go for it? A threatening sky put an end to our equivocation. What else to do on a wet Sunday in Mijas? And bloodless bull-fights, like free-range chickens, seemed just about acceptable to a liberal conscience. Besides, the show was to include a 45-minute display of dancing Andalusian horses, which we knew would delight Eleanor.

Sure enough, she was charmed, especially by the brace of ceremonially dressed ponies with bells round their necks. 'Look Daddy, jingle-bells ponies,' she cried. Then the bull trotted on. Or, to be more precise, the bullock. This was not one of the famous *toros bravos*, the fighting bulls, of Andalusia. This was a slight creature of almost endearing naivety, plainly bewildered to find itself goaded by a youthful matador. Jane recognised the matador. 'I'd know that little bottom anywhere,' she murmured. He was one of the four horsemen who had earlier entertained Eleanor, if not us, for there was a strict ten-minute limit to one's appreciation of equine prancing, especially when it is accompanied by a scratchy guitar version, played through an ancient loudspeaker, of 'I Just Called to Say I Love You'.

Slowly, it began to dawn on us that we had been suckered into something rather seedy. The small, century-old bullring at Mijas is almost absurdly photogenic, but not so the spectacle unfolding before us. We heard a distant rumble. It was either thunder, or Hemingway turning in his grave. But we consoled ourselves with the thought that the miserable bullock would be withdrawn, physically if not emotionally unscathed. Not so. The '*sin sangre*' line turned out to be a shameless lie. To our horror, the matador suddenly plunged his sword into the pathetic creature's back, concluding a contest that had never looked remotely even. For one mad, fleeting second, we assumed it to be a trick, retractable sword.

Except that the bullock, staring reproachfully at its nemesis, started violently spewing blood, before finally crumpling to the ground.

To add irony to injury, the corpse was then carted off right past us by Eleanor's jingle-bells ponies, while we told the children to look away and the matador bowed gravely to a civic dignitary, grandly referred to as 'El Presidente'. Three elderly locals applauded, while a hundred or so horrified tourists stampeded for the exit. Some of us stormed the ticket office, but it was firmly shut. In any case, my command of Spanish fell miserably short of what I wanted to say. I know the days of the week, but that wouldn't have helped.

For the rest of that holiday, Joseph in particular kept referring to the dying bull, and I wondered whether he would be emotionally scarred for life. Some fifteen months later, back in Spain, it was me and Jane and Jacob who ended up scarred, two of us emotionally and one physically. We sat down for lunch at El Pirata, with our friends Janet and Gabi, who lived in northern Andalusia and had driven down to see us. Jacob asked to sit at the end of the table, and we let him, without even registering that he would be nearest the precipitous drop. After all, it was still a walk to the window and I was next to him. It didn't cross either my mind or Jane's that there might be a risk.

Amid happy chatter, we scrutinised the menus and ordered our lunch. But when I turned to talk to Jacob I saw that he had dragged his chair over to the window and was looking out. All these years later I am still mystified as to how he managed to do that without any of us observing his determined little mission, but we didn't, and there was barely time to issue a warning shout before, with a flash of blue sandals and yellow socks that is seared into my mind for ever, he toppled out, headfirst.

I bellowed 'No!' and Jane screamed 'Oh my God!', shattering not just our own lunchtime conviviality but that of everyone in the restaurant. But we didn't dwell on the palpable shock around us, nor even look out of the window to see what had become of our baby – actually a highly spirited toddler but, in that moment, very much our precious baby. Instead, we made for the flight of stone steps leading to the beach, and I can remember forming the coherent thought in that short, frenzied dash that a child could not survive such a fall – forty feet onto rocks! – and yet how could we possibly have lost our beloved little Jakey?

We arrived on the beach to find a circle of twenty or so people, and in the middle of them, held tightly by a Spanish woman and crying lustily, Jacob. If the sight of his socks and sandals is seared into my mind, then so too is the joyous sound of him crying that day: it meant that he was alive and conscious. We pushed through the circle and Jacob, on seeing us, reached out instantly and needily for his mother, almost as if it was being held by a stranger that was making him cry, not that he had just plunged from a high window.

From the gathering around us we kept hearing the word '*milagro*', which means miracle, and he did seem to have confounded the laws of probability. We later realised that as he fell he must have bounced off the sheer stone wall, changing his headfirst trajectory and ensuring that he landed on sand rather than rock. Also, in all the analysing and agonising that went on over the following days and weeks, we learnt that if you are going to survive such a fall, it's best to be either a small child or paralytically drunk, which means that your body stays relaxed even at the moment of impact.

Yet it did seem like a proper *milagro*. Jacob had a few nasty grazes on his torso and a tiny cut behind his ear but there was no other obvious injury. All the same, and astoundingly, an ambulance arrived on the beach in under ten minutes. Even more astoundingly, there was a paediatrician on board. If you've ever been to Cape Trafalgar, you'll know how remote it feels, certainly by comparison with the over-developed coastline of much of southern Spain. We had to admit that if we'd been on a similarly desolate stretch of British coast, the response of the emergency services would have been rather more sluggish. On the other hand, no restaurant in Britain would have had an open window forty feet up. And nor in Britain, even on holiday, would we have been lulled into such complacency.

Which brings me back to the McCann parents, for whom I feel nothing but sympathy, because not only is there an often unwitting relaxation on foreign holidays of normal vigilance, but also, in Mediterranean countries especially, it's easy enough to fall into the local custom of applying the same rules to children as to adults. On the very morning of Jacob's fall we had seen a small boy standing on the front of a motor scooter driven by his father, neither of them wearing a helmet. And of course, the main piazza of every Spanish town is full of kids playing and eating tapas until all hours. There is scant place in their culture for dinosaur-shaped chicken nuggets and early bedtimes.

But it was our fault, not theirs. In fact I felt it was my fault, and nobody else's. When a Spaniard on the beach asked me, in hesitant English, whether I would like to consider legal proceedings against the restaurant, I dismissed the idea out of hand. He looked a little crestfallen; he was probably a lawyer himself, about to produce a business card from his tight Speedos (Spanish men, like Italians, still seem to favour the briefest of briefs). But the point surely was that the lapse in proper care and attention had been mine, not the restaurant's, although happily by this time the paediatrician had checked Jacob and, much to his ill-concealed amazement, declared him fundamentally undamaged. We carried him back upstairs to the restaurant, where we found six-year-old Joseph, alone at the big table, enthusiastically tucking – Archbishop of Canterbury-like – into his plate of pasta. Having established that his little brother wasn't dead, he saw no reason to skip lunch.

For the rest of that holiday – after a proper, shoulder-heaving cry the like of which I have had only two or three times in my adult life – I became the full-on father that Steve Martin was in *Parenthood*, playing endlessly with Jacob by the hotel swimming-pool and not even once wishing that he might get tired or bored. A couple of days after the accident he and I played paddleball for almost three hours, even though he couldn't sustain a rally for longer than about five shots; in fact, now that I look back, the foundations for his later aptitude for tennis might have been laid right there by that hotel pool.

Meanwhile, as relief swirled around us, we continued to be haunted by what might have been, and realised with a jolt of horror that if the worst had happened, we would have found little or no comfort in the presence of our other two children. From time to time, I am guilty, I imagine like many other people, of reading about the sudden death of a child with lots of siblings, and assuming that it can't be quite as devastating for the parents as the death of an only child. I remember fleetingly thinking that when the south London teenager Jimmy Mizen, one of nine brothers and sisters, was murdered in 2008.

But the thought didn't last long, because for Jimmy's poor parents (and I'll return later in these pages to his remarkable father, Barry) there was plainly a cruel equation that in more tragic circumstances might have applied to us: that the child you most want with you is the one not there. A female friend whose brother died young once told me that she still, decades later, felt that her elderly father, given the choice, would have preferred to have lost her rather than him. And I got a similar message from several readers after I had written candidly about the episode in the *Independent*. 'It remains my view that giving children too little independence is just as irresponsible as giving them too much,' I wrote. 'Nevertheless, the stark fact remains that we let our youngest child fall out of a high window.'

These days, I don't doubt that I would cop some vitriolic message-board abuse for being a crap father; like all journalists whose work is posted online, I am a target for some frankly unhinged ranting and raving from people who think they can be as obscenely unpleasant as they wish in the comfort of anonymity because, alas, in this cyberspace age of ours, they can. But in 2001 responses to newspaper articles still came largely via email or even by post, and I received some truly heartbreaking letters, including one from a woman whose toddler son had died after falling from the window of her first-floor flat. That had been twenty-eight years earlier, and yet she was still unable to take undiluted joy from the company and achievements of her other three children, although she admitted to me that she had tried to keep from them her crippling and enduring misery.

From our friends and relatives, too, when we got home from Spain and related the dramatic story, there was concern and understanding. Most of them very considerately raked up occasions in their own lives as mothers and fathers when a terrible accident had been narrowly averted by a twist of fate rather than good parenting. Even my mother recalled an incident she had long suppressed, telling me that, as a toddler, I had once crawled out of a window onto a parapet over the Kardomah café in west London. If I hadn't crawled back in, there wouldn't even have been a Jacob to fall out of the window of El Pirata a little under four decades later.

I suppose what all this shows is that, in times of need, judgementalism towards other parents and their way of doing things is supplanted by more generous instincts of empathy and support. There but for the grace of God, and all that. I might have failed in my fundamental job as a protector on that holiday, but the response from my fellow fathers was unequivocally supportive, suggesting, reassuringly, that when the chips are down, fatherhood is actually a kind of brotherhood.

14

One More Step Along The World I Go

Don't be paranoid – but beware the computer.

There is also, commensurately, a kind of sisterhood of mothers, but while the sisterhood is at its most sisterly (and also its most bitchy) when the children are small, it is when our beloved offspring hit their teens that fathers rely most on the brotherhood. After all, they don't just hit their teens, they also hit the bottle, even if it's only the mascara bottle. And that, I think, is when fathers most need the solidarity of other dads.

But it is really the onset of secondary school, not puberty, that marks the start of the second phase of fatherhood.

My theory is that for as long as children are at primary school, they seem like children. Elderly relatives might exclaim how big they are, how grown-up they seem, when they get to ten or eleven, but really, they're still kids, still helping to decorate friezes to go around the top of the classroom wall, still being met at the school gate, still playing kiss or dare in the school playground. Actually, at Farnborough Road Junior School in Southport, circa 1971, our rather more sophisticated version of the game was 'kiss, command, dare, truth or promise', and if by any chance the former Helen Plumtree is reading this, you might as well know that, aged ten, to kiss you was my devoutest wish. But I think I always got lumbered with a dare, usually to take my trousers down or stick my tongue out at a teacher.

In any case, by September 1973 the exquisite playground pain and pleasure of kiss, command, dare, truth or promise was already just a memory for me, since that was when I entered a grammar school for boys only. Which is not to say that a spot of same-sex kissing didn't go on in the darker recesses of King George V School (ahead of me by a few years, with a little group of friends as camp as he was, was the future lead singer of Soft Cell, Marc Almond), but really, the point is that I knew when Eleanor started at secondary school in the autumn of 2004 that it represented a new beginning for me almost as much as for her; that even though she and her new classmates were fresh-faced eleven-year-olds, they would now be making the friends with whom they would, more than likely, encounter all the pleasures (or vices, take your pick) that I did in my teens, and very possibly a few more. After all, sex had been dismayingly elusive for me even once I joined a co-ed sixth form, and my only experience of drugs amounted to a single nervous puff on a joint of cannabis which, like Bill Clinton, I chose not to inhale.

So, with the teen years approaching, what sort of father would I be?

I should think that most fathers and mothers of children just starting in secondary school can remember their own adolescence vividly, and therefore their own relationships with their parents at the same age. Remembering what we do of ourselves during and after the onset of puberty, the question is unduckable: shall we be the same as our parents were, or as different as possible? I have plenty of friends who resolved to be the very opposites, only to end up hearing daily echoes of their own mums and dads.

My own dad having died not long after my fourteenth birthday, before my balls had dropped or a single pubic hair had sprouted, his echoes were faint, and in any case, away from the dinner table his strictures hadn't extended far enough into my teens to remember many of them. As for my mother, she had dealt pretty admirably with my metamorphosis from child to adolescent. One day when

I was fifteen she found the three soft-porn magazines that, favouring convenience over secrecy, I kept hidden under my bed. But my mum didn't blow her top or even throw them out. Instead, she casually mentioned to me after school one day that she had added them to my stack of *Look and Learn*s – the entirely wholesome educational weekly to which I'd had a subscription for years – on the basis that they belonged under the category of looking and learning. I blushed a dark shade of puce, and chucked them out myself. I had obtained them in the usual way for a boy of fourteen or fifteen in the mid-1970s: trading a set of poker dice and 100 Bazooka Joes for two dog-eared *Penthouse*s, and adding a *Mayfair* from a schoolfriend who shoplifted to order.

This, as I saw it in September 2004, was the world Eleanor was now entering. Not that I remotely expected her to find a shoplifting friend, still less to do any shoplifting herself. But nevertheless it was a world in which she would increasingly assert her independence. And the truth was, she was ready for it. In July she had left a happy Church of England primary school in a village near Herefordshire's border with Shropshire, a parochial place to go to school in all the best senses of that unfairly maligned word 'parochial', but she was, without ever expressing it or even quite knowing it, champing at the bit for more freedom.

THE GOOD, THE DAD AND THE UGLY

At her primary school leavers' assembly, the departing pupils sat on the stage in the little hall and, swaying gently from side to side, some of them clutching teddy bears, performed Ozzy and Kelly Osbourne's version of the old Black Sabbath song 'Changes', the one in which Kelly sang to her dad that the two of them had shared the years, and shared each day, and that she loved him, but she'd found her own way. To which Ozzy sang back that the world is an evil place, but that his baby was grown now, and ready for its challenges. I've never been sure that it's right for a father to send his offspring out into the world with the message that it's full of evil, exactly, but all the same, if ever there was a cue for watching fathers to blub behind their video cameras, that was it. Certainly there were some tears shed, by mums as well as dads, and by some of the more overwrought children on the stage.

Eleanor, though, stayed resolutely dry-eyed, partly because it was only two years since she'd left her previous set of primary school friends behind, when we'd moved out of London, and the overriding emotion she was feeling this time was excitement, at the onset of the long summer holiday and the prospect of a new school at the end of it. I stayed dry-eyed too, and concentrated hard on suppressing laughter at the most transparent attempt to get an audience weeping buckets since Walt Disney killed off Bambi's mother. Even Jane, who has discovered over the years that her tear ducts can hardly ever withstand the sound of children singing, remained unmoved.

In fairness, it was different for the parents who had seen their little darlings go all the way through the school from reception class. Back in London, on the day that Eleanor finished St Mary's Infant School and she and her little friends had trilled 'One More Step along the World I Go', Jane as well as not a few fathers had ended up awash in great puddles of tears. But this transition from primary to secondary school seemed more a case for celebration than tears, albeit laced, particularly on my part, with apprehension.

That summer, we bought Eleanor her first mobile phone. She would be travelling to school in Hereford every day by train, and getting to and from the station would entail a walk across the city. It wasn't a long walk, Hereford being a small city, but we still felt that a mobile phone was now a necessity rather than a luxury, if admittedly for our own peace of mind rather than hers. Maybe she would miss her train, or lose her way to the station.

Back in the Jurassic 1970s, of course, Jane and I had somehow navigated our way through secondary school without mobile phones. I had to get to school by bus as well as train in those days, but the only necessity foisted on me by my mother was a navy-blue Pac-a-Mac that was permanently mildewed, on account of my habit of stuffing it into its own hood, which doubled as a little sack, without letting it dry out first.

Whether I would have had a mobile even if they'd been invented by 1973 I very much doubt, however, my mother generally being of the opinion that anything remotely state-of-the-art was not for me. My first pair of rugby boots were borrowed from our next-door neighbour, Mrs Watson, whose son Giles had worn them a decade or so earlier, and had almost certainly been handed down to Giles by his grandfather, if not his grandfather's grandfather. They were made of cracked brown leather with huge steel toe-caps and lethal studs the size of small bollards, belonged only in a museum devoted to the life and times of William Webb Ellis, and have entirely informed my own approach to my children's sporting needs. I'm all for recycling, and have tried never to lavish things on the children for the sake of the make or the label, but whenever I balk at the cost of tennis racquet A and sway towards the substantially cheaper tennis racquet B, those ancient rugby boots clomp into vision and I dig deeper for the better, more expensive piece of kit.

It is intriguing, this dimension of fatherhood, whereby we strive part of the time to give our children what we had as children and part of the time resolving to give them anything but – whether in terms of books, clothes, toys, holidays, or of more profound commodities such as values and affection. Fathers who were never hugged or kissed by their own fathers tend to be either exactly the same with their own kids, or more tactile than a department-store Santa Claus (before laws came in to keep department-store Santas safely at arms' length).

On a more prosaic level, I wanted my children, especially my sons, to read the books that had engaged me at the same age. As a kid I was devoted to the gently comic novels of Anthony Buckeridge, whose stories about Jennings, Darbishire and their classmates at Linbury Court Preparatory School delighted me endlessly, even though I wasn't at all sure, aged ten or eleven, what a preparatory school was. I excused Eleanor on the basis that they were stories more likely to appeal to boys, but as soon as Joseph was old enough, I banged the drum as loudly as I could for *Jennings*, and also other books I'd loved at the same age, in some cases even foisting on him the very copy I had read myself decades before. It gave me untold pleasure to see Joseph and subsequently Jacob reading my battered Puffin edition of Richard Carpenter's *Catweazle*.

Nevertheless, my success rate in this matter was not high. Joseph was every bit as voracious a reader as I had been, and I should probably have settled for that, rather than trying to interest the Harry Potter generation in the sorcery of *Catweazle*. Nor was Linbury Court much of a rival to Hogwarts. But he generously indulged me by reading *Jennings Goes to School* and even claimed to have quite enjoyed it, which of course represented another milestone on the great journey of fatherhood: the point at which this child, whom you have pretended not to see in endless games of hide-and-seek, whom you have allowed to get the better of you in countless games of I-Spy, starts treating you with mild condescension.

I can remember treating my own father that way myself. I was ten years old, and my best friends Jem and Chris Sykes had been given a spy game, which required us all to have aliases. For some unknown reason I asked my dad to think of a secret name for me, and for some equally unknown reason he suggested William Piping. That was more than forty years ago – and he's been dead more than thirty-five years – yet I can still remember my thought processes. Should I tell him that William Piping was a rubbish name? Or, to spare his feelings, should I adopt it? I took the latter course, convinced that he'd be hurt if I didn't, which meant that my two fellow spies got to be called Jett Black and Aztec Starr, and I was saddled with William Piping.

As I recall, our spy cell communicated via two empty

yoghurt cartons connected by a long piece of string, which seemed to act as a kind of rudimentary walkie-talkie – as long as we shouted into them loudly enough to be heard anyway. I suppose it would have been less fun if we'd each had a mobile phone. Games console addicts might disagree, but technology has removed an awful lot of imagination and invention from childhood fun.

As for buying my own first child her first mobile phone, it was a small rite of passage for us both, since it meant, for the first time in her eleven years, that she could effortlessly make contact with a world beyond the family. This fact came crashing home to me on holiday in north Cornwall the summer before she began secondary school. One day we walked with some friends up to the lighthouse on Trevose Head, to admire the wonderful view, and I was aghast to see Eleanor with her head bowed towards her new and already beloved Motorola for almost the entire walk, frantically texting and cheerfully oblivious to the glorious sight of huge Atlantic breakers crashing onto the rocks beneath us. Naturally, I remonstrated. Not everyone loves a view, but I'm a sucker for a seascape, and a sunset, and have always tried to get my family to share the joy. Again, this sets me up for more condescension, whereby they oblige me with a fleeting ooh or aah, then get back to more pressing matters, like *The Simpsons*, or the Motorola.

Later, of course, I would get exceedingly, gloomily familiar with the spectacle of Eleanor furiously texting, and find it a source of wonder as well as annoyance that she, like practically every other girl of her generation (though not all boys), could somehow manage to hold a conversation, consume a meal or watch a television programme while simultaneously messaging twenty friends. But on Trevose Head came the first inauspicious step into this new world, one in which my daughter, even while notionally in my company, would be far less interested in anything I had to say than in the messages pinging to and from her mobile phone.

Once she started at secondary school, I also found myself dunked into the dark and mysterious waters of social networking. With Facebook in its infancy, the networking site favoured by eleven-year-olds in 2004 was called Bebo, which I didn't even begin to understand. A little later, Eleanor and her friends turned to MSN instant messaging, which I didn't understand either, although at least I got the letters in the right order, unlike our lovely Canadian friend Joanna, a fast-talking, modern-day Mrs Malaprop who calls piccalilli 'Piccadilly', refers to her Sloggies underwear as 'soggies', and to whom MSN was always S&M. 'She's spending an awful lot of time on S&M,' said Joanna, worriedly.

Joanna's daughter Sarah was one of Eleanor's friends,

and frankly, a revelation that they and their other mates were into S&M would have been only marginally more worrying, to some parents, than the reality of their obsession with MSN. Even at the Bebo stage, there were concerns that our impressionable daughters were being groomed by middle-aged paedophiles pretending to be fellow schoolchildren. These were fed by a few media stories of just such sinister deeds, with the consequence that parents already inclined to be neurotic about the dangers of the modern world – which Jane and I weren't, unduly – seemed to lose the power of rational thought. To some, the very name Bebo, apparently an acronym for 'Blog Early, Blog Often', began even to sound like that of a predatory monster in a contemporary version of a Grimm Brothers fairy tale: they talked as if there were no greater threat to their kids than this malevolent Bebo.

All this added up to the overwhelming irony of twenty-first-century parenting, that as our children were allowed less and less to roam unsupervised in the great outdoors, and encouraged more and more to stay inside where they wouldn't be prey to nasty men or endless other risks, the biggest perceived threat to their emotional and physical well-being was suddenly right there in their bedroom or the living room or the kitchen: the computer.

There had been a similar wave of angst during my

own childhood about the television set. I even knew one or two households where there was no television, lest it curdle the brains of younger members of the family, and several others in which viewing was restricted to BBC One and Two, the feeling being that ITV was a wholly malign, downmarket influence. As I recall, these decisions were always taken, unilaterally, by dads, yet a generation later it tended to be mums who fanned the flames of the Bebo paranoia, which I suppose says something about the changing domestic role of the father since the 1960s and 1970s. Broadly speaking, he is no longer the paterfamilias that his own father was, and that is almost certainly for the best.

All that said, it was me who in 2008 instituted the hunt for whoever in the Viner household had been looking at a website called Red Hot Lesbos. I found it while looking for something else in Google History, and made a list of potential culprits. It was a short list, and just to crank up the intrigue I added our middle-aged cleaning lady to it, but in the event all the evidence pointed towards nine-year-old Jacob, not least the fact that, aptly enough, he went red and hot when I mentioned it.

'Jacob, have you been looking at things on the computer that you shouldn't have?'

'What do you mean?' he said, with a passable stab at indignation.

'Well, have you been looking at a website called Red Hot Lesbos?'

'No!'

'Are you sure?'

'Yes!'

'Positive?'

He flushed. It never took much interrogation to make him wilt.

'It was Josh's idea,' he said.

Josh was his schoolfriend, and nine going on nineteen. It added up.

I wasn't sure how cross, how red-hot under the collar, to be. Nine seemed a bit young for boys to be looking at Red Hot Lesbos; in my day it was at least fifteen. But the 'in my day' train of thought was itself worrying. Since when had pornography been a conduit for misty-eyed nostalgia? Still, I clearly remembered friends with older brothers – and one whose father had a stash of 'naughty' magazines in his garage – showing me *Mayfair*s and *Penthouse*s when I wasn't much older than nine. If we'd been able to access internet porn, I suppose we would have done. But that didn't mean I should condone it now. I told Jacob that I didn't want him looking at 'rude' websites, and that if he did it again, I would be much crosser. 'I won't, I'm sorry,' he said.

We left it at that, with Jane and me in agreement that

there was no point raising hell. A week or so later, however, at a dinner party in London, I told the female friend sitting next to me about the website episode, treating it as something more amusing than worrying. Jane overheard and, as we walked back to our hotel, both with a little too much good wine inside us, lambasted me for it.

'That's not something you should be telling our friends,' she stormed.

'Why not? She's got children too. We're all parents. These things happen.'

'Yes, but it's not right to make a joke of it.'

'I wasn't. I was just treating it light-heartedly.'

Those were just the early broadsides in a row that intensified and raged late into the night. In twenty mostly contented years of marriage, underpinned by proper mutual love, respect, shared values and – just as important – the ability to make one another laugh like drains, we have only had a handful of really furious differences of opinion escalating into full-scale shouting matches. But that was one of them. And it was the Red Hot Lesbos that started it.

When we were friends again, we agreed on the need to police the use of the computer. On the other hand, as with the telly decades earlier, it was plainly naive to see this machine purely or even largely as an instrument of depravity. I hadn't got my knickers in a twist over the Red Hot Lesbos – if you, and they, will forgive the metaphor – and eventually, too, knickers untwisted with regard to social networking and instant messaging. Clearly, they were going to loom as large in twenty-first-century adolescence as endless repeats of old episodes of *Friends*, and there was no point wishing them away.

Moreover, the benefits of Eleanor's mobile phone became clear, not least when it also became clear that in eleven years on the planet she had not quite learnt to tell the time, which I suppose was our failing rather than hers. We certainly assumed that she knew, yet on her way from school to the train station she would phone us to ask whether it was yet a quarter to five, which I must remind her about next time she and I have a chuckle affectionately at the expense of another girl, a good friend, whose mum called her on her mobile at the end of one school day in that first year of secondary education to deliver an urgent warning.

'Darling,' she said. 'There's a big pile of dog poo just outside Waterstones. Please be careful not to step in it.'

Maybe this was something about growing up in rural Herefordshire, albeit in Eleanor's case only from the age of nine, that had made her and her friends such apparent innocents abroad, requiring telephone contact with their parents to help them tell the time and navigate their way round steaming heaps of dog shit. It was, I felt, a vindication of our decision to move out of London, the prospect of our children staying childlike for longer.

Certainly, even in the not-overly mean streets of London N8 and N10, Crouch End and Muswell Hill, kids often learn the hard way that it's not a great idea to hold a mobile phone to your ear on the way to or from school, lest it be forcibly removed by members of a passing gang. Of Eleanor's contemporaries at primary school in north London, an extraordinarily high percentage would end up being mugged for their mobiles or iPods. All that could be said for it was that it made them streetwise in a way that Eleanor wasn't.

Despite the increasing amount of time she was spending texting and MSN-ing, Eleanor remained a cheerful, biddable child. But there were more and more signs that she had left her primary-school self behind, starting with her name. She had always been Eleanor, to friends as well as family, but seized on that opportunity for reinvention that secondary school offers to call herself, from day one, Elly. I was torn. I didn't want to be one of those fathers that I'd frequently encountered myself over the years, who answers the phone and responds to your request to speak to Mick with a resounding 'Michael!' Better still, I'd had a friend at university whose name, as far as everyone was concerned, was Bill. We were astonished when it emerged that his actual name was Rupert. When I phoned him at home during one summer vacation, and asked for Bill, his dad told me firmly that I must have the wrong number.

To us, our daughter had always been Eleanor, or Els. Elly didn't sound right. Yet I knew full well that there were greater trials ahead. The teen years were heading our way like distant but approaching thunder, and I wondered just how stormy they would be. It seemed to me that I had weathered the challenges fatherhood had set me so far, but that this one, even taking into account Joseph's five years of wakeful nights, might just be the most turbulent yet.

15

Anything You Do To Her, I Do To You

Forget the birds and the bees.

My journalistic career has yielded many privileges. As a sports writer for the *Independent* I played tennis with John McEnroe, golf with Seve Ballesteros, snooker with Ronnie O'Sullivan, darts with Phil 'The Power' Taylor. And before that, writing a regular column in the *Mail on Sunday* called 'Brian Viner's Telly People', I got to spend one-on-one time with some of Britain's most celebrated entertainers.

Once, in his hotel suite near London's Marylebone Station, an elderly Norman Wisdom did his famous shadow-boxing routine just for me, being punched across the room by an imaginary assailant until he lay spread-eagled and panting on the bed, tie and jacket askew. Another time, I sat across a table from Harry Enfield, who acted out some of the characters he had conceived for his forthcoming television sketch show. So I knew about Kevin the Teenager before the nation did, and realised at once that he would strike a chord not only with anyone who had ever been the parent of a teenager, but indeed with anyone who had ever been a teenager. He was, is, Enfield's simplest yet cleverest comic creation, and his unveiling was a small work of TV genius: the twelve-year-old who is helpful, friendly and polite to his parents until midnight strikes on the day of his thirteenth birthday, when he becomes at a stroke sullen, rude and obstreperous, retaining his niceness only for the parents of his friend, Perry (marvellously played by Kathy Burke), who is similarly lovely to Kevin's parents, yet contemptuous of his own.

It is a metamorphosis that the comedian Jack Dee, a father of four, summed up nicely in a stand-up show that I saw in Ludlow in November 2011. When his son was twelve, said Dee, his suggestion of an outing to a firework display was gleefully welcomed. 'Yes, PLEASE! Can I hold a SPARKLER!?' Yet the following year, the same suggestion was met with a markedly different response. 'NO, it's so GAY!'

There are, of course, plenty of mitigating factors in this process. Hormones start whizzing and crashing round the body like vehicles in a stock car race, and spots begin forming on previously unblemished skin, cruelly at a time when one's looks are of unprecedented concern. Meanwhile, schoolwork is getting much tougher, and peer pressure is building, not least to try forbidden substances, whether alcohol or drugs, or both.

That all adds up to a lot to handle, and to put the tin lid on it, those boring old farts at home expect you to do your share of the washing-up, go to bed at a sensible hour, keep your bedroom tidy, and be nice to your siblings. In some ways, it's less surprising that so many teenagers are obnoxiously unpleasant to their parents than that more aren't. But as even Harry Enfield would acknowledge, all this doesn't necessarily kick off at thirteen. Some kids undergo this transformation when they're eleven, some when they're fifteen or even seventeen, and some not at all. Some actually become easier to deal with in their teens than they were before: Kevin the Teenager turned on his baseball-capped head.

Eleanor's early teen years were relatively untroubled and untroublesome, to the extent that we congratulated ourselves, albeit while remembering that we had also given ourselves a resounding pat on the back for getting her to sleep through the night at an early age, only for Joseph to show us that it was more about good luck than good parenting. Who knew what his entry into the teen years, and later Jacob's, would presage?

Moreover, for all that Eleanor remained, on the whole, an amiable presence in the house, the process continued of me, as a father, becoming more dislocated from her everyday life. At least I had shared with Jane the experience of her becoming a little more independent of us when she started secondary school in Hereford. But with puberty, inevitably and properly, came more distance. Buying her first bra, talking to her about menstruation; obviously these were tasks for her mother, not for me. Nor would it ever be my job, either with Eleanor or her brothers, to raise the thorny issue of sex. Television and the internet had helped to make them a sight more knowing than I was at the same age. They would probably tell me that if I considered it thorny, I must be doing it wrong.

I don't know when the birds and the bees breathed their last, as examples for the ritual parent-to-child talk about reproduction. But it was certainly a welcome development when the nation's schools started shouldering more responsibility than parents for sex education. While they were still at their Herefordshire primary school, our children and their classmates were visited by a friendly, witty nurse who talked frankly about breasts and penises and vaginas. Jane's equivalent, in the early 1970s, was a film of a Labrador having puppies. And if I had an equivalent, I've either forgotten it or blanked it out.

I can't remember how old I was when I first understood the mechanics of sexual intercourse. I do, however, have a vivid memory of asking my dad – I must have been ten or eleven – what a 'johnnie bag' was. My friends Jem and Chris, who were older than me and a little worldlier – which wasn't difficult; there were umbrellas worldlier than me – had had great fun on the way home from a kickabout on our local recreation ground discussing a johnnie bag, and I had chortled along, not knowing what the hell they were on about.

It saddens me, incidentally, that even pubescent boys have stopped talking, and laughing, about johnnie bags. By my mid-teens I knew them as johnnie bags, johnnies, condoms, Durexes, Fetherlites and Black Shadows, without knowing whether there was any distinction between these names, and certainly without ever having used one for anything more exciting than a water bomb.

Anyway, for some reason, my memory of the 'johnnie bag' exchange with my father is etched on my mind, to the extent that I can even recall where it happened: in the car – a brown Ford Granada that was strikingly and thrillingly similar to the one used by Jack Regan and George Carter in *The Sweeney* – on the drive over Hillside

Bridge, close to our house in Southport. The conversation went something like this:

'Dad, what's a johnnie bag?'

'It's something very rude. I don't want you using language like that. I wonder what mum's cooked for our lunch?'

That was the closest to a sex education lesson that I ever received from my father, and the barren wastelands of my knowledge didn't get much in the way of cultivation from my boys' grammar school, either. I wasn't alone, though. I remember our biology teacher, Mr Greenhalgh, holding up a diagram of a human male's sexual organs, and asking us – thirty adolescent boys – to identify the most prominent part of the package.

'Who can tell me what this is?' he asked.

Silence. We were all too embarrassed even to say the word, except for a lad called Stephen Twigge, who put his hand up and, with what seemed to me like audacious bravery, said: 'It's a penis, sir.'

A generation later I didn't want my children to be as clueless as I had been, and yet, the very fact that thirteen still seemed too young to me for a girl to know all about sex, not to mention sexually transmitted diseases, doubtless meant that I wasn't the right person to deliver the information at any age. What I did know by the time Eleanor turned thirteen, and had known for at least a couple of years before that, was that it was no longer appropriate for us both to be in the bathroom at the same time.

For the first six or seven years of her life, I had shared her bathtime as often as possible, sometimes climbing in with her but more typically sitting on a chair nursing a much-needed beer or glass of sauvignon blanc and indulging her fondness for creating little playlets with a variety of plastic and rubber animals. Joseph was usually in there too, and what fun we had with all those improbable, improvised stories involving a sheep, a llama, an eagle, a buffalo and a squirrel. As in most family bathrooms, there was no watershed moment when either Eleanor or I decided that we should bring these communal bathtime larks to an end; they just sort of faded out.

Of course, there is scarcely such a thing as privacy in some households, whereas in others it is held sacrosanct. In a majority of families, I should think that it just evolves, more or less unspoken, although I do recall Jane suggesting one day that thenceforth, before either of us (meaning me) walked into Eleanor's bedroom, we (meaning me) should probably knock. She was entirely right, but it represented one more tiny increment in the growing gap between Eleanor's existence and mine.

This is how it should be. I'm all for physical warmth and emotional candour between fathers and their teenage daughters, but too much of either seems a little weird to me. Or maybe I'm the weird one, because I've never really bought into the notion that there should be anything more special about the relationship between dads and their girls, or for that matter mums and their boys, than between fathers and sons and mothers and daughters. I realise that this puts me out of step with lots of people. 'Obviously you really love your daughter, but you just completely adore your son, don't you,' a female friend of Jane's once said to her, referring to herself and her own two children, to which Jane responded with a slightly queasy, noncommittal smile. She, like me, is uneasy with the mixed gender dimension, feeling that there is something faintly Oedipal about it. Why can't you love and adore all your children equally?

It was Sigmund Freud – who else? – who came up with the idea of the Oedipus complex, named after the mythical king of Thebes who murdered his father and married his mother. I suspect that old Sigmund, were he still around, would tell us that his theory has been greatly misunderstood, and the adjective 'Oedipal' widely misused. But he's not, so we can say what we like. In general parlance, Oedipal has come to mean a slightly unhealthy relationship between a son and his mother or a daughter and her father, and maybe the best way to deal with such an uncomfortable phenomenon is to joke about it, as Joan Rivers did when she said that she had been shocked during one of her comedy performances to see a woman in the fourth row breastfeeding her son. 'I wouldn't mind, but the boy was fourteen years old,' shrieked Joan.

It is unsettling to detect the faint whiff of Oedipus in your friends' relationships with their children. One pal of mine eventually had to tell his daughter, who was demonstrably aware of her sexuality even at the age of eleven or twelve, to stop habitually sitting on his knee and nibbling his ear. On her part it was an exercise in manipulation, pure and simple, and maybe it's true that, more often than not, the female of the species learns those so-called womanly wiles from her relationship with her father. Jack Dee marvelled at the ways in which his daughter wangled money out of him, for example by cheerfully announcing that she'd be absolutely fine walking home, on her own, through the woods, at the end of a night out. It was, he declared, nothing short of extortion.

This emotional blackmail – or emotional leverage, if you prefer – can be deployed at all ages and for all kinds of reasons. A friend of mine, a documentary filmmaker, tells a story about an incident a year or so after 9/11, after he'd spent the best part of a fortnight in New York making a programme about the British victims of the outrage.

It was the first time he'd been away from his six-year-old daughter, an only child, for more than a few days, and he'd missed her intensely, as she had missed him. But he arrived back from New York late at night, after both the child and her mother were in bed, and took himself to bed in the spare room, naked as was his habit, having first locked the door. He had already left a note on the kitchen table asking to be left asleep until 1 p.m. Jet lag was never a problem for him, as long as he could sleep it off as soon as he got home.

At around 8.30 a.m., however, there was a firm knock on the door. 'Daddy,' came a plaintive little voice. 'Daddy, I know you're in there. Daddy, I've missed you so much. Daddy, please let me in. Daddy, I love you so much and I've missed you, I want to see you before I go to school.' Knowing that to wake up would clobber him for the next few days, but that if he slept on he would be able to pick her up from the school gate that afternoon feeling entirely refreshed, he tried to ignore his daughter's voice in the hope that she would give up. But she didn't. 'Daddy, please, please, please let me in!'

There was nothing for it but to pad over to the door, starkers, and open it. And there in front of him was not his daughter but an unfamilar little boy in full school uniform complete with cap and carrying a satchel, having just been dropped off by his mother who'd asked if he could possibly have a lift to school. Appalled, my friend covered his genitals and, turning round, dived back for the sanctuary of the bed. At which point came the satisfied voice of his daughter.

'There you are, Freddie. I told you you'd see his bottom.'

We have to hope that Freddie isn't still scarred by the experience. As for the supposed special bond between fathers and daughters, I've read academic research conducted in the United States to suggest that the quality of the early father–daughter relationship influences romantic liaisons that the daughter will later have, although, as so very often with academic research, the conclusions – presented to the Annual Convention of the Association for Psychological Science, no less – look not so much like the consequences of rigorous study as the application of plain common sense. To wit, conclusion 1: girls with good communication with their fathers also had significantly better communication with their boyfriends when compared with girls with low communication with their fathers; conclusion 2: girls with high levels of trust with their fathers also had significantly better communication and trust with their boyfriends. It took a survey of seventy-eight teens and young adults to find that out. I'm sure I could have saved them the bother.

Whatever, the irony of this is that plenty of fathers would prefer their teenage daughters not to have sexual relationships at all, rather than be told that their own healthy father–daughter interaction has had a positive impact on their daughters' relationships with boyfriends. There are endless examples in popular culture of fathers eyeing with deep suspicion, if not outright hostility, young men with designs on their daughters. In 2007 the American singer Rodney Atkins had a number one in the country music charts with 'Cleaning This Gun (Come on in, Boy)', in which a father instructs his daughter's boyfriend to have her home by 9.30, while ostentatiously polishing his shotgun. And a father's hostility more or less constituted the entire plot of the enjoyable comedy film *Meet the Parents*, while in the rather less enjoyable comedy *New in Town*, Harry Connick Jr's character waves his daughter off to her first dance with the menacing warning to her escort: 'Just remember, anything you do to her, I do to you.'

This is art imitating life. Bruce Willis once said on Jonathan Ross's talk show that when the time came for his eldest daughter to go out with boys, he would tell her date that he'd better bring her back in the same state she left 'because you're a young guy and I'd hate to have to kill you'.

But life also imitates art. In the epic TV serial *The*

West Wing, when Charlie, the aide to Martin Sheen's President Josiah Bartlet, asks permission to take out Bartlet's youngest daughter Zoey, the President says: 'Just remember these two things: she's nineteen years old, and the 82nd Airborne works for me.' A few years later, the real and yet eerily Bartlet-esque American President, Barack Obama, issued a remarkably similar warning to a boy band, the Jonas Brothers, concerning his own daughters. 'Sasha and Malia are huge fans, but boys, don't get any ideas. Two words for you. Predator drones. You will never see it coming.'

Now, if two such paragons of civilised liberalism as Jed Bartlet and Barack Obama can allude to their daughters' well-being by invoking the military might at their disposal, however jokingly, then maybe there is something in the concept of a particular father–daughter bond. They wouldn't make the same tongue-in-cheek threats if it were their sons consorting with older women. On the other hand, neither Bartlet nor Obama fathered sons, so their only relationships as parents were – are – with girls. I'm sure I would be just as quick to respond to a distress call from Joseph or Jacob in the middle of the night, as I would be if it were Eleanor needing my help.

That said, the underlying, often unmentioned, dimension to the father's protectiveness towards his daughter concerns sex. Directly or indirectly, seriously or genially, that's what Bartlet, Obama, Willis and Connick were getting at, and of course the father's anxiety on his girl's behalf often springs from the vivid recollection of what he wanted from girls at the same age.

Even as my own daughter progressed through her teens, however, and started blossoming into a beautiful young woman, I recognised the pitfalls of casting her as the virginal innocent and all the boys in her orbit as potential predators. Surely, the job of a father, as well as trying to equip her with confidence and self-respect, is to take a leaf out of those rather predictable research findings presented to the Annual Convention of the Association for Psychological Science, and foster the kind of relationship with his daughter that will, whether she recognises it or not, boost her chances of enjoying fulfilling relationships with other men. After that, if things go wrong, at least he's done his best, and if there's a song that should be adopted as the definitive father–daughter anthem, it's not 'Cleaning This Gun (Come on in, Boy)' but Paul Simon's lovely, and helpfully titled, 'Father and Daughter', in which he promises to stand guard over her – 'though I can't guarantee there's nothing scary, hidin' under your bed' – until he leaves her with a sweet dream in her head.

That's certainly more apt than another song often associated with fathers and daughters, 'Somethin'

Stupid', simply because it was most famously performed by Frank and Nancy Sinatra. I mean, they did it very nicely, Frank and Nancy, but it's quite the wrong kind of love song for a man and his daughter to sing together.

In 2000, coincidentally, I interviewed Sinatra's other daughter, Tina, who had just written a book, *My Father's Daughter*, about her relationship with the old man. She was in London, staying at the Savoy, and I remember taking her a bunch of delphiniums for no other reason than that I knew how much it would have tickled my own late father, a big Sinatra fan, to think that his son had bought flowers for the daughter of Ol' Blue Eyes.

Tina's own eyes, rather disappointingly, were brown and somewhat lifeless. After giving several interviews back to back she was a picture of weariness, as if she had done a long shift in a coal mine; in fact she was so weary that when I arrived with my flowers she could not quite haul herself from her armchair but merely offered a limp if beautifully manicured hand. 'Thank you, how sweet,' she said, somehow cranking up the energy to glance at the delphiniums before passing them to the ever-obliging publishing PR person.

I asked her, just to break the ice, of which there seemed to be rather a lot, whether she was currently seeing a psychotherapist. Los Angelenos don't mind that question. It's like asking Londoners whether they use the

Tube. 'No,' she said, flatly, 'but I used to, in my teens.' That I already knew. After all, the odds were against her growing up emotionally balanced even before her father left her mother for Ava Gardner, when Tina was just a few months old.

As so often happens with people giving newspaper interviews to publicise their books, Tina Sinatra was a good deal less candid in person than she had been in print. The book put the frank into Sinatra, relating colourful details even of an incident in the early 1970s, when she was twenty-two, and unmarried. She went into hospital for an operation on an ovary, during which the surgeon, Red Krohn – 'gynaecologist to the stars' – discovered that she was pregnant. She came round to find her father at her bedside – Krohn evidently thought that Frank should know before Tina. There was clearly no question of keeping the baby. But Krohn declined to perform an abortion, instead inducing a painful miscarriage in a surgical procedure that lasted five hours. Her father's gift to her during her long recuperation was a colour television set. She was pleased enough with it, until she found out that he'd also given a colour TV to the surgeon, Red Krohn.

Anyway, here's the real point of recalling my encounter with Tina Sinatra. Nancy has described her younger sister as the keeper of their father's flame, and indeed

Tina seems to have assumed that role with a passion verging on obsession. No psychological expertise is required to understand that her preoccupation with Frank's memory and the failure of her two fleeting marriages might just be related. 'I married the wrong men,' she told the *Daily Telegraph* in 2004. 'Was it difficult for them to compete with my father? You bet.'

For good or ill, for sons as well as daughters, and for poor as well as for exceedingly rich, the legacy of the father is lifelong. Tina Sinatra also dated Dodi Fayed for a while, and she referred to him in that 2004 interview as 'the son I never had – he was so cute, but damaged'. No wonder he later hit it off so well with Diana, Princess of Wales, who was also cute, and also damaged, and had also, like Dodi and Tina, been very young when her parents divorced. Unlike Tina, Diana and Dodi were both raised – doubtless with a bit of help from nannies – by their respective fathers, which in their particular cases goes a long way towards explaining why they were so screwed up.

Still, the 8th Earl Spencer could at least take satisfaction in the fact that, as the world knew, the youngest of his three daughters was still a virgin when she married Prince Charles. It might have stood her in better stead had she not been. The sowing of a few wild oats prior to settling down with one person never hurt anyone outside

Victorian novels, and while it might have disqualified her for the hand of the heir to the throne (as it had her older sister, Lady Sarah, a previous girlfriend of the Prince of Wales), that wouldn't have been such a bad thing, either. She'd have had a much longer, happier life.

But it's all very well recommending the sowing of wild oats to people who aren't your own children. I wouldn't want my kids to stay uninitiated, either, but it's not something I want to think about, and it's certainly not something they want to think that I might be thinking about. This is where the brotherhood of dads comes in so handy. Having assumed for so long that there was nothing much I could tell Joseph that he hadn't already learnt at school, or from the internet, or from films starring Hugh Grant, when I did start wondering whether it might be time for a father-to-son chat, I asked my mate Will, my fellow-traveller in the matter of table manners and whose kids are older than mine, whether he had ever raised the subject of sex with his boys.

Only once, he said, and that was after finding a condom in his son Tom's wallet, when Tom was sixteen. He waited until he was driving Tom home from a football match on a Sunday morning a few days later. Will was the coach, and Tom had made a solid contribution to a welcome victory, so with both of them feeling pleased with themselves, and with good father–son bonding vibes all around, he decided that he should seize the moment.

'Tom, erm . . . I happened to be looking through your wallet the other day, and . . . I found a condom.'

The good bonding vibes melted like ice-lollies in the sunshine.

'What were you doing looking in my wallet?'

'I found it lying around. I just happened to look inside it. And found a condom . . . and I just wanted to say, that if you want to have a chat about anything . . .'

'WE ARE NEVER HAVING THIS CON-VERSATION!'

There was a short silence.

'Anyway,' Tom continued, moving from attack to defence. 'It's not mine. I've been keeping it for a friend.'

'Keeping it for a friend? What's he going to do? Phone you at 11 o'clock at night and say, 'Come round, quick"?'

'No! It's not like that!'

And that was more or less that. The subject had been broached, and buried, all within the space of a few traffic lights. And I remembered Will's story when a few years later Joseph set off for a university open day with a friend of his, a girl. I didn't know whether there was anything between them – he had kept his cards tight to his chest – although I did know that they would be sharing a twin room that night. But Joseph was cut from the same cloth as Tom: he would no more welcome a friendly chat from his dad about sexual matters, and responsible behaviour, than he would a sudden poke in the eye with a very sharp stick. At the same time, I felt I needed to say something. So I dropped him off at the station, breathed a deep fatherly sigh, and said, 'Be good.'

16

Happy Birthday, Sweet Sixteen

Force your children to visit elderly relatives
occasionally.

I have leapt ahead in time and must now leap back. As Eleanor – now Elly – moved through her teens, and Joseph – also now at secondary school, and now mostly Joe – moved into them, it became clear that if underage sex wasn't likely to become a major source of parental anxiety, underage drinking would. In the summer of 2008, the summer that Elly turned fifteen, we had a family holiday just outside Porto Venere on Italy's dramatic Ligurian coast, and took with us Elly's best friend T.J. By then we were already well aware of the preoccupation with alcohol among British teenagers, and the willingness among some of their parents to provide access to it. Even at fourteen Elly had gone to parties where the booze was free-flowing.

It was both uplifting and dispiriting, therefore, to sit in Porto Venere's delightful harbourfront restaurants, as we did night after night, watching large gaggles of Italian teenagers, at least fifty of them in total, most of them two or three years older than Elly and T.J., having loads of fun with not a beer or Malibu and pineapple between them. True, more than a few of them were smoking. But it was thumpingly clear that none of them was reliant on alcohol to have a good time. They ate ice-cream, laughed, shouted, chatted, sang, hugged and occasionally snogged late into the evening, troubling nobody. It was impossible – literally impossible – to imagine fifty British kids of sixteen, seventeen and eighteen hanging out every night for a week in a seaside town, sometimes beyond midnight, in the same wholesome manner. There might be laughter, shouting, chatting, singing and snogging. There might even be ice-cream. But there would also be heavy drinking, crying, vomiting, maybe a bit of fighting, and more than likely a few stomachs pumped.

There isn't much point dwelling for too long on the reasons for this. It's basically down to entrenched cultural differences between Mediterranean countries and northern Europe, influenced, in part, by climate. Those same British teenagers, in many cases, have seen their parents having more fun pissed than sober, and also, whether at home or in pubs, drinking for drinking's sake, not to slake a thirst or accompany a meal. In that respect, I'm as guilty as anyone of providing a poor role model.

All the same, it was shocking to me as the father of teenagers to see how early the drinking culture began, certainly earlier than it had when I was an adolescent, and no great surprise when in March 2012 I read in the *Daily Telegraph* that according to the latest research, British teenagers were among 'the world's worst' for both binge drinking and underage sex. In a league table of forty countries, England had the fourth highest percentage of youths who had been drunk by the age of thirteen, with Wales fifth and Scotland eighth. If only the home nations were ranked so impressively in the international football league table.

There is, alas, as we've established, no point pretending that adults are not in some way complicit in this early exposure to alcohol. In December 2008, Elly asked whether she and T.J. could co-host a pre-Christmas dinner party at our house, for them and sixteen schoolfriends. She wouldn't be sixteen until the following June, and T.J. was two months younger, but there was clearly no question, once we had agreed to them having the dinner, of these kids drinking orangeade.

In any case, they were well over the minimum age at which children in the United Kingdom are permitted to drink alcohol 'at home or at a friend's house with the permission of a parent or a legal guardian'. That age, which perhaps you know but I didn't until I wrote this book, is, wait for it, five years old. Five! Moreover, ours is apparently the only country in the world with a minimum legal age for drinking alcohol at home, which surely says something significant about our place in those drinking league tables, though I'm not entirely sure what. Other countries presumably don't see the point in passing legislation either because it wouldn't occur to anyone to give even a heavily watered-down alcoholic drink to a small child (e.g. the USA), or because it wouldn't occur to them not to (e.g. France).

We could, of course, have insisted on a no-alcohol policy at Elly and T.J.'s dinner party. But that would have exposed them to the ridicule of their friends, and thoroughly undermined their image of themselves as sophisticates, which was to be firmly compounded by the dress code: posh frocks for the girls, black tie (or tuxes, that dreaded Americanism – and more, later in these pages, of that phenomenon) for the boys. In any case, it seemed enough to insist that Jane and I, and T.J.'s mum Debbie, be present all evening. We bought a limited amount of sparkling *rosé* for them, but didn't

– oh, the naivety! – allow for the fact that many of the guests would smuggle in extra reserves.

It was, to put it mildly, an interesting evening. Jane, with Elly and T.J.'s somewhat notional help that afternoon, had prepared simple but tasty starters of goat's cheese on bruschetta; then followed by chicken wrapped in prosciutto, with roast potatoes and Mediterranean vegetables. The first sign that the assembled guests might be more interested in drinking than eating, however, came when Elly wove a determined course into the kitchen after the starters and said, 'Mummy, I don't think anyone's, like, hungry any more.' Jane, who was standing with Debbie and me putting the finishing touches to eighteen plates of chicken, gave her a furious glare, which Elly was still sober enough to recognise. 'No, actually, they are,' she said, hastily backtracking. Yet it was clear enough that while we had been lovingly roasting vegetables and carefully wrapping chicken breasts, they had been getting steadily plastered.

As for my admission that I smacked my children a few times, I have no doubt that some readers of this book will think me an irresponsible parent for allowing my fifteen-year-old daughter and many of her friends to get drunk more or less under my nose.

Still, there was never any point in writing this book without being honest. And besides, Jane and I have always given regular parties for our own friends in our home, and have encouraged our kids to do so for theirs. It pleases us that they want to, and pleases us to be able to oblige. At least we can keep an eye on them.

By the end of that evening, we'd realised that it hadn't been nearly enough of an eye. By then I'd removed all the alcohol I could find, but I was turning the key in the stable door with the horse already galloping over the horizon. One of Elly's friends sat in an untidy heap outside the loo, wailing that she'd let herself down. And without going into details, Elly herself was in no fit state even to bid people goodbye. At around 12.30 a.m., parents started arriving to drive their kids home. That's the thing about living in the country, in our case five miles from the nearest town: until your children are old enough to drive themselves (a story for a later chapter), every night out ends either with a parent standing on the threshold jiggling his or her car keys after driving half-way across the county, or with a sleepover.

A word here about sleepovers. My friends and I didn't have them when I was a child, or at least, on the very few occasions we did, they certainly weren't called sleep-overs. At least we haven't started calling them slumber parties, not yet, and yet sleepover is still another Americanism, which I suppose accounts for the follow-ing Wikipedia entry:

Sleepovers are usually held at one participant's house, with other guests sometimes bringing their bedtime things, such as pillows or sleeping bags. Common activities include playing board games or video games, having pillow fights, watching movies, midnight feasts, playing party games such as Truth or Dare?, Light as a Feather, Stiff as a Board, and Spin the Bottle, building forts out of pillows and blankets, or having a spa night, in which participants polish their nails and toes and put on facial masks. Apart from bedrooms, sleepovers can be conducted in tents, trailers, and on trampolines.

Much as British children continue to ape their transatlantic counterparts, I'm not sure that the trampoline sleepover will ever catch on over here. And what the hell is Light as a Feather, Stiff as a Board? It sounds more like an after-dark adult game to me. Anyway, the point is that the sleepover is yet another example of how, over the course of a generation, childhood has become more fun than it used to be, and parenting has become commensurately more indulgent. There will be those who dispute this, insisting that their own childhoods thirty or forty or fifty years ago are memorable for long hot summers filled with carefree days out of doors, and snowy winters filled with sleigh bells and sledges, but surely these memories don't really stand up to scrutiny?

What, for instance, became of the unutterably boring Sunday afternoon outing to see the aged relative, sitting in an overheated room smelling of musty antimacassars if you were lucky, and wee if you weren't, the single highlight being a slightly stale four o'clock custard cream? That was at least as much a part of my 1960s and 1970s childhood as the Space Hopper and Spangles sweets and Suzi Quatro, and of Jane's too, and I suppose it has diminished partly because of a general diaspora, whereby ever-increasing numbers of us are bringing up our children in a different part of the country, or even the world, from where we were raised ourselves. But it is also because, as asserted earlier in this book, we prioritise our children's contentment more than our parents did ours. On the other hand, maybe the present generation of under-eighteens could do with a few more obligatory visits to elderly relatives; it might teach them something about duty, and of course give them a taste for stale custard creams.

I'm ambivalent about all this. None of my children have ever had to spend five consecutive days of a summer holiday with nothing to do: Jane, far more than me, has always made sure that there is a sports course somewhere, or a trip to an outward bound centre, or just a friend coming round, to be followed, almost inevitably, by a sleepover. Yet cycles of five days with nothing to do in the summer of 1975 enabled me to watch every ball of an Ashes series on television. It is a sadness to me that Joe and Jacob haven't learnt to cherish five-day cricket, and the commitment it takes to follow a Test match from first delivery to last. Their lives are too full. Some accommodating emptiness is required.

So, now that I've got that off my chest, let me reluctantly return to those painful moments towards the end of The Great Dinner Party Fiasco when Elly's friends were collected by their parents, who swiftly enough realised that too much drink had been taken. Had we known all of the other parents, we might have managed to laugh it off, and bantered about chalking it down to experience. But many of them we didn't know, and while they were all too impeccably middle-class to berate us, there was palpable, tight-lipped disapproval as young Alex or young Caroline made for the front door with a slight but perceptible stagger, and thanked us slurringly for our hospitality. One of Elly's friends, the girl who had earlier wailed that she had let herself down by drinking too much, weaved up to me before she left and, meaning to thank me for my tolerance, said: 'Mr Viner, thank you very much. You've been very tolerable.' Practically on the spot, it became a family saying.

There were other enduring benefits. A male friend of Elly's ended the evening not only completely sober but also playing the guitar, and thirteen-year-old Joe, who was keeping an impressionable eye on proceedings, thought to himself: 'That's the guy I want to be when I'm older.' He's given up guitar lessons now but continues to regard alcohol with circumspection. Which is not to say that he doesn't enjoy a cider or two at parties, but as far as we know he resists the peer pressure to get hammered, which in his social circle very often involves a 'dirty pint'.

This is a revolting and explosively potent mixture of alcohol, and, *in extremis*, other substances, which is meant to be drunk as a forfeit. The last time Joe was handed a dirty pint at a gathering of his friends, he later reported, matter-of-factly rather than boastfully, that he declined to touch it. I was proud of him for that, and if it is true then I suspect he won more respect than opprobrium from his peers, who recognised that it took more strength of character to say no than to say yes. If it isn't true then he can expect some stick from his mates if and when they read this. Either way, what do I know? I'm just his father.

Whatever, it is hard for many of us dads to take a zero-tolerance or even a zero-tolerable view of our children's consumption of alcohol, if only because we remember our own teenage transgressions. Some of us even remember the prejudice we felt towards us as teenagers.

I don't know whether anyone has ever coined the word teenism, so let me. Most -isms have become socially unacceptable, and our world is a better place for it. In the company of most decent, fair-minded people, casual racism, sexism, and ageism too these days, are frowned upon or, better still, not tolerated at all. But teenism, though of course a form of ageism, is an acceptable -ism, because we've all been on the receiving end. Every adult – black, white, male, female, straight, gay – has been a teenager and therefore prey to the assumption, whether directly or indirectly, individually or by association, that he or she is temperamentally prone to certain kinds of behaviour. That's why teenism doesn't seem to carry the whiff of bigotry that makes those other -isms so unpalatable. Besides, as so cleverly exploited by Harry Enfield, this assumption about teenagers is perfectly true; many, maybe unsurprisingly given the emotional and physiological changes they're going through, are thoroughly horrible to their parents.

It is thought that the word 'teenager' entered common everyday parlance, initially in the USA, in about 1944. It had appeared in print before then – the writer of a feature in an April 1941 edition of the American magazine

Popular Science Monthly declared that 'I never knew teen-agers could be so serious' – but it wasn't until well after the Second World War that it really caught on this side of the Atlantic.

Here, though, there was a problem from the start. The word had really been coined to represent all-American optimism, a kind of antidote to the word adolescent, which had also been introduced in America, by the psychologist Granville Stanley Hall, but implied a more anti-social component of society. American teenagers, by contrast with American adolescents, and despite the paradox that they were one and the same, were by the 1950s considered a Good Thing, the trainee architects of a brave new affluent world. Remember the TV series *Happy Days*, set in the 1950s? Admittedly it was a product of the 1970s, and one probably shouldn't cite the Fonz as part of any lesson in social history, yet *Happy Days* evoked perfectly the generally benevolent attitude towards teenagers in Eisenhower's America.

In Britain, there was no such benevolence. The late 1950s and early 1960s produced angry young men and to a lesser extent women, increasingly at odds with their parents' generation, and the word 'teenager' acquired a pejorative sense that it has never wholly shed. In 1977, in his Father's Day column in *Punch*, the ever-astute Hunter Davies put his finger on it. 'My dad knew what it was like to be me because society hardly changed in those days, but I've no idea what it's like to be Caitlin,' he wrote, referring to his thirteen-year-old eldest child. He was absolutely right, and yet in the last twenty years or so, as mine – and Caitlin's – generation have become parents, that gulf in understanding between parents and teenagers has contracted again.

That's why I try to take a relaxed view of teenage drinking. I don't condone it, and I would rather British teenagers were like their Italian contemporaries, but it would be downright hypocritical of me to condemn it – as one or two of my friends reading this book might testify.

Nevertheless, it is a curious phase of fatherhood, that period when your children become old enough to indulge in the same vices as yourself. On the flip side, they also become old enough to relate to you on an adult footing, the missing dimension in my relationship with my own father. It's rather wonderful when you realise that your children can make you laugh, not simply by doing or saying funny, childlike things, but with a sense of humour as sophisticated as your own. Shortly after she turned sixteen, Elly treated us to her (or possibly Michael McIntyre's) splendid theory that if you put on a posh enough voice, practically any random noun can be turned into an adjective to mean a state of extreme drunkenness.

Try it; it works. 'Yah, I was, like, absolutely budgerig-ared!' 'Oh God, he was just so totally lawnmowered!' 'Darling, she was completely greengrocered!'

To mark her sixteenth birthday, almost exactly six months after the controversial dinner, Elly asked if she – again sharing with T.J. – could have a party in our back garden, this time for eighty people, ranging in age from fifteen to eighteen. After due consideration of the high probability, if not outright certainty, that several of these kids would end up budgerigared, lawnmowered or greengrocered, we gave our consent. Strict warnings were issued, and we insisted on being present through-out. It really did seem like no time since we had been organising Pass the Parcel at our children's birthday parties, not trying to stop Pass the Vodka.

Like all parents of teenagers, we were also keenly aware of stories such as that of Raj and Nishi Shukla of Kingston upon Thames, who were away for the weekend when their sixteen-year-old son Aneesh threw a party he'd advertised on Facebook. They came home to find that 100 people had crashed the party and trashed the house. Six police cars and two ambulances were required to quell the chaos, and the obligatory 'shocked neigh-bours' reported that at the height of the party, people were urinating out of first-floor windows. Within just a few weeks, there were remarkably similar reports of another set of horrified parents, Michael and Nichola Ross from the Wirral, returning home from a wedding to find that their fifteen-year-old daughter Rachel had also made the mistake of posting details of a modest social gathering on Facebook.

'Suddenly from being a small party for her and her mates from school it turned into a riot, with men in their late twenties turning up in cabs,' her shocked father told the *Sun*. Again, the party-crashers trashed the joint, and yet it could have been worse; there could have been decapitations. 'Michael's ornamental samurai swords had been thrown around the house like spears and some were left embedded in walls,' reported the *Sun*. 'The TV remote was microwaved, and bubble bath was poured into the television. Yobs had urinated in their youngest child's bed.' And so on, literally *ad nauseam*.

At least we were going to be on hand, but even so I had nightmarish visions of a banner headline across the front page of the *Hereford Times* – 'Birthday Party Turns into Rave: Three Thousand People Turn Up from as Far Afield as Swindon: Bewildered Parents Blame Facebook'. Happily, that did not come to pass, and yet the deal in these rural parts is that teenagers invited to parties sleep in tents pitched in the adjoining fields, so by the time the thing got under way there was a mini-Glastonbury situation over the fence where the sheep usually are, making it even harder to keep tabs on alcohol consumption.

All the same, I was determined to register an adult presence, so ambled around with T.J.'s dad Patrick trying, and probably failing, not to look like two constables on the beat. I invoked Parental Power only once, relieving an eighteen-year-old boy of a large bottle of gin which he appeared to be drinking neat. I told him in what my wife and children call my Victorian voice – Enforcer Dad – that if he carried on swigging neat gin, he would kill himself. The following morning, looking surprisingly and frankly rather annoyingly bright-eyed, he asked, unashamedly, if he could have it back. I later learnt that he'd taken it from his parents' cocktail cabinet. Whether with their blessing or not, who knows?

It's a strange and probably uniquely British thing, this uneasy relationship triangle involving parents, children and booze. And maybe some of us send out confused signals, occasionally using alcohol as a way of treating our growing teenagers like young adults, offering them a glass of wine or a bottle of beer as a means of bonding with them at home or over Sunday lunch in the pub, but then, when they're going out with their mates, telling them not to drink too much. Very often, of course, they say no to the fatherly offer of an alcoholic drink, and the more deluded of us ascribe this to their maturity, or to a healthy circumspection about alcohol, whereas it's more likely that few of them consider their dads to be ideal drinking companions, and would no sooner choose to swig a beer with him than listen to a new album with him.

And that's another thing: music. It is still the inalienable right of fathers in particular to raise an eyebrow at their teenage children's taste in music, as well as clothes and choice of television programme – I do it myself, if only to wind them up – but I don't ever hear us undermining their affection for a particular pop or rock star by saying, either in mock or genuine uncertainty, 'Is that a man or a woman?' Our own fathers did, as predictably as the sun rose. In the 1970s scarcely anything emphasised the chasm-like generation gap quite like Top of the Pops, and dads walking into the room and annoyingly questioning the gender of Dave Hill of Slade, or Sweet's lead singer Brian Connolly, before walking out again. But our teens, significantly, also coincided with the punk movement. Teenagers who grew up listening to The Clash were never likely to become the kind of parents their own parents had been, lambasting their children for the 'god-awful racket' produced by the Kaiser Chiefs, for example.

As a teenager myself, I was much more into sport than music. Goodison Park and Old Trafford cricket ground were my places of pilgrimage, not Glastonbury and

Knebworth. However, I still went to see Elvis Costello and the Attractions in 1978, and The Specials the following year. My own dad had passed on by then, but his idea of musical nirvana had been Louis Armstrong, the Count Basie Orchestra, and Billy Eckstine duetting with Sarah Vaughan, so it wasn't hard to imagine what he would have made of 'Too Much Too Young', let alone the Sex Pistols. Things are different now. That gulf in understanding has contracted because the cultural gap has contracted. Dads are actually allowed to enjoy the same music as their kids without it seeming either pathetically ingratiating or a desperate bid to appear youthful. And one other thing; they're allowed to wear jeans. When I was thirteen, nobody's dad wore jeans, except possibly to do the gardening.

17

Fools In Old-Style Hats And Coats

Philip Larkin had a point.

To what extent do our childhoods, and by extension our parents' childhoods, and their parents' childhoods, and so on in ever-more diluted fashion back through the generations, forge our personalities? Not many of us can ascribe the way we are to the privations of the Warsaw Ghetto, like my friend Bill, and thank Heavens for it, but all the same, Ignatius Loyola, the sixteenth-century Spanish knight who founded the Jesuits, was surely onto something when he said, if indeed he did say: 'Give me a child until he is seven and I will show you the man.'

It is this notion that has become the guiding principle of the brilliant documentary series that began with *Seven Up!*, the idea that not only your place in society but also your lifelong character are essentially determined by your first seven years of life. In April 2012 I interviewed the illustrious director Michael Apted for the *Radio Times*. As a junior member of the production staff at Granada Television he had assisted in the making of the original *Seven Up!*, and had then directed all the subsequent films, including the one he'd just made, *56 Up*.

We talked about most of the participants, those fourteen people whose lives had been documented every seven years – or hadn't been, in the case of the few who withdrew either permanently or sporadically from the project – since 1964. In every case, he said, it was possible to look at the original film and see the 56-year-old adult in the seven-year-old child, and vice versa, meaning not just physical but also emotional characteristics. This even applied, he said, to the Liverpool-raised Neil Hughes, the most written-about of the subjects, who as an aspiring astronaut at the age of seven was about as cute and engaging as it is possible for a seven-year-old to be, yet later had to cope with mental health issues, homelessness and loneliness that nobody watching him in *Seven Up!* could possibly have foreseen.

If there is an oversight in the *Up* films – and finding fault with them feels a bit like criticising the ceiling of the Sistine Chapel, or *The Complete Works of Shakespeare*, so I'm happy to accept that there might not be – it is the absence of the participants' parents. Rarely are they mentioned, but meeting them, or just hearing about them, would surely have shed more light on how those children had grown into the people they were, and the people they became. In Neil's case, it might have explained the reasons why he was so sparky at seven, so full of life and hope, and why seven years later the light in his eyes literally seemed to have been extinguished. Could his parents have explained it? They were still around, and still together, because he talked at fourteen about going to church with them on a Sunday morning. Were they in some way the cause of the changes that befell him in those years?

Whatever, the second seven years of a child's life are usually more revealing than the first seven in showing what kind of adult he or she will be. That's manifestly true of Neil from *Seven Up!*, anyway, and it sort of makes sense in terms of the child's developing relationship with its parents. If the first seven years of childhood, as a parent, are about helping to lay the foundations of the child's character – teaching him or her to distinguish right from wrong, good behaviour from bad, and other guiding principles such as treating others as you would want to be treated yourself – the second seven years, as your son or daughter becomes more independent, will offer a pretty good indication of how successful you've been.

Of course, not all parents bother with those lessons, or indeed, by their own actions and lifestyle, teach their children the very opposite. Either way, even in the most loving households, in which parents discharge their responsibilities ably and diligently and children respond happily and healthily, there is always going to be some truth in Philip Larkin's famously provocative 1971 poem 'This Be the Verse'. Your mum and dad fuck you up, reckoned Larkin, but then, in mitigation, they 'were fucked up in their turn/ By fools in old-style hats and coats'.

On the assumption that Larkin's poem is the best-known and most widely reproduced piece of verse on the subject of the parent–child relationship, this seems like an appropriate place to quote a dyspeptic American comedian called Doug Stanhope, who considers children to be just like poems: 'They're beautiful to their creators, but to others they're just silly and fucking annoying.'

It's a good joke, and while I was writing this book it was also quoted in the *Guardian* by a columnist called Tim Jonze, who declared himself alarmed at the number of babies being born to people in his social circle – 'suddenly and without warning, they are falling from the sky . . . so frequently are they arriving that I imagine them hitting the ground with a "thwump" noise' – and confessed to being 'petrified' by the prospect of becoming a dad himself, for which he could find no good reason at all beyond the instinctive biological urge to procreate.

Would he understand the mystifying appeal of children once he had them himself, he asked, calling it 'a momentously risky gamble'. He also quoted a recently published book called *Why Have Children? The Ethical Debate*, by the splendidly named academic Christine Overall, which challenges the convention in modern Western society whereby people are more often required to justify the decision not to have children than they are to justify having them. This, says Overall, should be turned on its head: it is the choice to have kids, rather than the choice not to have them, that should be subject to considered justification and reasoning. 'Children are not essential to all good lives,' she writes, 'nor are having and rearing children prerequisites to becoming a good person.'

This is indubitably true. And yet I still find it faintly disconcerting when I meet men of roughly my age in a long-term heterosexual relationship who have chosen not to become fathers, rather than having tried and been unable to conceive. I wouldn't ever register this disconcertion to them, of course, and sometimes scarcely to myself. I can also see that it is my flaw, and that of society in general, rather than theirs. Why should I leave a business lunch, as I did one spring day in 2012, after a long chat with the charismatic man next to me who turned out to be married and childless, thinking it a pity that he wasn't a father as he'd have made a good one? If he didn't want it, why should I have wanted it for him?

That modern assumption that parenthood is the middle-aged adult's natural condition is what Christine Overall's book is all about, and the hundreds of online responses to Tim Jonze's *Guardian* column showed how emotive the whole subject is, as well as proving how snidely unpleasant message-boarders can be from under the comfortable rug of anonymity. Jonze asked, probably for no better reason than that he had a 900-word article to churn out, why, given all the good reasons not to, anyone would have children. 'If only your mum and dad had taken the same advice, Tim,' went one response, 'there would be one less shit article in the world.' Nice. Imagine the stick Philip Larkin would get if he were still around to post 'This Be the Verse' on the internet.

Incidentally, it was Larkin's father – autocratic, racist and misogynistic, and those were his good points – who clearly fucked him up a good deal more than his mum. In 1979, the poet admitted in an interview that the holidays he took with his father, Sydney, 'sowed the seed of my hatred of abroad'. It wasn't altogether surprising. In 1937, when Larkin was fifteen, his father took him on holiday to Nazi Germany, of which Sydney was such an admirer that on the mantelpiece of the family home he kept a small statue of Hitler, which performed a Nazi salute at the push of a button. He also kept Nazi regalia in his office, and only took the swastika down in 1939, on the day war was declared.

Larkin was by all accounts a pretty strange cove himself, but I'm not sure he inherited too many of his father's characteristics. Very often, it's not until you become a father yourself that you realise how much like your father you've become, and Larkin never did. As for me, I don't know how many of my character traits I owe to my own father, because I only had his company for fourteen years. Admittedly, fourteen years is long enough for a parent to have a profound and long-lasting impact on a child; we know not only from Michael Apted's remarkable films but also from the evidence all around us that if not by seven then certainly by fourteen a human being's personality is pretty well established. But I don't think I knew my dad for long enough to know now, beyond my attempts to instil good table manners in my children, how many of my traits, quirks and prejudices were also his. He was warm, funny, gregarious, stylish and popular with his friends. A proper man's man, as many of them told me at his funeral and in the months following. He also had an addictive personality (gambling, horses and poker being his particular weaknesses), with a streak of intolerance that seemed to be aimed quite whimsically at certain of my friends, certain of my mother's friends, and certain people in the public eye such as, bizarrely, the actor Stewart Granger, for whom he reserved special disdain.

The other reason for not knowing how many character traits I picked up from him, as I've also recorded, is that I was adopted, aged all of two weeks. So when, in my thirties, I met my biological father for the first time, my biological mother having unexpectedly tracked me down with the help of a post-adoption agency, I became a one-man case study for the Nature v. Nurture debate.

In his book about the dynamics of the child–parent relationship, which in homage to Larkin he titled *They F*** You Up*, the psychologist Oliver James used the story of John Hinckley to illustrate the complexities of the nature–nurture thing. Hinckley was the disturbed young man who developed an obsession with the actress Jodie Foster, and in March 1981, as a demonstration of his love for her and to show himself worthy of her, tried to assassinate Ronald Reagan. In 1985, Hinckley's parents published an account of their life with him. Their central thesis, understandable enough in the circumstances, was that their son's pathological personality was all to do with nature, pre-determined by his

DNA, and nothing to do with nurture. Nothing that they had done as parents, they insisted, could possibly have turned him into a mad fantasist who was prepared to murder the American President as some sort of warped billet-doux.

James asserts that, in the view of most bright people, what makes people tick is partly nature and partly nurture. But this, he claims, is wrong. In his persuasive opinion, the circumstances and environment of a child's upbringing are hugely more influential in determining its character than its genetic make-up. Nonetheless, the debate endures, as it has for generations. According to James there is even a political divide between those who believe in nature as the overriding influence, and those who stick up for nurture. He cites a survey from as long ago as 1949 which showed that politically right-wing people tend to favour genes as the dominant factor in who we are, while folk on the political left identify the environment. It is the same today, he suggests: 'The right will tend to argue that the hierarchies of society reflect genetically given talents, so that the rich are there because they have better genes, the poor are poor because they come from less good genetic stock. Likewise, women should be at home caring for children because genetic evolution has equipped their sex better for this role. For the left, these things are seen as the effect of society, something that can be changed.'

I don't know what Oliver James's politics are (though I do know, from having once worked in the same newspaper office, that he looks strikingly and disconcertingly like the actress Zoë Wanamaker), but his is the typically left-wing view that nurture trumps nature. And yet, if I might present myself as exhibit A in the case against, I'm not convinced.

My biological father turned out to be a ceramicist, extremely illustrious and indeed rather famous out there in the world of pottery. My birth mother too was flamboyantly artistic, a 1960s' hippie chick with a vast and valuable collection of textiles and jewellery from central Asia that she had assembled during her many extended visits there, and which was important enough to be displayed in the Victoria and Albert Museum, although when the V&A asked her to give a talk about her cultural immersion in Afghanistan in the 1970s and 1980s, she replied sweetly that she couldn't remember anything about it, having been stoned most of the time.

After giving me up for adoption she had gone on to have two other sons, who by the time I got to know them were a professor of Russian politics, author of some highly regarded academic textbooks, and a successful, wonderfully idiosyncratic artist, based in New York. My

two half-sisters and one half-brother through my birth
father also, to one extent or another, worked with their
hands. So there was clearly a creative gene in me, demon-
strable throughout my schooldays when I had no idea
who my blood relatives were and assumed I never would,
and then in my choice of writing as a career.

Writing, moreover, is a skill and interest that has
informed my life, helped to shape my personality. Yet, if
I had been the natural, biological child of my mum and
dad, I doubt whether I would ever have become a writer.
They were bright and articulate people, but not really
artistic or creative. Whatever natural talents I might
have had that they didn't were certainly nurtured and
encouraged, but it's clear that my particular genetic
inheritance determined my professional destiny, and to
an extent my personal life, since it was through journal-
ism that I met Jane.

What, though, of my particular foibles as a father?
Can they be traced to the father I had for fourteen years,
or to the biological father I didn't know until I was in my
mid-thirties? Or both? Or neither? Maybe even my
preoccupation with table manners was innate.
Intriguingly, it turned out that my birth father had been
strict with his three legitimate children, and something
of a martinet at mealtimes.

I suppose that if I were ever to succumb to

psychoanalysis, something might be made of the fact that of the two fathers I've had in my life, one forsook me by dying and the other by giving me up for adoption (not that I attach any blame to either of them, let me hastily add). This brings me back to an assertion made much earlier in this book: that the first and most important challenge of fatherhood is simply to stick around. But maybe it's time to consider what tends to happen to people who are deprived, early in life, of their fathers.

It needn't have a negative influence, indeed a disproportionate number of American presidents, including George Washington, Thomas Jefferson, Barack Obama and Bill Clinton, grew up either without a father on the scene at all, or having lost him in their impressionable adolescence. There is plenty of evidence to show that men who for one reason or another were separated at an early age from their fathers are statistically more likely than those who grow up with an ever-present paternal presence either to succeed spectacularly in life, or to fail spectacularly. Or, in the cases of Adolf Hitler and Josef Stalin, both.

In *They F*** You Up*, Oliver James explores just this phenomenon, citing Mahatma Gandhi and Leo Tolstoy as further examples of 'a lifetime struggle to repair damaged self-esteem and to prove his worth to the world'. According to James, the early loss of a father makes a boy feel inadequate and exposes him to the danger of deep self-loathing because he cannot replace the source of stability, the family breadwinner. After that, suggests James, his life becomes one long battle to overcome his inadequacy, and to replace his dead father.

I don't think I'd own up to that one myself, but maybe stretched out on a sufficiently comfortable couch I might. I certainly don't mind being in a club with Gandhi and Tolstoy, not to mention Isaac Newton, another high achiever who grew up fatherless, although the club looks less appealing when you find Hitler and Stalin on the membership list. For Oliver James, all these men, as a deep-seated response to losing their fathers at such a young age, 'used the control of fellow humans as the means of expressing their need for mastery'. Gandhi and Tolstoy did so benignly, Stalin and Hitler malevolently. Then there was George Frideric Handel, whose stern father wanted him to take up law as a career rather than music. Handel was only eleven when his father died and the psychoanalytical view is that the major guiding force in his remarkable subsequent deeds was a desire to prove the old man wrong.

Who knows for sure? I don't, and I don't suppose that Oliver James does either, really, though I admire the breadth of his research, and I definitely admire any book that in adjacent paragraphs can summon Jean-Paul

Sartre and Tracey Ullman to elucidate the same theory. In his autobiographical work *The Words*, Sartre considered the impact of the loss of his father Jean-Baptiste, when he was only two years old. 'Making his moods my principles, his disappointments my pride, his quirks my law, he would have inhabited me . . . the death of Jean-Baptiste was the big event of my life,' wrote Sartre, adding that his father's passing had left him soulless and rootless, which clearly informed all those existential musings on the nature of nothingness while wearing his beret at the Café de Flore, before going home to bonk Simone de Beauvoir, doubtless still in his beret.

As for Tracey Ullman (from whose eponymous show *The Simpsons* was a mere spin-off, unbelievable as that now seems), she was six years old, being read a bedtime story by her father, when he suddenly had a massive heart attack and died. Apparently, it was the little comedy routines she did to cheer up her bereaved mother, in the months and years following that traumatic episode, that made a comic actress of her.

So, the point is that fathers don't even have to be breathing to exert a powerful and enduring influence over their children's lives. But the problem I have with the fatherhood theories of psychologists such as Oliver James, and for that matter anyone's theories, including my own, is that we're all wired differently. Plainly, two people might lose their father at a young age and develop in entirely different ways. In fact, such theories can be downright dangerous, because people who don't seem to conform to them often start worrying that they're out of step with the world.

In fact, the more I think about it, the more redundant almost all parenting theories seem. The dear old Earl of Rochester hit the nail on the head all those centuries ago, with his line about having no children and six theories, and in due course, six children and no theories. After all, six children means six different personalities and sets of needs, in relation to each other as well as to their parents. Thus, everyday fathering can require the kind of diplomacy, and conflict resolution skills, that people look for in your average secretary-general of the United Nations.

This is another area in which it is useful to hear from other dads about their headaches, to cast some perspective on your own. And the need for conflict resolution strategies is by no means restricted to the fathers of young kids. My friend Simon once came back from a skiing holiday with his three children, then aged twenty-one, nineteen and eighteen, and was so utterly aghast at how the holiday had been blighted by their constant bickering that he resolved to find the Latin for 'when in doubt, be an arsehole' and incorporate it into a handsome new family coat-of-arms.

It is principally their middle child, apparently, whose demeanour tends to dictate the mood of family gatherings. If he's feeling upbeat, everything goes with a swing. If not, a kind of gloomy irritability infects everyone. There is someone with this influence in plenty of families, and I suppose it's more often the mother or father than a child. But if it is a child, and if that child has siblings, then again the nature v. nurture debate becomes relevant. Why should his or her mood flavour an entire afternoon or evening? Is it innate, or is it learnt behaviour? And if it's the latter, then how come the other siblings haven't absorbed the lesson?

Jane has a female friend who every Sunday morning used to look anxiously out of the kitchen window, waiting for her husband and teenage son to arrive home from football. She could tell instantly from her son's expression and body language whether the team he played for had won or lost, and therefore knew at that moment whether Sunday lunch would be a pleasure or a trial. It's easy enough to say that his father, himself a forthright character, should have used the car journey home to tackle the situation, and point out how inappropriate it was to cast gloom when so much effort had been put into preparing the Sunday roast. But teenagers are often immune to that kind of reasoning. They consider themselves victims of unfairness, not perpetrators, and even when they know they're acting unreasonably they are powerless to stop, like highly strung runaway horses that would quite like to stop galloping, but can't.

Joseph, our own middle child, will have to forgive me for using him as an example of this phenomenon, but here goes anyway. It was a Sunday lunch too, though at our local pub, the King's Head, rather than at home. Joe, then aged sixteen, at first asked for a steak, but just before going outside to kick a football around with Jacob, called over that he would have a burger instead. Unfortunately, for some reason I didn't process this change of mind, and ordered him a steak. Which was cooking by the time I realised the mistake.

'I'm sorry,' I said, when he came back in. 'I forgot you'd changed your mind, and I ordered you a steak.'

His face darkened. 'But I told you I wanted a burger,' he said.

'I know, but I forgot.'

'But I'd only just told you.'

'Well, I've said I'm sorry. It's not such a disaster, is it?'

And that should have been that – the kind of prosaic exchange with which most families are familiar. But Joe couldn't shake off his annoyance, speaking only when spoken to, and then sullenly. In turn, his anger engulfed me. What kind of nonsense was this, a child resentful at being served an £18.95 steak? It was all I could do not to invoke starving children in Africa, an appeal to a child's sense of proportion that practically all parents make from time to time, and which is always a mistake, since they hardly ever respond to it as we hope they will, making us even crosser. Joe certainly wouldn't have done.

The meal continued in this fug of crossness, and when we got home I exploded, telling him he was an ungrateful wretch and in return getting cold-shouldered for the rest of the afternoon and most of the evening. But before he went to bed that night he apologised profusely and sincerely. And Jane reminded me that we had been there ourselves as teenagers, she and I, trapped in that cocoon of irrational contempt for the rest of the family and sometimes the wider world too, and unable to break out of it. If there were Ten Commandments for fathers, maybe that should be the first one: Remember Thy Own Childhood And Do Unto Your Children As You Would Have Had Done Unto You. And yet, of course, we would break it all the time.

18

The Sky-Diving Years

We have to trust them to keep themselves safe.

Rolling back through the decades to your own teens can be a torment as well as a help to a father of teenagers. Especially when it comes to matters of personal safety. All the stupid things you did, the risks you took, that feeling that you were indestructible. How agonising it can be to realise that your children are entering the same phase of life.

That said, I never dreamt of jumping out of a plane. Yet in mid-October 2009, Elly, then sixteen, casually announced to us one day that she intended to do just that – a sky-dive in aid of a Hereford-based charity called Concern Universal. We blithely assumed that this was a vague ambition for some time in the middle-distant future, but then she added matter-of-factly that it was all fixed for 31 October, just a fortnight later.

'If I was going to jump out of a plane,' I said, a little sourly, 'Halloween is probably one of the two dates I'd avoid, along with Friday the 13th.'

'Ooh, I hadn't realised it was Halloween,' she said. Fleetingly, she pondered whether she could carry a broomstick, just to make the pictures better for her Facebook page.

I was torn between pride and anxiety. All that time spent diligently strapping her into her car seat and her Maclaren pushchair, and here she was intending to plunge 13,000 feet from an aircraft, albeit strapped to the front of an instructor. I knew, however, that there was no point trying to dissuade her. Besides, I didn't really want to. It pleased me that she'd be raising money for Concern Universal, a fine charity, although I braced myself for universal concern from the extended family.

Sure enough, one of her grandmothers mused that sixteen seemed a bit young for sky-diving, and I felt much the same, at least until I saw that week's *Hereford Times*, which carried pictures of ninety-year-old Maggie White, wearing her mother's 1927 flying helmet, on a sponsored sky-dive to raise funds for an extension to her Quaker Meeting House. There was something rather splendidly British about a nonagenarian raising funds for a Quaker Meeting House by jumping out of a plane, and afterwards the redoubtable old lady told the *Hereford Times* that she would cheerfully have another go. 'Perhaps not tomorrow but maybe next week,' she said, and it struck me that one sky-dive probably wouldn't be enough for Elly, either. Or that she would insist on doing the next one solo, or maybe bungee-jumping off the Severn Bridge or something.

A bungee jump was certainly on her agenda. One of her friends had recently come back from a gap year in Australia enthusing about his jump in Cairns, although just as he was taking off into thin air, the guy supervising said urgently, 'Hey, wait a sec, mate, I'm not sure you've got your fore-buckle properly fastened . . . oh no . . .'

It was just a wind-up, of course. There isn't even such a thing as a fore-buckle, and the story reminded me of my father-in-law Bob, who on reporting for his first day's work at a South Yorkshire colliery in the 1940s was sent to the workshop for a Long Stand. There's no such item as a Long Stand, either. He was made to wait in a corner and after forty-five minutes reminded the bloke why he was there. 'Aye, tha's 'ad tha long stand, tha can bugger off nah,' he was told.

Her friend's story about the mythical fore-buckle did not put Elly off the idea of jumping from a great height, and I wondered whether actually the nature–nurture thing wasn't a complete red herring in analysing your children, for I didn't see how either nature or nurture had produced a female adrenaline junkie.

I doubted whether her younger brothers would follow in her slipstream, but then Jacob had already done his sky-dive, out of that restaurant window in Spain. It must have been seven or eight years after that episode before I stopped getting sweaty palms whenever I saw him at the top of a high stairwell. Or anywhere above ground level, really. Even now there are times when we're close to a precipitous drop that I have to fight the urge not to grab a fistful of T-shirt, most recently at the top of a tower in San Gimigniano, Italy, when he was fourteen years old. Good parenting, it sometimes seems to me, is a triumph of sense over impulse.

But then there's parenting, and there's parenting of teenagers. And where we live, in the wilds of the Welsh Marches, a part of England where you don't need a time-table so much as a five-year diary to know when the next bus is due, the parenting of teenagers involves looking through your fingers at the news pages of the *Hereford Times*, where almost every week there is a story about a fatal car crash involving the under-twenties.

Round here, as doubtless in other parts of rural Britain, children yearn to start driving the instant they turn seventeen, and then pester you to either buy them a car, or lend them yours, or let them buy their own banger barely fit for a scrap yard. In towns and cities they can assert their independence with the help of public transport, but in these parts they either learn to drive, or continue to rely on mums and dads for lifts, which isn't ideal for anyone but does statistically increase their chance of arriving at their destination in one piece. With her birthday falling in June, Elly hadn't even got her L-plates before some of her friends had suffered their first accidents.

Mercifully, none of them were injured, but one of them wrote off the family car, and I was reminded of my schoolfriend Pete, who in Southport in the autumn of 1979 – with 'Cars' by Gary Numan at number one in the charts, just to add vinyl to injury – was driving his mother's little olive-green Fiat home in triumph, having twenty minutes earlier passed his driving test at the first attempt when he saw a lad walking along the pavement whom he recognised as another schoolfriend of ours, 'Bugsy' Everett. Waving excitedly, Pete fleetingly took his eyes off the road, and was rewarded with a sudden unexpected impact and that horrible dull sound of splintering metal. He'd back-ended the vehicle in front of him, completely written off his mum's car and, after all that, it turned out that the bloke on the pavement wasn't even Bugsy.

I told Elly this sad and salutary tale, presenting it as the best illustration I knew of how a new driver's technical proficiency and fluency in all aspects of the Highway Code are countered by a potentially disastrous lack of experience and road sense. She looked at me with that expression with which all fathers of teenagers are familiar, a look combining scepticism and boredom, and loyally insisted that the accident had been absolutely no reflection of her friend's driving ability.

'In fact,' she said, 'he's a very good driver.'

'I'm sure he is,' I said soothingly, 'but you have to admit that he's not very experienced.'

Elly would admit no such thing. 'He's really experienced,' she said, indignantly. 'He passed his test at, like, the beginning of the Easter holidays.'

Our anxiety over the sky-dive – which in any case had passed without incident, albeit with me watching from the ground wearing a sickly smile of false confidence and bonhomie – seemed piffling compared with our worries about her turning out of our drive on her own. We also, as it turned out, had to shepherd her through the emotional maelstrom of failing her test. Failure was a relative stranger to Elly, and this was comfortably the biggest challenge she had ever flunked. When, after duly commiserating, I gently theorised that failing her driving test was a fair indication that she wasn't yet ready to drive, she took considerable umbrage. It wasn't that she was protecting her dignity and secretly knew I was right. She knew, in fact, that I was wrong.

When eventually she did pass, and was about to set off down the drive on her own, in my car, I had to wrestle with that eternal parenting conundrum: how to warn her about life's perils – in this case, the perils of other drivers overtaking on blind bends and crests, for which our two local major roads, the A44 and A49, are grimly notorious – without presenting the world as one great big bag of terrors. In truth, we had always tried to encourage all three children to look at the outside world and see stimulation and opportunity, rather than pitfalls and danger. I didn't want any of them to think, as Ozzy Osborne sang, that it was full of evil. Which is not to say that the evil and the dangers aren't real, and children should be made aware of them, but just as you can make a neurotic out of a five-year-old for warning her never, ever to speak to strangers, so you can unnerve a fifteen-year-old by giving her a rape alarm.

Jane goes further than me in this regard. Like Blanche Dubois in *A Streetcar Named Desire*, though without being anywhere near as doolally, she tends to place the utmost faith in the kindness of strangers. And similarly, she has always trusted Elly's driving ability, worrying only about the irresponsibility of other drivers on the road. I'm more inclined to bang on about the need to keep under the speed limit, and of course the need not to have even a single alcoholic drink in the course of an evening. Do I practise what I preach? Of course not. But when was that ever a tenet of fatherhood?

My good friend Mark will not mind me, at this juncture, telling a story at his expense. One day, aged nineteen, he borrowed his mum's car, and as we were all wont to do in those days, drove it like the clappers along the coastal road in Southport, at least until he reached the back of a long line of cars. After a while chugging along at 40 mph, he decided to overtake the entire line of about eight vehicles, regardless of the approaching bend. Reaching more than 80 mph, he just managed it, but had to swerve sharply to avoid a head-on collision with an oncoming car. By now he was at the front of the line of eight cars, and glancing in his rear-view mirror just before he accelerated out of sight, realised to his dismay that the vehicle at the front of the line was his dad's, the old man rigid at the steering-wheel having realised that the car that had just performed a madly risky manoeuvre more worthy of the Indianapolis 500 than the Southport coast road was in fact his wife's. Not that he entertained the idea for more than a split-second that she, a singularly sensible and genteel woman, might have metamorphosed into Emerson Fittipaldi. For Mark there was, of course, hell to pay.

THE GOOD, THE DAD AND THE UGLY

I've told my children many stories of the high jinks my friends and I used to get up to at school and university, but I've carefully edited out all the tales of irresponsible driving. I wouldn't want them to think, even subliminally, that if their dad did it and got away with it then so can they. But will they make the same mistakes anyway, which in my case, and Mark's, mercifully never resulted in disaster?

Probably not. Happily, it is clear that the current generation of young drivers are far better educated than we were about the dangers of recklessness at the wheel. Joe came home from school one day, while in the fifth form, and said that his year group had that afternoon been given a spellbinding talk by a man who'd been an extremely promising golfer, a boyhood contemporary of Nick Faldo, Ian Woosnam and Sandy Lyle, and almost as good as those guys, with a glittering career as a professional seemingly ahead of him. But then he drove while drunk and killed someone, and served a two-year prison sentence. His talk, so eloquent and powerful about the catastrophic effect this had had on his life, made an enduring impression on Joe. I wished that someone had done the same for me at the same age; not that I habitually drove while over the limit, but I can't pretend that it didn't happen occasionally, in my late teens and early twenties.

It wasn't until 1989, however, when I was twenty-seven and certainly old enough to know better, that I was stopped while driving over Putney Bridge in London for the solid reason that it was 1 a.m. and I had no headlights on. The reason I hadn't switched my lights on was, frankly, because I was pissed. I certainly hadn't intended to drive, but I'd been at a party with a woman I fancied, and when she announced that she was feeling unwell and wanted to go home, with no mini-cabs available for more than an hour and black cabs scarce in that part of London so late at night, I stupidly decided to take the risk. I was positively breathalysed and in due course, at West London Magistrates Court, fined £180 and banned from the roads for fifteen months. But it was in Fulham police station that I got the pep talk I could have done with years earlier. A kindly sergeant pointed out a drunk sprawled on the floor.

'We picked him up shortly before we stopped you,' he said. 'He was staggering across Putney Bridge, lurching off the pavement and into the road, and a few minutes earlier you might have hit him. It wouldn't have been your fault, but if you'd killed him, while over the limit, you'd be going to jail. As it is you're going to get a fine and a ban, which might seem like a terrible thing, but it could have been much, much worse.'

I've never told my kids that story and I hope I never

have to, and yet fatherhood is perhaps more about deploying your failures and embarrassments for the benefit of your children, than your achievements and triumphs.

I have a friend, a charismatic and highly successful man, well known in the entertainment industry, who early in his career was an alcoholic and a cocaine addict. It is getting on for twenty-five years since he kicked both addictions – like all recovering alcoholics he knows how long it is practically to the minute since he last had a drink – and while I was writing this book I talked to him about that, and about his own father, who committed suicide while suffering from a debilitating disease, and about being a dad himself, to three sons and a stepdaughter.

His eldest boy was approaching the age at which social gatherings could be expected to involve alcohol, and so I asked my friend – I'll call him Tommy – how he thought he might deal with this. Would his own history make him more or less tolerant of adolescents getting pissed?

'If one of my sons demonstrates a character defect that I know runs florid within me,' Tommy replied, 'I can say to him, "Look, I'm a bit like this, you know, and I've found in life it can scupper you now and again."'

He hadn't intended, though, to share with his sons the tragic details of his father's death, at least not until they were eighteen or so, but there is scant hope, in this internet age, of anyone of even modest renown keeping any aspects of their personal lives away from their children. And at twelve years old, sure enough, his eldest son did a Google search which revealed elements of the story, although not the whole truth.

'He asked me about it,' Tommy told me, 'and so I told him. My feeling is that if a child is old enough to ask a question which speaks of a vacuum in his knowledge of his father then if you don't fill that vacuum with the truth, he'll fill it with sinister thoughts. Asking the question meant he was old enough to get the answer.'

That certainly hadn't been my own father's approach to parenting, which is why when I asked him on Hillside Bridge what a johnnie bag was, he swiftly changed the subject to what my mother might have made for our lunch. But it's a healthy philosophy, and it enabled Tommy to talk at length about his father, whom his son had never known.

'He was a good father and I loved him,' he had concluded to his son, following which there was a pause, and then the son said, 'You're a good dad as well.'

That story made me well up with tears hearing it, and I'm welling up again telling it. Poignant stories of father–son relationships almost always move me if not to tears, then somewhere close, though I prefer there to be at least the promise of a happy resolution. That was emphatically not the case in the almost unbearably tragic tale of Dominic Crouch, a fifteen-year-old boy from Gloucestershire who in May 2010, little though his parents knew it, was the target of homophobic bullying. On a school trip to the Forest of Dean one weekend, he had been dared during a spin-the-bottle game to kiss another boy, and did so, but another pupil took a picture on a mobile phone, which allegedly was circulated around the school on the Monday of the following week.

On the Tuesday morning Dominic's older sister Giulia drove him to school. He hadn't mentioned the incident and there seemed nothing wrong. Yet that lunchtime he walked to the top of a nearby six-storey block of flats and jumped off. Dominic, who was dyslexic, left a note that said: 'Dear Family I'm so sorry for what i'm about to do. I hav been bullied alot recantly and had alot of shit! made up about me that ain't true. I'm sorry for what i have done and what has happened. This led me to commit suicide. Love Dominic Crouch'.

There is much that is heart-rending about that letter, but what I find almost more poignant than anything, for some reason, is that he signed his full name. In fact he did not die instantly, but lived on in intensive care for several hours with multiple fractures and massive internal injuries. His mother Paola, father Roger, and Giulia sat with him, and two years later Paola told the *Mail on Sunday*: 'Giulia talked to him. I couldn't talk. I couldn't breathe. The shock as he died was . . . I couldn't take it in. When he died Roger just wailed. You could hear him for miles . . .'

At Dominic's funeral, Roger spoke movingly and brilliantly about bullying issues. 'Sadly, we all know people in this world who so lack real self-esteem that they have to steal it from others, too often from people like Dom,' he said. Four weeks later, Roger took an overdose. Paola found him in time and called an ambulance. He rallied to become an indefatigable anti-bullying campaigner, touring schools and meeting MPs, talking about what had happened to Dominic. In November 2011 the gay equality charity Stonewall gave him their Hero of the Year award. Neither he nor Paola thought that Dominic had actually been gay, more that he'd been innocently playing a high-spirited game, but partly as a consequence of his dyslexia had found himself unable to frame quick retorts to the subsequent taunts. Whatever his sexuality, homophobic bullying is endemic in Britain's schools. A report commissioned by Stonewall concludes that 98 per cent of secondary-school teachers have witnessed it.

And in this terrible instance, it claimed not one life but two. Just a few weeks after receiving the Stonewall award, Roger Crouch hanged himself. 'When Domi died, it was like a black box opened up inside his head,' Paola later told the *Observer*. 'It seemed to be the beginning of the end . . . I don't think Roger meant to kill himself. I think he meant to stop the pain.'

It's hard for any father to know how he might react to the death of a child, whether in those tragic and avoidable circumstances or any other. In 2008, Barry Mizen, fleetingly mentioned earlier in these pages, lost his sixteen-year-old son Jimmy to a random murder following a row in a south-east London bakery. Like Dominic Crouch's father, he dealt with the grief by turning himself into a robust campaigner, in his case against casual violence, yet he did not fall prey to, or perhaps more accurately was able to fight off, the demons that compelled poor Roger Crouch to take his own life. Outside the Old Bailey, following the conviction in March 2009 of Jimmy's nineteen-year-old murderer, Barry Mizen talked with dignity, passion and great common sense. 'This country stands apart from most other countries in the world,' he said. 'It is a country of civility, fair play, fairness and safety. But we are rapidly losing that. We are becoming a country of anger, selfishness and fear. It doesn't have to be like that. Let's together try and stop it.'

Amen to that, and yet the sad truth is that in the time

it has taken you to read these chapters, similar tragedies will have befallen other blameless fathers of blameless teenagers. It turned out, incidentally, that Roger Crouch had been bullied himself as a schoolboy. He knew what it felt like and he would doubtless have been able to help, had he only been aware of what Dominic was going through. In fact, that was one of his most painful torments, the feeling – understandable, if unwarranted – that it had been within his power to prevent his son's death. And there lies one of the great challenges of fatherhood: as your children move into and then through their teens, they become more and more independent of you (which is not quite the same as becoming less and less dependent). This is a natural, overwhelmingly positive development in the lives of both parent and child, and it was ever thus, but it also means that the father is increasingly unable to exercise the protectiveness that is his natural instinct. We can't keep them safe if we don't know where they are and what they're doing; we have to trust them to do it for themselves.

19

Dad Things

'Love is proved in the letting go.'

In October 2011 Elly went to university. Just as she had been ready to leave primary school for secondary school, and unable to join in with the sentimental blubbing among her little eleven-year-old friends, so – for all that she hugely enjoyed secondary school and made some marvellous friends there – was she clearly ready to take the next step along the pavement of life. For us, just to switch metaphors, the departure of our eldest chick resulted in the first tingle of empty-nest syndrome.

This, I knew, could be a trauma for fathers as well as mothers. The author J. G. Ballard, who had brought up his three children on his own following his wife's sudden death from pneumonia in 1964, once wrote of his own empty nest, that 'childhood has gone and in the silence one stares at the empty whisky bottles in the pantry and wonders if any number of drinks will fill the void.' Yikes.

Another writer, Jack Rosenthal, despite still having the engaging company of his wife Maureen Lipman, took it even harder, seeking some kind of catharsis in his wonderful television plays *Eskimo Day* and *Cold Enough for Snow*. For the poet Cecil Day-Lewis, the most painful wrench had come earlier, when his son Sean went to school for the first time, though it took him another eighteen years to write his evocative poem 'Walking Away', which concludes:

> I have had worse partings, but none that so
> Gnaws at my mind still. Perhaps it is roughly
> Saying what God alone could perfectly show –
> How selfhood begins with a walking away,
> And love is proved in the letting go.

Is there a better, more moving or more succinct way of summing up the central paradox of both childhood and parenthood, that their fulfilment is marked by walking away on the one part, and letting go on the other? None that I know. And of course that process of letting go builds in increments throughout the child's life, starting in earnest with the stage Day-Lewis described, and culminating when they leave the family home to make a life under another roof.

In fact, Jane found it harder than I did when Elly left for university, which may have had something to do with finding herself the lone female living with three males. She and Elly had – have – a powerful bond based to a large extent on Elly talking nineteen to the dozen about the minutiae of her life, and Jane listening with unfeigned interest. Suddenly she faced more than the occasional evening with nobody to talk to while her three menfolk, and even the two dogs, watched football on the telly.

But I was as happy as Jane when, one weekend in May 2012, Elly came home from university with four girlfriends for a spot of rest and recuperation, it being so draining to get up day after day for 10 a.m. lectures. And in return for their bed and board, and unrestricted access to my supply of white wine, I asked these assembled girls of eighteen and nineteen if, for the purposes of this book, I could chat to them all about their relationships with their fathers. They generously agreed, and there ensued a more intense and revealing session than I think any of us had anticipated. It wasn't as though I'd met Elly's friends more than once before, and in the case of one of them, never before, yet they were candid to the point of it seeming, to me as well as to them, almost like therapy. They were perfectly happy for me to use their names, too, but at risk of hurting their dads, I'm changing them.

I started by asking what their fathers moaned about; whether there were things that seemed to annoy their dads beyond reason, but weren't particularly perturbing to their mums?

'He hates it when I say "like",' said Alice. 'He's always trying to get me to, like, complete a sentence without using the word "like".'

Elly and I both smiled in recognition. From the time she was about fifteen her apparent inability to string ten words together without saying 'like' had driven me to distraction. I had tried any number of fiendish devices to stop it, including a fines system – a five-pence levy for every unnecessary 'like' – and an immediate interjection by me of the word 'cabbage' every time she said it. For a while it seemed as though the cabbage trick might work, except that we both started finding it even more annoying than her saying 'like' all the time, so my cabbages petered out.

It was interesting to find that Alice's dad was similarly exercised, while it didn't really bother her mum. I was aware of many other households where the same dynamic applied in relation to language and vocabulary. The mothers in those families might be driven mad by discarded clothes on bedroom floors or dirty dishes left in the sink, to which fathers might turn a blind eye, but sprinkle a few superfluous likes into a sentence and he'd hit the roof.

In my case, what particularly riles is my children's unwitting collaboration in the Americanisation of our language, which I realise makes me sound like Victor Meldrew, if not Alf Garnett, but there we are.

I love America. I've been dozens of times on both business trips and holidays and also lived there for a year in the mid-1980s. I have lots of American friends, some of whom will read this book, and so it is with half an apology to them that I say that Americanisms infuriate me. I hate hearing British children talking about their forthcoming school 'prom'. I realise that the 'school disco' died out with flared jeans and home-knitted tank tops, but what's wrong with 'party' or even 'ball'?

Hearing my kids talking about tuxes instead of dinner jackets, and diapers rather than nappies, and 'New Year's' with the emphasis on the New instead of 'New Year's Eve' with the emphasis on Eve, has the same effect on me as the 'like' habit. There was even one terrible day when Jake referred to his closet rather than his wardrobe. It is the grim legacy of all those years watching the Disney Channel, and since everyone else's children talk the same way there doesn't seem much I or any other grumpy father can do about it.

Why this should be principally a Dad Thing I don't

really know, although actually it was a mother – the actress Emma Thompson, in proper Nanny McPhee mode – who in September 2010 most forthrightly aired her loathing of the 'like' epidemic, telling the *Radio Times* that she had been to give a talk at her old school, Camden School for Girls, and hearing the pupils' likes and innits had driven her 'insane'. She told them that it made them sound stupid, even though they weren't, which was just my beef with Elly. Yet some linguistics experts sprang to the defence of the like-mongers following Thompson's broadside, suggesting that it was just the English language evolving and really nothing to get too steamed up about. Maybe they're right.

Maybe, also, I and other dads should take a more relaxed view of table manners. It was reassuring, though, in my session with Elly and her friends, to find that this was a preoccupation of some of their fathers too. Gaby said that her father explains it by saying that he wants her to know which fork to use, and how to use it, in case she ever has dinner with the Queen. 'Like, when is that ever going to happen?' is her not-unreasonable response. It is her dad, too, rather than her mum, who enforces other areas of protocol, insisting on her and her two sisters sending thank-you cards whenever they have received hospitality somewhere, or been sent a present. It's the same in our house. Dad Things, not Mum Things.

We started on topics like those, but gradually the conversation became more emotionally profound. When I asked them what lessons they had learnt from their fathers, Alice said that there was much about her dad that she disliked, which enabled her to recognise and address the same flaws in herself. More poignantly still, Hattie said that she had learnt from her dad how important it was to cherish your spouse, which she felt he had failed to do with her mum. Her own relationship with him was good, she added. The youngest child, with two much older siblings, she felt certain that she was his favourite, and he made her feel as though she was capable of anything in life. Yet she hated the fact that he showed her mum insufficient respect. 'I sometimes think I shouldn't love him as much as I do,' she said.

Minnie, too, had a few issues with her father. Like Alice's dad, and like me, he was hung up far more than her mother on her use of language. He was French, and her mother was English, so a kind of household Franglais had developed which drove him mad, she said. He was always on at her and her three siblings to speak either French or English, rather than a hybrid of both. She offered an example – *'il est vraiment stingy'* – of the kind of construction that maddened him. Yet he had many habits that were even more maddening, she said. For example, he would routinely treat her like a much younger child, unnecessarily telling her how to do simple things, yet when she failed to discharge some responsibility or other, would say: 'I can't believe you're nineteen!' 'It's so paradoxical,' she complained.

Nevertheless, she was 'really proud' of him, and loved introducing him to her friends because he was full of fun, while at the same time needing always to be the centre of attention, and to have people tell him how great he was. 'He is such a drama queen,' she added. 'And he's selfish. When he's in a bad mood he makes life horrible for everyone. For instance, he's always unhappy at Christmas. I think it's something to do with his childhood.'

The ghost of Philip Larkin doubtless issued a thin smile at this unwitting reference to Minnie's dad being fucked up in his turn by fools in old-style hats and coats. Perhaps, too, there was something in the childhood of Gaby's father that made him protective of his three daughters to a degree that sounded suspiciously like obsessive-compulsive behaviour. 'I've had to tell him that he doesn't still have to check the bedroom windows every time he says goodnight to me,' she said, adding that it wasn't all that long since he stopped checking that she was breathing before he left for work in the morning. 'We are everything to him,' she said. 'All he needs is us, and the dog. You can just tell by the stuff that he does that he couldn't function without us.'

Was this sweet or unhealthy? I wasn't sure. Maybe a little of both. He texts her and her sisters every day, saying: 'Morning darling, have a great day, I love you,' and more often than not at night, too. Elly would think I'd either taken leave of my senses or had succumbed to a fatal illness if I started texting her twice or even once a day telling her that I loved her, and yet listening to Gaby talking so affectionately about her dad I wondered whether I should maybe text my student daughter more often than the little conversational flurry we exchanged once a fortnight or so, often when I happened to be passing somewhere near her university on the train. But then, that was how we operated, how our relationship had evolved, from a powerful wellspring of love, of course, but in a way that suited her personality and mine.

I carried on asking questions, and they carried on answering them with tremendous candour. It turned out that the fathers of both Hattie and Alice had in fairly recent times been made redundant, and that seemed to have affected the family dynamics. Tellingly, Hattie said: 'I used to love seeing him come home from work in a suit.' And now he doesn't. Instead, he looks after the house and cooks 'amazing' meals. 'But he always wants thanks for it,' she said. 'He should just, like, do it.'

Alice's father too had looked after the home since losing his job, and I wondered, from what she told me, whether he was perhaps suffering from depression. She said he didn't seem to have much confidence, didn't have many friends, spent an excessive amount of time talking to the dog. I ventured that maybe ten or twenty years hence she and Hattie might understand their dads better, might feel as though they should have been more sympathetic towards them? There was an eloquent silence.

As for Elly, I encouraged her to speak just as frankly as her friends, though doubtless she was keen to spare my feelings.

She took a deep breath. 'It annoys me,' she said, 'that every time I leave our house for a night out, you tell me to be careful and not drink too much. And every time I take the car, you tell me to drive carefully and keep to the speed limits. Mummy never does it.'

She reckoned that this bespoke a disappointing lack of confidence in her. I would dispute that. I'm articulating my concern for her safety, not a belief that she really needs a pep talk before she steps out of the door. Still, if she thinks that it's a show of no-confidence, then it might as well be. Either way, underlying much of what I talked to Elly and her friends about that night were the differences between mums and dads. They are certainly many and varied, and one of them is that on the whole we have different lengths of fuses, and they are lit in different ways.

For example, in the spring of 2011 I took Jake, then aged twelve, to the Forte Village resort in Sardinia for three days. I'd been invited on a press trip to write about a new enterprise called SuperSkills Travel, which had been set up by the former England rugby players Will Greenwood and Austin Healey, the concept being that they, and other celebrated sportsmen, would give kids specialist coaching as part of a family holiday. It was the first time Jake and I had been away on our own together, and I resolved that there would be no arguments between us. At twelve, as now, my youngest child was hugely characterful, a wonderfully vibrant but strong personality, and we sometimes sparked each other off. Jane was more tolerant of his wilfulness than I was. But I promised her, and promised myself, that I would stay serene in the face of any provocation, a walking practitioner of Zen and the Art of Fatherhood.

That's exactly how the trip unfolded, too, and we had a great time together, until half-way along the A14 on the long drive home from Stansted Airport. We were both ready for some lunch, and so I pulled into a service station, whereupon Jake expressed huge and voluble disappointment that there was no Marks & Spencer outlet there, on the basis that his favourite thing to eat in the entire world, when on a lengthy car journey, is a pack of M&S Honduran prawns with cocktail sauce dipper.

So I grudgingly, but with moderate good cheer, agreed to get back into the car and drive on to the next service station, where I knew there was an M&S. We duly stopped at the next services.

'Actually, Dad,' he said, spotting a Kentucky Fried Chicken counter, 'I think I'd quite like a KFC instead of Honduran prawns.'

This was before Joe's intense brooding over the Sunday lunchtime burger that never was at the King's Head, but recalling both incidents now, it strikes me that food is probably the most common denominator in me getting cross with my children, and them with me. Anyway, remembering my resolution not to lose my temper with Jacob, I chose to indulge his change of mind with nothing more than a sigh, even while feeling my good cheer dissipate and my fuse shorten by half. I just wanted to get home.

However, I continued indulging him at least until we'd been standing in the KFC queue for almost ten minutes – it being lunchtime, there was only one person on the till. At that point I insisted on leaving the queue for M&S, and he trudged along, more disconsolate than any child who hasn't just had his bike stolen, his birth- day party cancelled, and his pet rabbit murdered, has any right to be. That we were now in the shop he'd wanted to go to in the first place, faced with more

Honduran prawns than there probably were in all of Honduras, caused him no satisfaction at all. While I chose things I wanted to eat, he dithered and sulked, claiming that he simply couldn't make up his mind, until finally I blew my top, banging down my basket on the floor, and storming out of the shop and back to the car, with him in tears alongside me.

It was a response, I like to think, with which 90 per cent of fathers reading this book will sympathise. I'd done my best, been as accommodating as possible, then finally been driven to the end of my tether. Here's the thing, though: his mother would have dealt with the situation differently, and more successfully, preserving the happy holiday mood. She would have let him queue for his blessed KFC for as long as it took, while shopping for herself at M&S, or sitting down with a coffee and a magazine. It wasn't that Jane was a pushover. She is no more tolerant than I am of inappropriately rude or stroppy behaviour. But she is more willing than I am to see tiredness and hunger as mitigating factors in a child's crossness, and more skilful than I am at avoiding such confrontations in the first place. In fact, she wouldn't have even bothered turning into the other services first. Jake's fondness for Honduran prawns with cocktail sauce dipper would have been uppermost in her mind, whereas uppermost in my mind was grabbing a quick bite and getting home. This, I think, as far as one can generalise, is another fundamental difference between fathers and mothers.

I have touched on quite a few of these differences already in this book, and perhaps at their root is the physiological distinction enshrined in conception and pregnancy. Many thousands of words ago I quoted Jim Keeble, the man who did not feel the immediate surge of adoration for his newborn son that he had assumed he would. I hazarded that maybe the reason for this was the zeal with which he had embraced the role of the expectant father, because when all that expectation finally erupted into reality in a birthing pool, he felt disconnected, 'suddenly conscious of being inherently, clumsily, ignorantly male in a wholly female world of blood and birth – a hapless, useless bloke watching women making the world turn'.

That was sort of how I felt, though maybe not as deeply, when Jane gave birth to Jacob in our Crouch End bathroom, and Margaret the midwife sent me to the washing-machine. Back we go to what I wrote in the prologue of this book, that perhaps only in the very moment of conception does the father take more of the strain than the mother.

It is now, at the time of writing, almost twenty years since my own first child was conceived. After nearly two decades as a father I like to think that I am properly engaged with my children's lives, and yet I'd be deluding myself if I claimed to be anything like as engaged as their mother. Just as I once marvelled at how Jane stood at the school gate saying hello by name to every other mum and every other child – of whom, on a good day, I could name about two – so I marvel now at how she knows each of her children's mobile phone numbers. They are stored on her phone, of course, as they are on mine, but that hasn't stopped her memorising them. And this is not because she has more time than me for immersing herself in their lives.

Jane is a full-time novelist, and also does the bulk of the cooking, shopping, cleaning, washing, ironing, dog-walking and assistance with homework, as well as monitoring (and worrying about) our finances, paying (and worrying about) the household bills, and running (and moaning about) our two small holiday cottages. What do I do? I used to put the bins out once a week, but that important role has passed to Joe and Jake. I'm still the major breadwinner, in that quaint old expression. I, and I alone, clear up dog shit from the garden. It's usually me who mucks out the chickens. We have high ceilings, so it's me who clears the cobwebs from remote corners of rooms. On long journeys, I drive. It tends to be me who organises and plans family holidays. But if there were a league table and points dished out for who contributes most to the well-being of our three children, she would be Manchester City and I would be Hereford United. Possibly even Hereford United reserves.

Every family is different, of course. If I've learnt anything while writing this book, it's that fathers fall into so many different categories that they can scarcely be categorised. Of those student friends of Elly's, it is in two cases the dads, not the mums, who know their mobile numbers by heart. But if I've earned the right to generalise, then let me say this: fatherhood is the most challenging and also the most rewarding job I've ever done, or ever will do. But motherhood is harder.

20

Absent Dads, Single Dads

Some fathers make good mothers.

If motherhood is harder than fatherhood, where does that place single motherhood? And single fatherhood? After all, people die. Fathers die young leaving single mums, and mothers die young leaving single dads. Or single parenthood arises out of separation, divorce or abandonment. Over my many years as a journalist I have interviewed well over a thousand famous high-achievers – mostly from the worlds of sport and entertainment – and it's amazing how many of them came from single-parent families. And within that disproportionate number, a striking amount were abandoned by their fathers. Former *Countdown* queen Carol Vorderman, for example, has always kept the surname she was born with, yet it was given to her by her Dutch father, Anton Vorderman, who left the family home when she was three weeks old. She didn't see him again until she was forty-two.

None of this means, of course, that it's desirable to spend your childhood without a mum or a dad on the scene, on the basis that it necessarily increases your chances of success in life. Probably, in truth, and despite that high proportion among my interviewees, the opposite applies. But it was still unsurprising to me to find the statistic about people who grow up without a father being more likely to become risk-takers in adulthood . . . whether the kinds of risk that end in prison sentences, or in multi-million pound fortunes, or indeed in lovely Carol Vorderman, closer to her sixtieth birthday than her fortieth, stepping out in such revealing frocks.

In my own case I can say without too much equivocation that I have always found it easier to bond with older women than older men, and the reason for that, I think, is that for most of those formative teen years, as I developed from a boy into a man, I was used to grown-up company predominantly in the form of my mum and her female friends.

As a consequence, I generally got on better with the mothers of my own friends than with their fathers, which certainly had its benefits (not that you should read between the lines and assume that I was sexually initiated by a friend's mother, which I definitely wasn't, more's the pity in one or two instances) but I just as certainly missed out, not having a dad to guide me into adulthood.

Maybe that's also why fatherhood interests me so much, because my own experience of it as a child was cut short. And maybe, too, that's why I'm interested in the reverse phenomenon: men who go through most of their lives with their fathers still alive and still sending out positive role-model vibes. Of course, it takes two for a role model to have a beneficial effect. The actor David Soul – Detective Ken Hutchinson of the Los Angeles Police Department for those of us old enough to remember *Starsky & Hutch* in its original, 1970s' incarnation – was in his mid-sixties when his father died, and talks about the old man with unabashed adoration.

'He was the kindest, dearest, most giving man I think I've ever known,' Soul told a newspaper interviewer in May 2012. 'He was the kind of guy you just wanted to turn to. No matter how old you get – and I'm 68 – you're still somebody's kid and when I'm feeling desperate now I think of my pop and it's enough for me to think: "Come on, David, buckle up, get your shit together."' Clearly, even in death, his pop is his role model. And yet in life,

Soul Senr (Dr Richard Solberg, actually) had one marriage, to Soul's mother, lasting sixty-four years. Whereas Soul, at the time of writing, has been married five times. I was going to write 'an impressive five times'. But one time is surely more impressive.

What, though, of those fathers whose marriages or partnerships are cruelly abbreviated by death or divorce, and who must then raise their children alone – or, in the case of my mother-in-law Anne's late father Colin, farm them out to be raised by relatives? I'm happy to say that in my own immediate circle of friends there is nobody in that predicament, and it's far, far less common in society generally than it used to be, for the general reason that we all live longer, and the specific reason that women rarely die in childbirth any more. But there are still men who take on the mother's role as well as the father's in their children's lives, as one of the better known of this kind of parent, J. G. Ballard, was aware. 'Some fathers make good mothers, and I hope I was one of them,' he wrote, in later life.

So much of this book has drawn from my own experiences of fatherhood, but now that it's nearing a conclusion, I want to turn to the experiences I have never had, and in the case of Jeremy Howe, fervently hope I never do have. As I've attempted to explain, my brand of fatherhood feeds off Jane's brand of motherhood. I can't imagine doing it without her, but then nor could Howe, a BBC radio executive, before his 34-year-old wife Lizzie, an academic, was murdered by a laboratory technician high on vodka and drugs in her study on the University of York campus on 25 July 1992. The lab technician's name was Robin Pask and he slit her throat. It was a random, motiveless crime. The Howes' daughters, Jessica and Lucy, were aged six and four. 'Jessica, Lucy and I were nearly swept away by the force of what hit us,' wrote Howe in his poignant book *Mummydaddy*, published in 2012. 'Nearly 20 years on, all three of us are again normal people leading normal lives. How on earth did we cope?'

They coped because the coping mechanism is one of the human psyche's most powerful bits of kit, if that doesn't sound too corny or crass. But of course in the days following Lizzie Howe's death, he had no idea how they would cope. He just busked it, and tried his hardest to do the parenting jobs that she had always done.

'I learnt to have pockets full of Sudocrem, Elastoplasts, tissues and hair scrunchies,' he wrote, 'but could rarely produce the right thing at the right time. I could get the girls out the door efficiently, but never with the right clothes for the weather. When it came to food and household items, it was feast or famine, so that by Friday we'd be short of an evening meal but have enough toilet rolls to last the siege of Leningrad. And there were always five boxes of chicken nuggets frozen solid into the freezer compartment, which could be prised out only after a twenty-minute attack with a sharp knife and a saw.

'In the winter, the girls always had chapped hands, because the art of keeping gloves in pairs was an insoluble mystery. However, they learnt how to throw good, firm snowballs, had no fear of scary playground rides, climbed trees like monkeys and became ferocious card players who played to win. Despite my best endeavours, though, they were pretty rubbish at football.'

That passage from *Mummydaddy* sheds more light than any psychology thesis on how the sudden removal of one parent changes the dynamics and intensifies the challenges of parenting. The book explains powerfully how Jessica and Lucy adapted to the situation forced on them, learning to brush each other's hair because their dad wasn't very good at it, and generally developing their own maternal instincts much sooner than they would have otherwise. But that is to gloss over how difficult it all was for all three of them. And Howe's job – head of drama at Radio 3 – provided no real respite. He started taking more and more leave.

'On holiday, I felt alive,' he wrote. 'I was able to relax and really enjoy my daughters' company. If I'm honest, I felt none of these things at home: I was in a permanent state of anxiety. Friends and neighbours helped, of course; but whenever we visited another family, I felt like an imposition. Boy, did I learn the meaning of "singing for your supper" – I'd tell funny stories, do the washing-up, make coffee, and make sure I never burdened them with my multiple woes. Once, I tried going to a single-parent support group. But it seemed more like a dating agency – such a scary prospect that, having walked through the door, I walked straight out again.'

Nick Hornby chose just that – a single-parent support group – as the starting premise for *About a Boy*, his novel about an unmarried, childless man in his mid-thirties, Will, who as a fiendish ruse to meet and woo a sexy but vulnerable woman of about the same age has the bright idea of attending a support group (to which Hornby gives the splendid acronym SPAT – Single Parents Alone Together) claiming to be the single dad of an entirely make-believe two-year-old boy. It's also worth noting that Will was played in the film version of *About a Boy* by none other than Hugh Grant, whom we have already met in these pages and whose status as a new dad in November 2011 attracted so much coverage in the British press.

Grant is another single father, if not exactly typical of the breed, and not surprisingly it is the mother,

Tinglan Hong, who is their daughter's principal carer. In a rare newspaper interview four months after the birth of baby Tabitha, however, he insisted that he had firm ideas about how he wanted her raised, intending to be 'incredibly strict' on a few key issues such as good manners. He also declared his intention not to set up Tabitha financially when she reached maturity. 'There are few things in life I believe in 100 per cent,' he said, 'but one is not giving your children money. I see nothing but fuck-ups among my trust-fund friends. It's like 99 per cent fuck-ups. So I would not want to do that to my children, no.'

It was a perfectly reasonable, indeed admirable sentiment. But we'll see. When Tabitha is eighteen, Grant will be almost seventy, and probably wondering what to do with his fortune. It won't be easy to resist feathering the nest of his doubtless beautiful daughter, and if he succumbs he will certainly be following in the tradition of many other rich, older fathers.

Take Bernie Ecclestone, over whom the celestial chequered flag will almost certainly have waved by then. I have interviewed Ecclestone, who was one of the trickiest customers I have ever encountered with my tape-recorder: brusque and unwilling to make even the most fleeting small talk. Even as we cursorily shook hands he gave every indication that he resented the potentially valuable time it took up, while every nuance of his conversation and body language screamed tough, self-made billionaire. Plainly, here was a man who neither suffered fools nor needed friends, as his many offensive off-the-cuff remarks down the years suggest. In 2005, asked whether the American IndyCar driver Danica Patrick might have a future in Formula One, he said: 'You know I've got one of those wonderful ideas . . . women should be dressed in white like all other domestic appliances.'

This was hard, uncompromising, charmless and of course profoundly sexist talk, yet when we turn to the two daughters he fathered in his fifties, well, Petra Ecclestone (born when Bernie was fifty-eight) rather unwisely told the 'Life in a Day' people at the *Sunday Times Magazine* that her day – in the Los Angeles house that used to belong to television mogul Aaron Spelling, and is thought to be America's most expensive private home – starts with her butler bringing her breakfast, prepared by her cook. At twenty-three, she was about as far from being a 'domestic appliance' as it is possible to get. In fairness, it is said to be mainly Bernie's ex-wife Slavica who lavishes untold millions on their two daughters, and it was Slavica who paid for Petra's £12 million, three-day wedding in Italy. Bernie likes to make a big deal of grumbling about the extravagance. But he's kidding nobody. He's the son of a hard-up Suffolk trawlerman and his daughter lives in an $85 million palace in LA. From wrasse to riches in two generations. Without the slightest doubt, it gives the little old man a great big kick.

21

Older Dads, Step-Dads, Grateful Dads

If you want to stay fecund, try camel milk.

I fathered my first child at thirty-one years and eight months, and my third and last at thirty-six years and ten months, which rather boringly puts me splat in the middle of the national average. Yet that average has been creeping up. In Britain since 1980, there has been a 30 per cent increase in the number of men over forty fathering children, and a 20 per cent decrease in the number of men under thirty.

As long ago as 1997, of fathers aged over thirty at the time of the child's birth, a quarter were over forty. And the number of older dads has increased since then, although of course they're not all first-timers. For every Gordon Brown (who became a dad for the first time aged fifty-four), there is a Tony Blair (who was forty-five when the mother of his three children rather unexpectedly bore him a fourth) or a Paul McCartney (who marked his ill-starred second marriage to Heather Mills by fathering baby Beatrice at the age of sixty-one). Not to mention Rupert Murdoch who in 2003, at the age of seventy-two, became a father for the sixth time. I know someone who once spotted the media tycoon cavorting in a New York playground with his two young daughters by the third Mrs Murdoch, Wendi Deng. Apparently it looked quite alarmingly disorientating, like seeing Keith Harris and Orville testifying at the Leveson Inquiry.

More often than not, and as in the cases of Murdoch and McCartney (which sounds oddly like a company of Edinburgh solicitors), it is the consequence of a second – or third, fourth or fifth – marriage to a younger woman that produces these babies relatively late in a man's life. For obvious reasons, there aren't too many blokes over fifty who become dads with the woman they've been with for years, although I did play golf once with a fellow in his mid-fifties who had three children, aged twenty-five, twenty-three and one, all with the same wife. He still looked in a faint state of shock.

According to a man called Jack O'Sullivan, co-founder of an excellent organisation called Fathers Direct, there are more advantages to late fatherhood than disadvantages. 'Research shows that old fathers are three times more likely to take regular responsibility for a young child,' he says. 'They are more likely to be fathers by choice and this means that they become more positively involved with the child. They behave more like mothers, smiling at the baby and gurgling – although young fathers are probably better at getting down on the floor for physical play.'

These gurgling oldsters have included David Jason (sixty-one) and Charlie Chaplin (seventy-three), both already celebrated in this book, as well as John Humphrys (fifty-six), Mick Jagger (fifty-seven), Michael Douglas (fifty-eight), Warren Beatty (sixty-two), Rod Stewart (sixty-six), Luciano Pavarotti (who fathered twins, no less, at sixty-seven), and the Nobel Prize-winning novelist Saul Bellow at a whopping eighty-four. Alas, but not surprisingly, Bellow only lasted another five years. Which, though Jack O'Sullivan sensitively didn't mention it, is surely the one major disadvantage of being an older father: the scant likelihood of watching your child grow up for longer than a few years.

Apparently, the world's oldest-recorded father (if we overlook Abraham, who fathered Isaac at the age of 100, well and truly putting the old testes into Old Testament), was an Australian mine worker called Les Colley, who was slightly older than the twentieth century when he fathered a son, Oswald, in 1992. He'd met his Fijian wife through a dating agency a year earlier, and told newspaper reporters: 'I never thought she would get pregnant so easy, but she bloody well did.' At least Oswald Colley, wherever he is now, probably has dim memories in more ways than one of the old man, who was only four months short of his hundredth birthday when he succumbed to pneumonia.

Then there was Rajasthani farmer Virmaram Jat, eighty-eight when his forty-three-year-old wife gave birth in July 2006. Like Pavarotti's partner Nicoletta Mantovani, she produced twins. Virmaram claimed to have intercourse every night between the hours of 2 a.m. and 4 a.m. He was a vegetarian who had never touched alcohol and had been drinking camel milk every day since childhood, which might be a higher price than most of us are prepared to pay should we be tempted to do whatever it takes to stay virile into our late eighties. Viagra might be a better bet than camel milk, which reminds me of the joke about the man who asks his pharmacist if he stocks Viagra pills. The pharmacist says he does. 'Can I get it over the counter?' the man asks. 'Only if you take six of them,' the pharmacist replies. But that's not a joke Virmaram Jat would have understood. He had never heard of Viagra.

Also in 2006, a writer called Tom Leonard anticipated

his impending status as an older dad in an article in the *Daily Telegraph*. His own father had been fifty-one when he was born, he wrote, so he had grown up associating fathers with naturally rather than prematurely grey hair. He was also writing in the week that a woman called Patti Farrant made headlines by becoming Britain's oldest mother – following expensive IVF treatment in Russia – at the age of sixty-two. Leonard pointed out that there had been a great deal of collective tutting in the media about Mrs Farrant giving birth at sixty-two, yet the age of her husband John, who was sixty, had gone almost unnoticed.

'Even if John Farrant is confident his age won't matter,' wrote Leonard, 'I wonder if his son will always feel the same? I'm not suggesting he'll necessarily rush into his father's bedroom each night to check he's still alive – as an anxious young Agatha Christie did – but children can be self-conscious about older dads. It wasn't an issue with my own father, as visiting friends always assumed he was the gardener (which tells you all you need to know about where he liked to be at moments of high child density). But I used to feel sorry for a boy at my school every time other pupils mistakenly told him his grandfather was looking for him. He always looked crestfallen, as he knew they were talking about his father, who, I have to say, didn't exactly do a sensitive son any favours by looking, dressing and acting like doddery Private Godfrey from *Dad's Army*.'

I wouldn't dream of making the same observation of my friend Bill, who fathered two children in his fifties; he's more of a Corporal Jones than a Private Godfrey. But he does know all too well the indignity of being mistaken for his children's grandfather. On the other hand, he echoes O'Sullivan's line about there being more advantages than disadvantages. He has a teenage daughter from a previous relationship, and makes the same point as a lot of men who get a second crack at fatherhood later in life: that it offers him a welcome opportunity to change things he perhaps got wrong first time round, and certainly to be much more of a presence in his younger children's lives, having been preoccupied with his career during his firstborn's early years.

The flip side of all this, however, is mortality, not that the Grim Reaper is exactly hacking with his scythe at Bill's heels, but he is nevertheless acutely aware that his own father – the guy who'd been in the Warsaw Ghetto – passed away at fifty-one, and with vivid poignancy recalls being called off the rugby field at the Roman Catholic boarding school he attended to be given the devastating news that his dad had died suddenly. The news, incidentally, was conveyed not by the headmaster, or a teacher, or even matron, but by the school captain, one Brendan Lynch.

THE GOOD, THE DAD AND THE UGLY

Bill remembers Brendan giving him the news in the sixth-form Common Room, where 'Hey Jude' happened to be playing. To this day he can't bear to listen to 'Hey Jude'. Heaven knows why the monks who ran the place might have considered it appropriate for one schoolboy to be asked to tell another that his father had died, but then death elicits curious responses in people. I was kept off school for a fortnight following the sudden death of my own father in February 1976, and returned to find that my dad's passing went completely unremarked, one of my teachers having told my classmates that this would be the wisest course.

That was more than thirty-five years ago, and I can still clearly remember the relief I felt when one of my mates, Pete (the boy who three years later would write off his mum's car within half an hour of passing his driving test), took me to one side and said: 'I just wanted to tell you how sorry I am about your dad.'

It turned out that he had been uneasy with the teacher's directive and had consulted his own father, who told him he should say something. His simple decency that day cemented a close friendship that continues even now that neither of us will see our fiftieth birthdays again. And yet I do know the other boys were equally trying to do the right thing.

Returning to Bill, as well as being an older father he is

also a stepfather, to his partner Sue's two sons by her first marriage. When he came to stay at our house in the spring of 2012 the two of us saw off a decent bottle of Burgundy talking about the aspects of fatherhood that he had experienced and I hadn't, with stepfatherhood high on the list. He felt he had a reasonable relationship with Sue's two sons – one in his late teens, the other in his early twenties – which was founded partly on his determination not to try to woo them by relaxing his firm rules about how children, or in their case young adults, should behave.

Chiefly, this concerned the state of their bedrooms and their approach to meals. Their father, who lived nearby, with whom they lived most of the time, and to whom they were tremendously close, had a much more liberal approach to household etiquette. His view was that they were big boys who were entitled to eat what, when and how they wished, and also to do whatever they wanted in their bedrooms. Bill, however, took the view that in his house they must abide by his rules, the more so in the presence of his impressionable younger children. He told them that he would instruct the cleaning lady to stay out of their bedrooms unless there was a modicum of tidiness, and that they would observe family mealtimes or not eat.

This, remember, is the man whose own father's family

perished in the Auschwitz gas chambers. He finds it hard not to impose some of the discipline he experienced as a child on his own children. But imposing it on his stepchildren is harder. 'I'm very conscious that they're being set rules by someone they didn't ask for in their lives,' he told me. And yet the rules are set, regardless.

Being a part of somebody's life who didn't ask for you, or in some cases actively didn't want you, is the essence of step-parenthood, I suppose, or at least the essence of the problems that can arise. Jimmy Mulville, the hugely successful and influential television producer, is eloquently fascinating on this subject. He married his third wife, Karen, when her daughter Paige – by her first husband who had died tragically young of cancer – was no more than a toddler, and before he, Jimmy, had any children of his own. 'I wasn't just saying to Karen, "Will you marry me?"' he says. 'I was also saying to Paige, "Will you be my daughter?"'

Paige is now in her twenties and Jimmy, who subsequently had three sons with Karen, is in every sense except the biological one her dad. He loves her and she loves him. Yet she has only ever called him 'dad' when referring to him, never to his face.

'And I have never asked her to,' he told me, when during the research for this book I quizzed him on his relationship with Paige. 'As I said to Karen, the first man she called "Dad" left her. She calls me Jim. But two Christmases ago she said to me, "I've bought something for you and it will make you cry." Well, I cry easily. You're looking at someone who cries during *Casper the Friendly Ghost*, and when I go, I really go, shoulders and everything. Anyway, she bought me this . . .'

Jimmy fished in his pocket and brought out a silver money clip, on which was inscribed 'Dad'. 'And she was right, I did cry,' he said. 'But I genuinely felt I'd earned it. When my sons were born, I'd never met them before but I felt I knew them so well. Paige I met for the first time at Häagen-Dazs on the King's Road. But when she was about eight or nine, and she was kicking off with me, refusing to go to bed, she said to me, "My dad's in heaven, you're just my stepdad." I said, "Paige, what do dads do? Let's make a big list. They go to work, they take you on holidays, they look after you, they go shopping for you, they tell you to go to bed. And at the top of the list, they put a seed inside mummy to create you in the first place. Well, I do all those things, I just didn't do that thing at the top. But everything else, I do. So go to bed."'

Manifestly, the relationship between a stepfather and stepchild is greatly influenced not just by how he approaches the job, but also by whether or not there's a natural father around, and by when he arrives on the scene. Bill will never be the *de facto* father to Sue's boys that Jimmy is to Paige. On the other hand, if this book has established anything, it's that being the biological father, already there on the scene when the child arrives, implies some of the same challenges that confront a step-father as well as a whole raft of different ones.

Not all of those challenges have been explored in this book, indeed some of the toughest ones have been omitted, for the simple reason that, mercifully, I've never had to tackle them. I haven't had to deal with anorexia, bulimia, self-harming, truancy, petty crime, glue-sniffing or drug-addiction. My kids haven't fallen in with destructive or anti-social peer groups. Very rarely are they downright unpleasant to their mother or me. They don't suffer from autism, Asperger's or dyslexia. They are healthy and, like most fathers, I issue one *cri de coeur* above all others: let them remain so. They are also athletic, attractive, personable and bright. And yet, while there are plenty of reasons for me to be grateful, there are no reasons for me to be smug. Some of the challenges of fatherhood I have already flunked. Others I might flunk in the future. A few I might not know I have flunked until my children are parents themselves.

22

Blackpool Bloody Illuminations

Fathers turn into their own fathers.

Maybe, in fact, it won't be possible even to essay a proper estimation of my success as a father until my children look back on their lives, after I'm gone.

And that sobering thought brings me to the kind of father I will be as they grow into and through adulthood, and as I edge towards old age. Who honestly knows? Engaged and loving, I hope, and never a drain on their time or finances or plain goodwill. But I am entering that phase of life when a few friends are having to deal with parents with dementia, for instance, and none of us can say for sure that we will be spared either that or any of the other horrors that old age can spring on you, and which inevitably affect the parent–child relationship.

Besides, that relationship will evolve anyway, for better or worse or just for different. But if as a father you've got it more right than wrong for the all-important first twenty years, then at least you've got a strong bedrock on which to build the less important next twenty years.

I like what the writer John Crace, whose two children are about the same age as my older two, has written about the changing nature of fatherhood as one's children approach adulthood. It frees both parties 'to have a very different relationship. Not to be friends – who wants a dad as a friend? A dad should always remain a dad; someone to cadge lifts and money off, someone to turn to when things are shit, and someone to ignore when things are fine. But they are now able to see me as a person as well as a dad. I no longer have to pretend – too much – to be someone I'm not. They know my strengths and weaknesses almost as well as I know theirs and love me anyway. Well, they say they do . . .'

I echo all that, but what he doesn't address is the recognition of yourself in your children as the age gap appears to shrink. It was Elly's considered view during that session with her mates that no two members of our family of five are more alike – in terms of habits, temperament and quirks of personality, as well as looks – than me and our middle child, Joe. Now, whether he would acknowledge that, I don't know. As I write he is seventeen and a

generally even-tempered boy, considerate and good
company and properly interested in the world around
him, so I'll take it as a compliment even if he doesn't.

He is, of course, emphatically his own man, but if he
does take after me then happily for him he seems to have
my better qualities. He certainly focuses a great deal
more on his schoolwork than I did at the same age,
although that's not because of me urging him on but
because of a couple of inspiring teachers, and I'll name-
check them here with due gratitude and respect: Mr
Petrie and Mr Stanley. Indeed, as a wise friend of mine
once said to me, part of the experience of fathering sons
is the gradual realisation that, 'It will be another man
who lights your boy's pilot light.'

An even wiser man, the philosopher Bertrand Russell,
once asserted that, 'The fundamental defect of fathers is
that they want their children to be a credit to them.' How
very true. And how very unavoidable. Like his older
sister and younger brother, no more and no less, Joe is a
source of huge pride to me. I admire his work ethic enormously. Yet, for all that, I was horrified one day when he
came home and said that there'd been a quiz at school,
and that one of the questions had asked the date of the
Spanish Armada.

'Surely you knew that,' I said.

'I didn't have a clue,' he replied, and he really didn't,

indeed he couldn't name the century, let alone the year, and nor could any of his classmates.

Joe, I should add, was studying history as one of his A-levels, and was being encouraged by his teachers to try for Oxford or Cambridge. History had been one of his nine A-stars at GCSE. Yet he didn't know that the Spanish Armada unfolded in 1588. This troubled me, probably way more than it should have done. For when I was the same age in the late 1970s, certain dates were imprinted on the minds of every schoolchild: 1066 was one, 1588 another.

What had happened to dates? I recalled that Elly during her A-levels two years before had asked me when the First World War ended. Under interrogation, she admitted that she wasn't sure when it started, either. Which wouldn't have been so worrying if she hadn't been writing an essay titled 'The Causes of the First World War'. 'But Daddy,' she protested, when I spat out my tea, 'we don't learn about, like, dates.'

I phoned Joe's teacher, who confirmed that this was broadly true. It seemed that the teaching of history in British schools had increasingly been influenced by US methods of presenting the past thematically rather than chronologically. Thus pupils might study crime and punishment, or kingship, and dip in and out of different centuries. Consequently, dates lose their value. So 1605, which for me meant the Gunpowder Plot, for Joe simply meant that he was five minutes late for games.

Now, the point of telling you this is that there comes a stage in the lives of most fathers when they begin to remind themselves of their own fathers, and through my spluttering astonishment at Joe's inability to date the Spanish Armada I did pick up faint echoes of my own long-departed dad when he realised that after two years of secondary education I still couldn't do long division, or recite a single poem by Walter de la Mare.

Most of us, I think, end up hearing these echoes. For example, my friend Ian, the fellow who could not contain his blubbing on phoning his mum to tell her that he'd just become a dad, recalls in excruciatingly precise detail the Saturday night clobber he used to wear in the 1970s – 'Oxford bags, with six buttons on the waistband, so tight around the crotch that you could see each bollock, then a Penny Round collar shirt, and a vividly-striped tank top, and of course three-inch heels' – and how his dad used to poke fun at him for wearing it, much to his annoyance, yet how a generation later he poked fun at his stepson Milo for going out with the seat of his jeans hanging low and the vast majority of his Calvin Klein briefs showing, which doubtless Milo found similarly annoying.

I should think that most of us can think of examples of

the same phenomenon. In Britain, the average age of men fathering a child for the first time is thirty-two, but at thirty-two, you're only thirteen years out of your teens; accordingly, it's hard if not impossible to imagine yourself turning into the father you remember from your own adolescence. But middle age creeps up, and brings with it the gout or the bad back or the slight touch of arthritis that troubled the old man, and before you can say 'You're not going out dressed like that!' or 'Can you PLEASE turn that music down!' . . . well, it's too late, you've said it.

While writing this book I emailed a few of my friends to ask them at what point they started hearing their own fathers in what they said themselves, and for my mate Howie it was when he passed his daughter Ella on the stairs, when she was about eight and holding a bag of Maltesers. 'Don't eat them all at once,' he heard himself saying. To which she nonchalantly and guilelessly replied: 'No, I'm going to eat them one at a time.'

For most of my friends, the enjoinder not to leave lights on was what reminded them most of their own dads, and indeed the conservation of electricity, now that I think about it, generally seems to have been a preoccupation of fathers, rather than mothers, pretty much since Thomas Edison's light-bulb moment. Why is this? Is it because they are, on the whole, more careful with money than mothers? Or more environmentally aware? Or more intolerant of waste?

Traditionally, perhaps it was because they were the breadwinners, and hated the idea of being out at work all day if in the meantime the monthly salary was being eroded by lights and radios and Heaven knows what being left on at home. But men these days are less proprietorial than they once were about the household income, partly because more and more of their womenfolk bring home the bacon too, but also because they've been conditioned and educated into treating money as a shared resource.

So, it ought to follow that nagging about lights being left on should also have become a Mum Thing, especially now that the time-honoured complaint about it being a 'criminal waste of electricity' has been compounded by the more emotive image of massive carbon footprints. And yet all the evidence suggests it is still unequivocally a Dad Thing. Our friend Jane, who does not bring home much bacon (except from Sainsbury's), tells me that her husband James reminds her of both his father and hers when he arrives home to declare that the house looks like Blackpool Illuminations.

I use the Blackpool Illuminations line, too. Sometimes, Blackpool bloody Illuminations. I think all dads of my generation do it. And another friend, Chris, recalls that his dad was always going on at him and his siblings to 'turn those bloody lights off', and now he uses the same words in the same tone of voice. 'I understand every time I open the lecky bill what he was driving at!' he says. 'I try to soften it with the environment thing but essentially it's still about parsimony, and not wanting to see waste!' He once went so far as to work out a complicated system of financial penalties and rewards linked to their pocket money based on turning lights off, until he realised that it would cost him more than the wasted electricity.

In our house – and I might as well get this off my chest by writing it down, because nobody listens to me when I say it out loud – I am the only person who habitually turns the light off when I leave a room. The three children don't do it, and nor does Jane, and the dad in me that could just as easily be my own dad, or even his dad, wonders why they can't master that extraordinarily simple action of flicking or pressing a switch? It's not that they can't be bothered (because who honestly can't be bothered not to turn off a switch?), more that it just doesn't enter their heads.

All of which makes it hard to imagine that when Joe and Jake are my age and have teenage children of their own, they will be transformed into the family light-switch police. Yet, by some kind of miraculous osmosis, that is surely what will happen. It's part of the unwritten Dads' Charter, handed down through the generations, just as despair at a teenager's messy bedroom tends to belong more to the Mums' Charter. It is usually mums who bewail the level of their offspring's slobbiness, such as mother-of-two Tammy Cohen in a feature in *The Times* in November 2011, who claimed that following a burglary at her home a few years previously, 'A tutting CID officer looked into my daughter's bedroom and said, "Disgusting! Who'd do that to a little girl's room!?" It was the one part of the house that had been left untouched.'

Actually, I know plenty of families in which it is the father who leads the caterwauling at the state of the children's bedrooms, and Cohen herself cited a documentary about the late John Peel, in which the famously easygoing DJ 'was reduced almost to tears' when talking about the pigsty that was his teenage son's bedroom. In a subsequent interview with the *Observer*, Peel tried to explain this outburst, saying that he took a lot of trouble finding things for his kids that he thought they would like, and how distressing it then was to 'find them stirred into the soup on the floor'.

In remonstrating with his son, he almost certainly used the word 'pigsty'. When applied to a teenager's bedroom, 'pigsty' is another traditional favourite fathers' saying. It implies a lack of respect for the world, and perhaps, more painfully, for us. Also, according to the clinical psychologist Tanya Byron, this pigsty compounds our deep-seated fears as parents. Seeing our kids surrounded by squalor and chaos makes us worry about their futures, she suggests, while at the same time offering yet more evidence of them asserting their independence. So it is comforting, as with the issue of electricity, to think that this independence will probably end up with them bewailing the state of their own children's bedrooms. There will doubtless, in the 2040s, even be talk of pigsties, though possibly not of Blackpool Illuminations, which don't seem to have the status they once did as a veritable festival of electricity. I find this a little sad, after nigh on a century of dear old Blackpool promenade, a thoroughfare close to my heart, being invoked by so many grumpy dads.

Of course, it would be wrong of me to present the spectre of a man turning into his own father as being by definition a bad thing. For plenty of men it is nothing short of a life's ambition to emulate their own fathers, whether in terms of professional achievement, or personal happiness, or strength of character, or all the above.

Moreover, it is hard not to be moved when you see fathers and sons intensifying their emotional bond. It is, again, the sporting arena that offers me the best illustration of this, such as Pat Cash, after winning the men's singles final at Wimbledon in 1987, clambering over heads, and Centre Court protocol, to embrace his dad. However, I can think of no better example than that of the athlete Derek Redmond pulling up, distraught, with a popped hamstring during the 400-metre semi-final in the Olympic Games in Barcelona, and his dad, Jim, rushing down from the back row of the stand, pushing his way past spectators and officials and running out onto the track to finish the race with his stricken boy. Jim Redmond had no credentials to be on the Olympic track, except, more powerful than any badge, the credential of fatherhood.

If, on that summer's day in 1992, Jim and Derek Redmond encapsulated what the father–son relationship can be like at its healthiest, and in front of the biggest imaginable global audience, so twenty years later did internet images of a 44-year-old Chinese man called He Liesheng and his four-year-old son He Yide, represent just the opposite.

In January 2012, during a family visit to a wintry New York, Liesheng exhorted his son, who was wearing only trainers and underpants, to run through the snow and then do press-ups. On YouTube the boy can clearly be seen wailing and repeatedly asking his father to hug him, yet it was Liesheng himself who uploaded the film onto the internet, so proud was he of his parenting methods, which he said were designed to prepare his son for life's trials. Igniting inevitable comparisons with Amy Chua's controversial book *Battle Hymn of the Tiger Mother*, he described himself as an Eagle Dad, following the example of the eagle that pushes its young off the cliff top whether or not they are ready to fly. Time, I suppose, will tell whether He Yide will metaphorically soar or be dashed against the rocks. Either way, Liesheng clearly felt that he was being the best father possible, even as the vast majority of YouTube viewers – and as I write there have been almost two million hits – thought otherwise.

One Chinese blogger defended Liesheng, however, arguing that, 'Different families have different ways, so should be left alone.' If there were any truth in the second part of that statement, then social services everywhere might as well be disbanded. But there's no denying the first bit. Different families do indeed have different ways. There's Liesheng's way, and Jim Redmond's way, and my way. And of course Liesheng's wife's way, and Mrs Redmond's way, and Jane's way.

It's no wonder that we all do it differently, and yet for the overwhelming majority of us the objective is the same: if not to make happy, well-rounded human beings of our children, then at least to provide them with the tools to do the job for themselves. It might be a little fanciful to raise a football analogy here, but if a fellow can't be fanciful towards the end of his own book then when can he?

Football managers have varying ambitions for their teams – to win the Champions League, to win the Premier League title, to win promotion, to avoid relegation, or even just to tick along cheerfully, mid-table. So it is with fathers and their kids; we all have our own ideas of what constitutes success in fatherhood, but fundamentally we're surely all hoping for our children to achieve what might be realistically expected of them, if not a little more. Whether we choose 4–4–2, 4–3–3 or 4–3–2–1 as the best way to help them get there, or even 3–5–2 like Argentina in the 1986 World Cup, possibly means I am getting too carried away with my footballing imagery.

So let me instead turn back to music as an illustration of fathering methods. The Big Chill music festival takes place in the grounds of Eastnor Castle near Ledbury in Herefordshire, not half an hour away from where we live, and in 2010 Elly and Joe, then aged seventeen and fifteen, fervently wanted to go. Dozens of their schoolfriends were going to be there, and lots more people they knew. Teenagers descend on the Big Chill from all over the country, but in particularly large numbers from the Welsh Marches and the Midlands, driven there by their mums, dads and peer pressure.

Joe wanted to go because Sam, Ben, Alicia, Megan and any number of his other mates were going, so I drove him, Sam and Ben there, choosing my moment to issue what I hoped was a stern but not overwrought warning about the dangers of drugs and alcohol. Joe cringed with embarrassment, as I knew he would in front of his friends, but what kind of father would I be not to raise the issue? For that matter, what kind of father was I for letting my fifteen-year-old son spend four nights at a music festival, unaccompanied by adults, in the first place?

A middle-class liberal one was the answer, or at least my answer, and also one who trusted his teenage children not to do anything reckless. Nevertheless, when I posed the question and posited the answer in the column I then wrote in the *Independent* I got some almighty stick online, mostly from music festival regulars who suggested that festivals all over the country were routinely blighted by children too young to be there who drank or inhaled too much or ended up in a distraught, wailing heap because of a romantic break-up or unrequited crush. The cast-iron rule, said one of my message-board critics, almost audibly spitting contempt at my line about driving Joe and his mates to the Big Chill, should be that anyone not old enough to get to a music festival under their own steam shouldn't go.

I didn't respond; it's never a good idea to start an online dialogue with someone who's given you a lambasting. But if I had I might have piously ventured the suggestion that maybe drug dealers are a truer blight on music festivals. Joe and Elly both came home with stories of how easy it was to buy MDMA, commonly known as ecstasy, and other drugs. Some dealers peddled their wares cautiously; we heard about a middle-aged bloke wearing a respectable fleece and cargo shorts who walked past a bunch of teenagers and, without looking at them, or even breaking his stride, said, 'Ketamine'. His hope, clearly, was that they would catch up with him and complete a quick, discreet transaction. Instead, they politely said, 'Pardon?', which wasn't very Janis Joplin, and he hurried on with his cargo. 'I just thought he was, like, somebody's dad,' recalled one of the teenagers later. Maybe he was.

Other dealers were more overt. Elly said that loads of them lifted up the flaps of the tent she was sharing, at all hours of day and night, offering MDMA. The answer was always no, and they moved on. I should add that neither child, nor any of their friends, ever felt harassed or threatened. The E commerce unfolded in a cheerfully convivial atmosphere.

THE GOOD, THE DAD AND THE UGLY

Of course, I realise that reports of pills and powder at a music festival are not exactly shock-horror material. Heck, one of the Big Chill's headline acts that summer was Lily Allen, who sings all about her little brother in his bedroom smoking weed. But even taking drugs out of the equation, there was enough booze there to sink the *Ark Royal*, making me wonder whether my generation of middle-class liberals were really doing our children any favours?

It seemed ironic, certainly, that the same kids who'd spent the previous ten years not being allowed to play in the woods for fear of a paedophile strike or a pond disaster were now being packed off to music festivals, or to seaside resorts such as Newquay and Salcombe for a massive hooley when they'd finished their GCSEs, with their parents' blessings. Or better still, with their parents' gin. At the very least, we were guilty of giving them some seriously mixed messages. Yet if we didn't let them go, what kind of message was that? That, at large in the world, they couldn't be trusted?

Even though I've never been one of those who discouraged my kids from playing in the woods, I have no right to pitch my own tent on the moral high ground, for as a father I too have been known to dispense confusingly tangled messages. On holiday in Turkey in that same summer of 2010, I gave Elly a long, impassioned lecture about the dangers of drinking too much. Jane echoed this, but later quietly reminded me that we had spent the previous evening telling the children about something hilarious that had happened to us twenty years earlier when we were both, not to put too fine a point on it, thoroughly bladdered.

On another family holiday, to Rome, we took the children to the spectacularly macabre crypt beneath the church of Santa Maria della Concezione dei Cappuccini, on the Via Veneto. It is decorated with the bones of literally thousands of Capuchin monks who died between 1528 and 1870, and the names of four of the rooms, which doubtless sound slightly less weird in Italian, translate as the Crypt of the Skulls, the Crypt of the Pelvises, the Crypt of the Shin Bones and the Thigh Bones, and the Crypt of the Three Skeletons. The place makes the Chamber of Horrors at Madame Tussauds look like a Budleigh Salterton tea shop.

In one of the crypts there is a placard, which passes on a message from the dead monks. It says, simply if more than a little spookily, given the cowled skeletons in front of you: 'What you are now, we used to be; what we are now, you will be.' And that, it occurs to me now, rather usefully sums up the parenthood cycle too, assuming that our children will become parents themselves. Perhaps the challenges of fatherhood could be made slightly less testing by recalling more often how we challenged our own fathers, and invite our children to envisage being challenged by their children. I might even get some 'What you are now, we used to be; what we are now, you will be' badges made up for Jane and me, to give the children and us some pause for thought at moments of mutual incomprehension. But, as I look back over the last twenty years, and even as I look forward to the next twenty, I really wouldn't want to equate fatherhood with death. On the contrary, it is as a dad that I have felt most alive.

Acknowledgements

I am deeply indebted to the numerous friends and relatives who in many cases have shared with me their own stories of fatherhood, or in other instances, have raised no objections to their stories being told. I have tried to avoid compromising them, sometimes by using pseudonyms, but they all deserve to be thanked by their real names.

So, a huge and heartfelt thank-you to Doug Alexander, Rosie Alexander, Cathy Bartrop, Pete Bartrop, Joanna Bent, Stephen Bent, Marcus Berkmann, Ian Broom, Steve Canny, Ali Couch, Chris Couch, James Clayton, Jane Clayton, Lou Dalgleish, Patrick Henchoz, Avril Hill, Guy Hindle, Dom Howard, Ella Howard, Mike King, James Lello, Simon Lello, Sylvia Lello, Jimmy Mulville, Steve Ridley, Becky Rumsey, Anne Sanderson, Bob Sanderson, Roger Smith, Kim Staniland, Will

Staniland, Robert Stone, Mark Sutcliffe, Pete Venables, Sian Williams and Paul Woolwich.

To anyone I have inadvertently left off this list, my equally heartfelt apologies. I am tremendously grateful to the university friends of my daughter's, who talked so candidly about their dads, but I haven't included them here because I would hate this book to cause any hurt. If it does, despite my best efforts, then I am truly sorry. Fatherhood is an emotive topic, and I knew I'd be stirring some emotions in writing about it. My own, mostly, but perhaps not exclusively.

I have also referred here and there to other books about fatherhood, and to quite a number of newspaper articles. I think that in every case I have credited the author in the text, but I should add my thanks here.

My thanks too to the excellent team at Simon & Schuster led so ably by my editor, Mike Jones. They include Helen Mockridge and Abigail Bergstrom, while Katherine Stanton did a splendid job with the copy-edit, spotting various inconsistencies and some outright howlers. If any mistakes have made it into the final version, the responsibility is all mine. And hats off to Briony Gowlett, who thought up a cracking title when nobody else could.

At David Higham Associates, my agent Andrew Gordon has been, as ever, a source of unerring guidance and encouragement.